D1124391

THE
SHIPPING POINT

THE RISE OF CHINA
AND THE FUTURE OF RETAIL
SUPPLY CHAIN MANAGEMENT

THE
SHIPPING POINT

THE RISE OF CHINA
AND THE FUTURE OF RETAIL
SUPPLY CHAIN MANAGEMENT

Peter J. Levesque

WILEY

John Wiley & Sons (Asia) Pte. Ltd.

Copyright © 2011 John Wiley & Sons (Asia) Pte. Ltd.
Published in 2011 by John Wiley & Sons (Asia) Pte. Ltd.
1 Fusionopolis Walk, #07-01 Solaris, South Tower, Singapore 138628
All rights reserved.

No part of this publication may be reproduced, stored in a retrieval system, or transmitted in any form or by any means, electronic, mechanical, photocopying, recording, scanning, or otherwise, except as expressly permitted by law, without either the prior written permission of the Publisher, or authorization through payment of the appropriate photocopy fee to the Copyright Clearance Center. Requests for permission should be addressed to the Publisher, John Wiley & Sons (Asia) Pte. Ltd., 1 Fusionopolis Walk, #07-01 Solaris, South Tower, Singapore 138628, tel: 65-6643-8000, fax: 65-6643-8008, e-mail: enquiry@wiley.com.

This publication is designed to provide accurate and authoritative information in regard to the subject matter covered. It is sold with the understanding that the publisher is not engaged in rendering professional services. If professional advice or other expert assistance is required, the services of a competent professional person should be sought.

Neither the authors nor the Publisher are liable for any actions prompted or caused by the information presented in this book. Any views expressed herein are those of the authors and do not represent the views of the organizations they work for.

Other Wiley Editorial Offices

John Wiley & Sons, 111 River Street, Hoboken, NJ 07030, USA

John Wiley & Sons, The Atrium, Southern Gate, Chichester, West Sussex, P019 8SQ, United Kingdom

John Wiley & Sons (Canada) Ltd., 5353 Dundas Street West, Suite 400, Toronto, Ontario, M9B 6HB, Canada

John Wiley & Sons Australia Ltd, 42 McDougall Street, Milton, Queensland 4064, Australia

Wiley-VCH, Boschstrasse 12, D-69469 Weinheim, Germany

Library of Congress Cataloging-in-Publication Data
ISBN 978-0-470-82453-5 (Hardcover)
ISBN 978-0-470-82625-6 (e-PDF)
ISBN 978-0-470-82624-9 (e-Mobi)
ISBN 978-0-470-82626-3 (e-Pub)

Typeset in 10.5/14pt MinionPro-Regular by Thomson Digital, India
Printed in Singapore by Saik Wah Print Media Pte Ltd

TABLE OF CONTENTS

ACKNOWLEDGMENTS

I would like to thank my wife Lisa, my daughter Catherine and my sons Paul and Matthew for putting up with endless nights and weekends watching me work on my laptop from the kitchen table. They have been a constant source of unconditional support, and words cannot describe how much they mean to me.

I wish to thank the contributors to this book for their time and dedication in the midst of the global financial crisis that unfolded during the writing of this manuscript. Michael Jacobs from Toys"R"Us was instrumental in offering his insight and expertise in the technical aspects of dynamic supply chain models in China. Chris Robeson's international expertise in the area of supply chain innovation, particularly as it relates to postponement and delayed differentiation models, was invaluable to the development of the manuscript.

Tom Reilly from Next Horizon shared his perspectives on China's developing workforce and the future of business process outsourcing in China. I thank him for his insightful contribution. David Barnes from Clarkson securities in London provided valuable expertise on the container freight derivative market in Shanghai, and John Gouveia contributed his expertise in the area of geographical information systems. Special thanks to John Pattullo, chief executive officer of CEVA Logistics, for his introduction on the importance of leadership in supply chain management.

Thanks to Professor Steve DeKrey for sharing his expertise on the critically important role that leadership will play in building successful SCM organizations in the future. A special thanks to my former DHL colleague, Anne Schaefer, for her comments and suggestions during the development of the initial manuscript, to Gavin Dow from Modern Terminals Limited for his valuable review, and to Jonathan Beard PhD from the consulting group GHK, for sharing his insights on port development and cargo migration flows in China.

This book is the culmination of 20 years of experience in international supply chain management, including 14 years living and working in Hong Kong. There have been many wonderful people along the way. Thanks to David Starling, and Rod Miller from our time together at APL, also Robin Cheung and Kuang Siah, who I worked with in co-founding V-Logic Limited. And special thanks to Sean Kelly, Craig Grossgart, Charlie Wellins and Robert Sappio, who have made being in this industry so much fun over the years.

Thanks to Bill Aldridge, Maureen Saul, Lisa Schraer, May Ma, Shirley Pang, Mike Sullivan, Phil Trabulsi, Wayne Wan, and Caron Van Dyck from CEVA Logistics. A very special thanks to Margaret Li, whose administrative support and graphic design expertise helped make this project possible.

Much of the theme behind chapter one can be attributed to my former business school professor, Justin Yifu Lin, who later became the first Chinese chief economist at the World Bank. Another teaching mentor referenced in this book is Professor Keith Murnighan from the Kellogg Graduate School of Management, whose course on game theory made a lasting impression, and whose friendship over the years I very much appreciate. Thanks to the members of the American Chamber of Commerce's Transportation and Logistics Committee who have been a constant source of industry knowledge and discussion. I would also like to thank Nick Wallwork from John Wiley & Sons, for believing in the project and for getting it off the ground.

Last but not least, a special thanks to my parents, Paul and Mary Levesque, who taught me the importance of hard work, perseverance and leadership. And to David Scully, who for the last 20 years, has remained a constant source of mentoring and friendship. I am forever grateful.

ABOUT THE CONTRIBUTORS

Peter J. Levesque
Chief Commercial Officer, Modern Terminals Limited,
Hong Kong

Peter Levesque has over 20 years of international transportation and logistics experience and has been working in Hong Kong since 1996. Prior to joining Modern Terminals, Mr. Levesque served as senior vice president for CEVA Logistics and as regional vice president for DHL's International Supply Chain Group in Asia Pacific. In 2000, he co-founded V-Logic Limited, a niche 3PL company based in Hong Kong, and prior to V-Logic he held several management positions with American President Lines, including managing director of (ACS) APL Logistics for North Asia.

Mr. Levesque holds a BA in Political Science from the University of Massachusetts, and an MBA from Northwestern University's J.L. Kellogg Graduate School of Management and the Hong Kong University of Science and Technology. He has served as Adjunct Professor of Entrepreneurship for the Kellogg–HKUST MBA program, and the Hong Kong University of Science and Technology's MBA program.

Mr. Levesque sits on the American Chamber of Commerce's Board of Governors in Hong Kong and is a past chairman for the Chamber's Transportation and Logistics Committee. He also serves as Treasurer of The American Club in Hong Kong and sits on the Club's board of governors. His wife Lisa and their three children reside in Hong Kong and Falmouth Massachusetts.

Michael Jacobs
Senior Vice President, Logistics Toys"R"Us, Inc.

As senior vice president, Logistics, for Toys"R"Us, Inc., Michael Jacobs oversees worldwide distribution and customs compliance, global importing and exporting, fleet operations, domestic transportation, Asia operations and supply chain management for the corporation. Mr. Jacobs started his career at Toys"R"Us in 1997 as director of International Logistics.

Prior to joining Toys"R"Us, Mr. Jacobs enjoyed a career in the world of finance and supply chain management at PepsiCo and Melville Corporation.

Mr. Jacobs received both his Bachelors of Science in Finance and his Masters of Business Administration from Manhattan College. He also received a Masters of Professional Studies in Supply Chain Management from Penn State University. He lives in New Jersey with his wife Karolyn and his two sons Jonathan and Christopher.

Chris Robeson
Vice President, International Logistics Limited Brands, Inc. Logistics Services

Chris Robeson is vice president, International Logistics for the Logistics Services division of Limited Brands Inc. He joined Limited Brands in April 1991. In his current position, he is responsible for overseeing all international product flows. He returned to Columbus in fall 2006 following a four-year assignment in Hong Kong and now leads international air and ocean operations, customer service, and the Asia-based logistics associates residing in seven office locations globally.

Chris holds a B.S.B.A. in Marketing and Transportation/Logistics from Ohio State University. During his undergraduate studies he attended the University of Pittsburg-sponsored Semester at Sea program studying an international curriculum with associated global travel.

Chris has held board positions on the Columbus roundtable of the Council of Supply Chain Management Professionals. He has been a guest lecturer at Miami University of Ohio, and is a former member of the Hong Kong chapter of the American Chamber of Commerce.

Chris, his wife Julie, their three children, and their black lab, The Baron, reside in the Columbus suburb of Upper Arlington.

Dr. Steven DeKrey

Dr. Steven J. DeKrey has spent over 20 years in management education in Asia and the United States. He has an MBA degree from Kellogg School of Management and a PhD from the University of Iowa. He is senior associate dean of the Business School at the Hong Kong University of Science and Technology (HKUST) and is the founding director of the Kellogg-HKUST Executive MBA program, consistently ranked among the world's best programs. Professor DeKrey is active in community organizations and chaired the Board of Governors of the American Chamber of Commerce in Hong Kong in 2008.

LEADERSHIP & SUPPLY CHAIN MANAGEMENT

JOHN PATTULLO

It's been said that in business everything depends on leadership. The recent financial crisis has had a profound impact on the world we live in, and just as poor financial leadership helped create the crisis, transformational leadership, will surely help steer us out.

From a leadership perspective, times of turmoil often generate periods of intense focus, which if properly harnessed, can generate breakthrough innovation. Whether it's the development of radically more effective operations, or the invention of step change technology, innovation is often the byproduct of adversity. Leaders, who recognize crisis as a time of opportunity, can better anticipate the world that will emerge, and set a course for sustainable competitive advantage.

> **Shipping Point:**
> **"Inventory can be managed . . . people must be led."**

As a Scot, I am proud of the way that a small and poor nation has made an unusually significant contribution to global innovation. In my early school days, we were taught about Scottish technical breakthroughs from inventors such as James Watt, Lord Kelvin, Alexander Fleming and Alexander Graham Bell. These achievements were often driven by harsh economic necessity.

As chief executive officer of CEVA Logistics, I have seen the huge potential that is unleashed when talented people are empowered to lead, and to innovate. For all the technological advancement that has occurred in logistics over the last decade, supply chain management remains dependent upon the daily efforts of empowered people, supported by capable leadership.

Transformational leaders have the ability to galvanize individual efforts into team success. These leaders understand the creative potential that lies within the organization, and they enable a corporate culture that not only rewards success, but also learns from failure. Within this type of open culture, small successes build momentum and confidence, which in turn lead to larger successes, and ultimately to game-changing breakthroughs. Recognizing failure as an opportunity to learn, and a chance to start again, creates a culture of trust that rewards perseverance, and builds loyalty.

As supply chain models become more dynamic and complex, the demand for skilled logistics talent will continue to increase. Capable leadership will be critical for the recruitment, retention and career development of logistics experts around the globe. Talented recruits will expect the vision of the company to be well defined, and effectively deployed. Transformational leaders understand that their job is to cultivate more leaders, not to create more followers.

As we move beyond this most recent financial storm, we can be certain that new crises will gather on the horizon. But we can also be optimistic that the next decade will offer incredible opportunity to those who used this time of turbulence for positive change and improvement. Transformational leadership will play a critical role in the global supply chain over the months and years ahead, by unlocking the creativity and innovation of talented people to meet the rapidly changing requirements of clients around the world.

There is an old Scottish Proverb that says, "Twelve highlanders and a bagpipe make a rebellion." I believe this speaks to what is possible when you have a few motivated people, some capable leadership, and a small dose of inspiration. We hope that *The Shipping Point* provides you with a dose of inspiration, and that you find it to be a useful tool in navigating your team's retail supply chain strategy over the course of the decade ahead.

John Pattullo
Chief Executive Officer
CEVA Logistics, Amsterdam

INTRODUCTION

PETER LEVESQUE

There is an ancient Chinese curse that says, "May you live in interesting times." Looking back on the seismic events that occurred at the close of this last decade who could have imagined that Lehman Brothers would crumble, that home foreclosures would become routine in America's neighborhoods, or that the

> **Shipping Point:**
> **"A disaster is a terrible thing to waste."**
> *Jack Welch*

American automobile industry would suddenly rely on government programs like "cash for clunkers" to stay in business. Having experienced a global economic meltdown of a magnitude not seen since the Great Depression, there can be little doubt that we are indeed living in interesting times.

The global financial crisis touched everyone and everything, in ways that were unimaginable just a short time ago. When a speaker at a recent logistics conference was asked by a member of the audience how the shipping industry was performing "aside from the disastrous global economy," the speaker paused, and then replied, "You mean, aside from the shooting Mrs. Lincoln, how did you enjoy the play?"[1] It is near impossible to define any business situation today without relating it back to the turmoil experienced over the past two years.

During the peak of the crisis the once touted benefits of globalization, free trade, and the free flow of capital were increasingly scrutinized and in some cases vilified. Theories around de-globalization became increasingly popular, and protectionist policies found their way into the stimulus packages of both China and the United States. Mitigating global contagion associated with systemic financial risk, and balancing government intervention against the longer-term consequences of nationalization and moral hazard, remains a serious challenge for global policy makers today.

We discovered during the crisis that China's ability to "decouple" from the rest of the world's economies was more theory than reality. Evidence that China was not immune to the downside consequences of the global recession appeared early on when an estimated 20,000 factories in China's Guangdong Province closed their doors between 2008 and 2009, leaving some 20 million Chinese migrant workers unemployed. Hundreds of cargo ships that supported the Chinese trade were taken out of service, and over 570 ships were mothballed worldwide, representing more than 11 percent of the world's cargo ship capacity. In early 2009, at South China's Port of Yantian, over 350,000 empty cargo containers sat idle, waiting for China's factories to churn back to life. In 2010 most of the idle ships were put back into service and the shipping industry actually experienced a shortage in cargo containers due to the sudden increase in demand, highlighting the inextricable link between China and the global consumer.

When viewed through the narrow prism of recent events, the impact of the financial crisis on China may appear more pronounced. The reality is that in the midst of the financial crisis China continued to grow. It is critical that this relatively brief period of economic disruption not overshadow the broader narrative of China's historic economic development over the last decade.

The global economy is finally moving through a period of recovery. Unlike many countries in the West, however, China is emerging from the recent turmoil economically stronger and more influential on the global stage. An improving global economic environment should mean better times ahead for all. But while a rising tide lifts all boats, China's advantage in the years ahead, when compared to other world economies, will be that its boat is bought and paid for.

SECTIONAL FRAMEWORK OF THE BOOK

It is difficult to discuss where China is going without first understanding where China has been. In section one of this book we will discuss the re-emergence and rise of China as a global economic superpower and look at the impact that these developments are having on retail supply chain management (SCM). As China enters an exciting new phase of growth and innovation, it is developing world-class transportation infrastructure and technological expertise that will impact retail SCM over the course of the next decade and beyond.

China is also expanding its research and development capabilities, and there is a growing trend toward Chinese domestic retailing and Chinese domestic brands. As we will discuss further, some of these brands have already become internationally recognized. As China's original equipment manufacturers (OEMs) migrate from contract production to creating their own brand name products, they will require assistance with sales, marketing and distribution into not only foreign markets but also their own domestic markets. We will look at how this trend presents a niche opportunity for logistics service providers (LSPs) to exploit within the international logistics arena.

We will further discuss how international retail brands are increasingly looking to China not only for its ability to manufacture, but also for its enormous market potential. We will discuss how "selling to the source" (Li & Fung's terminology for selling products into the China market) will generate additional growth opportunities for global brands. We will also highlight the need for LSPs to expand beyond their traditional areas of expertise in order to meet the changing requirements of global retail customers.

China is not the only thing changing the dynamics of the global supply chain. Changes in consumer retail habits and retail business processes are also having a significant impact on the manner and speed in which products get to market. Traditional buyer/seller relationships are becoming a much more dynamic, tailor-made experience, requiring enhancements to supply chain strategy and design.

Section two will focus on the changing face of consumer retail, specifically the growing trend toward buyer participation in product development, where consumers are taking a more active role in the decisions that impact the functionality and design of the items they purchase. We call this trend "consumer-enabled design," and we will discuss what this trend means to the future of retail SCM.

While it is not reasonable to expect that all retail products will be tailor-made in the future, there will be enough retail customization in the market to warrant innovation in how retail supply chains are constructed. Further in section two we will discuss how the convergence of social networking and consumer-enabled design are challenging traditional product development, and how product differentiation is becoming more difficult to sustain, leaving retailers to differentiate more on supply chain process. We will highlight the issues involved with building supply chains that enable retailers to quickly source, assemble, and ship component parts across multiple geographies for final configuration, based on the unique requirements of each customer.

Sections three and four will focus on supply chain innovation and support in response to infrastructure developments in China, and the market shift toward demand-driven retail environments. We will show detailed examples of more dynamic and modular supply chain processes that provide greater flexibility for dealing with variations in demand. We will highlight the ways in which supply chain solutions in the years ahead will contain a more diverse combination of service offerings that combine functions and services previously considered unrelated to SCM.

The by-product of a demand-driven, consumer-enabled supply chain is complexity. The coordination of sourcing, purchasing, manufacturing, and shipping becomes exponentially more complicated as process variation is added, and the number of possible outcomes increases. We will look at developments in supply chain technologies that are being used to manage process complexity and visibility.

While systems technology will continue to be important in meeting the requirements of end-to-end transportation, it is the human element that will make the difference between success and failure in SCM. The sheer number of service combinations that will be possible within flexible supply chains will require clients to engage with LSPs beyond traditional service parameters, allowing LSPs to orchestrate business-critical decisions on the client's behalf. This will drive the need for more capable, responsible, and empowered logistics talent, together with the development of high performance logistics teams. We will highlight the need to balance investment in technology with investment in human capital and leadership. We will also examine the importance of human capital in building more resilient and sustainable global supply chains.

Many people claim to be experts on the China supply chain, but after 15 years of living and working in Asia, I have found that true China experts are few and far between. I am pleased to have as contributors to this book three proven experts in the area of SCM and leadership—each with years of hands-on experience in the Chinese market—offering their perspectives on leadership and supply chain best practice.

Michael Jacobs, Vice President of International Supply Chain for Toys"R"Us has been at the forefront of Chinese supply chain innovation and operations for many years, and was instrumental in the development of the Toys"R"Us cross-dock consolidation model and other advanced logistics solutions from China. His chapter on origin consolidation provides an in-depth look at the technical aspects of one of China's most dynamic retail supply chain models. This chapter outlines key industry definitions and looks at the critical components of a successful consolidation program within China.

Chris Robeson, Vice President of International Logistics for The Limited is an experienced China hand, having lived and worked in Asia for several years. His expertise in fashion logistics and his work in the development of greige supply chain processes are extensive. His chapter on innovative supply chains is a fascinating look at how the consumer retail landscape is driving the need for more flexible and modular supply chain strategy and design.

Dr. Steven DeKrey from the Hong Kong University of Science & Technology has written extensively on the subject of leadership in Asia Pacific. His chapter on the role of leadership in building successful SCM organizations in China is critical to understanding the importance of investing in human capital and talent development in order to support more complex supply chain models.

Supply chain management can be a difficult subject to write about without becoming consumed in complicated analysis and industry speak. We have tried to cover several topics on China and supply chain management in order to offer an interesting variety of subject matter for the reader. One of the problems writing a book on these topics is that events on the ground are often changing faster than the words can be written. In many cases we reference statistics from 2008 and earlier because the extraordinary events of 2009 were not representative of the true bigger picture. We hope that you will find the ideas and concepts contained in the following pages thought provoking and informative. Any errors or omissions are purely unintentional.

Visionary supply chain leaders will use the last two years of global economic disruption constructively, to foster innovation through product development, process improvement, and in the exploration of new markets. We hope that you are among those visionary leaders willing to take advantage of the recent global economic and political turmoil by turning it into something positive. As Jack Welch once said, "a disaster is a terrible thing to waste."[2]

Peter J. Levesque
Hong Kong

NOTES

1 The speaker's quip refers to the assassination of Abraham Lincoln, who was shot while watching the play *Our American Cousin* with his wife Mary Todd Lincoln, at Ford's Theater in 1865.
2 Attributed to Jack Welch – MSNBC panelist.

SUPPLY CHAIN ACRONYM QUICK REFERENCE GUIDE

3PL – Third Party Logistics
BCO – Beneficial Cargo Owner
BLP – Bonded Logistics Park
BOL – Bill of Lading
BPO – Business Process Outsourcing
C.A.F.E. – Coffee and Farmers Equity
CBM – Cubic Meter
CBP – Customs Border Protection
CFS – Consolidator Freight Station
CSI – Container Security Initiative
CTPAT – Customs Trade Partnership Against Terrorism
CY – Container Yard
DC – Distribution Center
DCF – Discounted Cash Flow
DHS – Department of Homeland Security
ECSW – Export Customs Supervised Warehouse
FCA – Free Carrier Alongside
FEU – Forty Foot Equivalent Unit
FFA – Freight Forward Agreements
FOB – Free on Board
FTP – Free Trade Port
ISF – Import Security Filing
LSP – Logistics Service Provider
NPV – Net Present Value
NVOCC – Non Vessel Owner Common Carrier

PO – Purchase Order
PRC – Peoples Republic of China
PRD – Pearl River Delta
RFID – Radio Frequency Identification
SCFI – Shanghai Container Freight Index
SCM – Supply Chain Management
SEZ – Special Economic Zone
SKU – Stock Keeping Unit
TEU – Twenty Foot Equivalent Unit
USDOT – United States Department of Transportation
VAT – Value Added Tax
YRD – Yangtze River Delta

THE RISE OF CHINA

CHAPTER ONE

CHINA'S GREAT COMEBACK

PETER LEVESQUE

There are numerous socioeconomic, cultural, and political theories for why China's civilization fell behind the West after the 18th century. The subject of European industrialization and its impact on China is extensive and goes far beyond the scope of this book; however, a brief overview is necessary in order to understand

> **Shipping Point: We can no longer define the world in terms of "The West" and "The Rest."**

some of the fundamental reasons for China's postponed industrial development relative to the West. It is also critical to understanding China's re-emergence as a global economic super power, and the implications this will have on the global supply chain in the years ahead.

The term "re-emergence" is appropriate when describing China's position in the world today, because in many ways China is an example of history repeating itself. To truly understand where China is today, and more importantly where it is going, it is critical to understand, at least on a basic level, where China has been both as a country and as a civilization.

For the so-called advanced countries it is sometimes easy to simplify the world into two camps; the developed West and the developing rest. Understanding the degree and complexity of China's development can be especially difficult in a world that tends to measure progress against Western criteria. When the Soviet Union collapsed in 1991 it appeared Western democracy had triumphed as the final form of government which the developing world, including China would eventually have to embrace. In Francis Fukuyama's famous 1989 essay, *The End of History*, he predicted that the fall of the Soviet Union and communism would mean a final victory for the Western form of liberal capitalist democracy. He wrote, "What we may be witnessing is not just the end of the Cold War, or the passing of a particular period of postwar history, but the end of history as such: that is, the end point of mankind's ideological evolution and the universalization of Western liberal democracy as the final form of human government."[1] China's ideological evolution toward "socialism with Chinese characteristics" was still being tested as the Soviet Union fell in 1991. Few could have imagined the extent to which China would develop in the amazing decades that followed.

The geopolitical turmoil and financial crisis that gripped the globe over the last two years has reminded us once again that political and economic stability can be fleeting, and that change is indeed constant. The growing power and influence of countries such as communist China increasingly challenges those who believe that the status quo in the West is comfortably secure. In fact, there is a growing emphasis on the need to recognize the realities of the developing world and to prepare for change. In a recent article for *Time* magazine Kishore Mahbubani, the Dean of Lee Kuan Yew School of Public Policy, National University of Singapore, described Asia's perception of Europe. He wrote that Asia views Europe today as "an inward-focused continent in danger of being left behind."[2] What is most noteworthy of his observation is that had Mr. Mahbubani been around in the 17th century, he may well have been describing the West's perception of Asia and China in particular.

Britain's 18th century industrial revolution, the expansion of European dominance through colonization, and the subsequent rise of the United States, may seem like ancient history in the eyes of many Westerners. But to the Chinese, with a civilization that dates back 5000 years, this era of Western dominance is viewed as a recent development. The Chinese have always taken the long view of history. In 1972, Henry Kissinger reportedly asked Chinese Premier Zhou Enlai about his thoughts on the consequences of the French Revolution. The Premier was said to have replied that he thought it was too early to say.[3]

From a Chinese perspective, taking the long view of history is perfectly understandable given the role they have played throughout civilization. Up until the 18th century it was China that led civilization in science, civil government and technology. Inventions such as gunpowder, paper, clocks, and the compass are just a few examples of Chinese ingenuity. China also had the largest global economy, and Beijing was the largest city in the world until it was replaced by London in 1850.[4] In the early 15th century during the Ming Dynasty (well before Britain ruled the seas) China was the greatest maritime nation in the world, led by the voyages of Admiral Zheng He, who sailed on massive wooden junks capable of holding up to 500 men.[5]

China was not alone in its early dominance as a civilization. India in the 16th century was also well advanced compared with Europe at the time. Alex von Tunzelmann captures the essence of just how advanced India was in his book *Indian Summer*:

> *In the beginning there were two nations. One was a vast, mighty and magnificent empire, brilliantly organized and culturally unified, which dominated a massive swath of the earth. The other was an un-developed, semi-feudal realm, driven by religious factionalism and barley able to feed its illiterate, diseased and stinking masses.*
> *The first nation was India, and the second was England.*[6]

Tunzlemann's description of 16th Century India could have just as easily been applied to China at the time. So what happened? How did China miss its own early industrial revolution? In reality, several factors contributed to China's postponed transition into the industrialized world. Part of the explanation has to do with how and where innovative ideas were developed in ancient China. Centuries ago, discovery and innovation were dependent upon the experiences of farmers and craftsmen thinking about ways to improve or simplify their daily work. China's large population of farmers and craftsmen gave it a vast resource pool for new ideas, and therefore a high instance of technological innovation and discovery in pre-modern times. But those discoveries were not easily communicated, or replicated, across the population because of China's immense geography.

Meanwhile in the 18th century the scientific methods of experimentation, replication and technological transfer were being used to invent and communicate new discoveries across Europe, making China's vast population less of a comparative advantage in the area of technological innovation.[7] As historian David Landes describes, "a significant area of European advantage was in the field of science, based on the growing autonomy of intellectual inquiry, spreading networks of scientific activity and the routinization of research and its diffusion."[8]

And while Europe was in the midst of its industrial revolution, China was to some degree being held back by its own inwardly focused culture and traditions. China at the time of Britain's industrial revolution was a meritocracy led by imperial rule. Social and economic advancement under Chinese imperial rule was available to males who could pass the arduous civil service examinations for admittance into the imperial court. Study for these examinations took many years and, among other subjects, involved memorizing the Four Books and Five Classics (*Sìshū Wǔjīng*) of Confucius' teachings.

The reward of social status and upward mobility that came with passing these examinations was so great, both for the student and their families, that China's best and brightest minds were naturally inclined to pursue this lengthy and difficult career path to the detriment of China's industrial development. As Professor Justin Yifu Lin explains, "The curriculum of china's civil service examination, which emphasized the moral obligations of government officials to the Emperor, and the built-in evaluation criterion along the ladders to officialdom, obstructed the incentives to learn mathematics and conduct experiments—both necessary for modern scientific research. Therefore, despite its early lead in scientific discovery and technological invention, China had no indigenous scientific and industrial revolutions."[9]

Memorizing lengthy Confucian texts for exams was only part of the problem. The Chinese also had the task of memorizing a complex written language. There are over 47,000 characters in the Kangxi Chinese Dictionary, though it is estimated you can be literate in Chinese knowing between 3,000–4,000 characters. Compare this with the effort it takes to learn the 26 letters of the alphabet and it becomes clear that learning to read and write Chinese takes a significant amount of time and effort just to be able to effectively communicate in writing.

Adding to China's postponed development was their "Middle Kingdom" mentality; the belief that China was the center of the universe, and that all others were merely outer barbarians (the further away from China, the more barbaric). Having twice been invaded and ruled by barbarians, first by the Mongols during the Yuan Dynasty (1279–1368) and then by the Manchus during the Qing Dynasty (1644–1912), the Chinese were in many ways isolationist, avoiding unnecessary interaction with the outside world. The maintenance of social order and civil control was a primary consideration for China's emperors and in fact remains a primary concern of Chinese leaders today.[10] The tributary system that developed in the Middle Kingdom involved the acknowledgement of China as the center of the universe by foreign countries, through the payment of tribute to the Chinese emperor.

As pre-modern China's development stagnated, it faced a rapidly growing population on the one hand, and rapidly depleting natural resources on the other. As Martin Jacques explains in his book *When China Rules the World*, "The pressure on land and other resources was driven by the continuing growth of the population in a time of relative technological stasis. Lacking a richly endowed overseas empire, China had no exogenous means by which it could bypass the growing constraints."[11] Europe also faced a growing population and suffered from its own limited resources, however colonization of the New World expanded their access to outside resources and labor (including slaves) that helped fuel their industrial revolution.[12]

Rather than a single cause, it was actually the combination of several key factors that contributed to the postponement of China's industrial development, even as Europe flourished. David Landes sums it up this way: "China had long slipped into technological and scientific torpor, coasting along on previous gains and losing speed as talent yielded to gentility . . . so the years passed and the decades and the centuries. Europe left China far behind."[13]

Fast forward to the year 1980 which in many ways represents China's economic turning point, thanks to the visionary leadership of Deng Xiaoping and his establishment of the three Special Economic Zones (SEZs) in southern China. The difficulty and political risk of turning a country, indoctrinated with socialism and communism, toward a market economy, cannot be overstated. In order to get around the potential pitfalls with calling it a move toward "capitalism," Deng referred to the initiative as "building socialism with Chinese characteristics." Deng was himself an entrepreneur and a businessman at heart, having opened his own restaurant, the China Bean Curd Shop, while studying in Paris in the 1920s.[14] His understanding of the entrepreneurial spirit helped shape the re-emergence of China on a grand scale as evidenced by cities like Shenzhen and Shanghai.

Deng's long-term outlook was instrumental to the success of the new SEZs. He staunchly defended his initiatives in 1988 when inflation ran rampant and price reforms became necessary. In 1992, at the age of 88

Source: Eightfish, Getty Images

Shanghai's Dramatic New Skyline

and with his political enemies taking aim, he headed out on his southern journey (*nanxun*) to Shenzhen and the Pearl River Delta to draw political attention to the great success that had been achieved in South China. Finally in 1992 the 14th Party Congress made the reforms official, by backing Deng and China's shift to a socialist market economy.[15]

The SEZs' locations were chosen because they had previously been neglected small farming and fishing villages that were considered far enough away from Beijing and Shanghai to cause any real harm. The SEZs were designed specifically as export processing centers for Chinese products that would entice foreign direct investment. The initiative worked. Foreign direct investment (FDI) grew from US$3.7 billion in 1990 to US$41 billion by 2000.[16] By 2008 FDI had reached US$92.4 billion.

Deng's great experiment was a major economic success. Between 1978 and 2000 China increased its foreign trade from US$36 billion to US$474 billion.

Per capita income doubled not once, but twice, from 1978 to 1996. Yergin and Stanislaw in their book, *The Commanding Heights,* note that, "it took Britain 60 years to double its per capita income; and the United States 50 years. . . . Deng did something that no one else in history has ever accomplished—he lifted upward of 300 million people out of poverty in just two decades."[17]

Deng died in 1997 at the age of 93. After his death was announced huge posters of the fallen leader lined the streets and buildings of Shenzhen, a city that just a decade before had been a small fishing village. The results of Deng's visionary initiatives will continue to have a profound impact on China's development for years to come.

Understanding China's history can also help us to understand some of the business issues that the country is trying to overcome today. Why, for example, despite such a large manufacturing base, have there been so few globally recognized Chinese brands in the market? Over the past several decades China's comparative advantage has been low-cost mass production where manufacturing was done to the design specifications and technical specifications that

Source: Kim Steele, Getty Images

A Chinese Factory Line

were provided by the West. It was not necessary for China to compete on creativity and innovation, and not possible given the skill level of its labor force. To be successful, China only needed the ability to follow technical specifications and assembly instructions from overseas. As the comparative advantage of low-cost labor in places like Vietnam becomes more widespread, there is now a fundamental shift toward the creativity and innovation that were once so prevalent in China leading up to the 18th century. Areas such as research and development, transportation infrastructure development, and product design engineering are seeing a vast resurgence in China today which is helping to drive the pace of China's overall progress.

Historically, the amount of time needed for countries to modernize has been continuously condensed, given the ease with which knowledge can now be transferred and experiences shared from previous modernizations. As fast as the industrial revolution in Britain (1780–1840) may have seemed at the time, it was relatively slow compared with that of the United States and later the Asian Tiger countries of Singapore, South Korea, Taiwan and Hong Kong.[18] We can see evidence of condensed modernization in China in simple things such as the leap-frogging of technology. While most Americans, for example, still have a home telephone, the Chinese skipped over the concept of home phones completely and went straight to cell phones. The United States national domestic freight transportation network started with the railroads, while China has up until recently placed a low priority on rail transport for cargo in favor of utilizing the largest road construction project in history.

While applying what they have learned from past modernizations the end result of China's rapid development and modernization may in fact look different than what the West expects it to look like. Martin Jacques explains that "We stand on the eve of a different kind of world, but comprehending it is difficult: We (the West) are so accustomed to dealing with the paradigms and parameters of the contemporary world that we inevitably take them for granted, believing that they are set in concrete rather than themselves being the subject of longer-run cycles of historical change."[19] Where the United States and Europe have typically measured the advancement of the developing world by each country's degree of Westernization, in the case of China's development, the world needs to prepare for something uniquely Chinese.[20] Knowing where China has been gives us a better perspective into where China is going. Regardless of what China's re-emergence as a global player may look like, we can be sure that whatever happens will impact the way we think about and execute international business and supply chain management in the future. We will discuss this in greater detail in the following chapters.

NOTES

1   Francis Fukuyama, *The End of History and The Last Man*, (New York: Avon Books, 1992).
2   Kishore Mahbubani, "Europe's Errors," *Time*, March 8, 2010, 34.
3   Martin Jacques, *When China Rules the World, The Rise of the Middle Kingdom and the End of the Western World*, (London: Penguin, 2009), 391.
4   Ibid., 80.
5   Ibid., 78.
6   Alex von Tunzelmann, *Indian Summer: The Secret History of the End of an Empire*, (New York: Henry Holt, 2007).
7   Yifu Lin, F. Cai, Z. Li, *The China Miracle – Development Strategy and Economic Reform*, (Hong Kong: Chinese University Press, 1998), 1.
8   David Landes, *The Wealth and Poverty of Nations: Why Some Are So Rich and Some So Poor*, (New York: W.W. Norton & Company, 1999), 210.
9   Yifu Lin, "The Needham Puzzle: Why the Industrial Revolution Did Not Originate in China," *Economic Development and Cultural Change* 43, no. 2 (1995): 269-92.
10 Jacques, *When China Rules*, 78.
11 Ibid., 80.
12 Ibid., 27.
13 Landes, *Wealth and Poverty*, 342.
14 Daniel Yergin and J. Stanislaw, *The Commanding Height, The Battle for the World Economy*, (New York: Simon & Shuster, 2002), 211.
15 Ibid., 198.
16 Ibid., 199.
17 Ibid., 204.
18 Ibid., 21.
19 Jacques, *When China Rules*, 8.
20 Ibid., 12.

CHAPTER TWO

THE DEVELOPMENT OF CHINA'S ECONOMY & INFRASTRUCTURE

PETER LEVESQUE

Little more than a decade ago the primary mode of transportation in China's major cities was the bicycle. Road infrastructure across much of China was sub-standard and poorly planned. Hotels were uncomfortable and English-speaking staff was a novelty. But there was a feeling of immense anticipation in China at that time. As construction cranes filled city skylines and welders could be seen working through the night, it was clear that something big was happening. China was modernizing at an incredible pace, and the 2008 Olympic Games was set to be the country's official coming-out party.

Source: OTHK, Getty Images

Shanghai's Maglev Train Travels at 268mph

Aside from the occasional inconvenience of obtaining a travel visa, much of the hassle associated with getting around mainland China has disappeared, at least in the major cities. Shanghai's high-speed Maglev train is an example of China's push toward state-of-the-art transportation. The focus now shifts toward building infrastructure that connects the hinterland provinces with China's urban centers. These Government initiatives will play a major role in reshaping both the international and domestic supply chains of tomorrow, determining where future production will take place, and how products will get to market.

First and foremost, it is important to understand that the Chinese view their infrastructure development as part of a national strategy for growing their economy, improving their competitive positioning, and promoting their national aspirations. A study conducted by the Federal Highway Department and the Department of Transportation (FHDOT) noted that, "the Chinese government at all levels, targets investments on those components of the transportation system that best advance national goals."[1] China's "Go West" strategy, for example, is geared toward incentives for manufacturing to be established in the hinterland to provide the same types of opportunity to rural workers that are currently available to those who relocate to the eastern port cities.

It is estimated that to maintain a growth rate of around 10 percent per annum, China would need to create approximately eight million new jobs a year in its urban centers, just to meet the demands of organic growth. Another 15 million jobs per year would be needed to absorb the migrant worker populations that are moving to the major cities annually.[2] The Chinese Government is keenly aware that as growth rates fall and jobs become scarce the likelihood of social unrest rises. Like the days of the Imperial Court, the Chinese Government today has a vested interest in maintaining social harmony.

> Shipping Point: "The Chinese view their infrastructure development as part of a national strategy."

Manufacturers are taking advantage of government incentives to migrate production to the north and to the west, as shown in Figure 2.1. Logistics service providers now need to develop a service network capable of transporting raw material and finished product to and from locations that are hundreds of kilometers inland. This will become easier as China develops its road and rail infrastructure throughout the country. China has invested

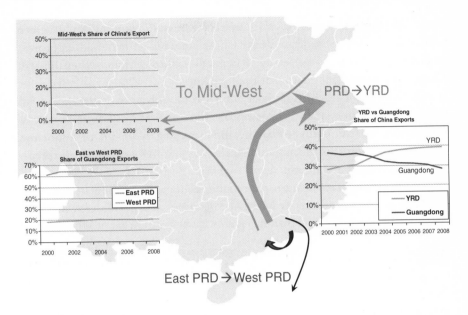

Source: Dr. Jonathan Beard—GHK Consulting

Figure 2.1   Manufacturing Migration

approximately 9 percent of its GDP in road and rail infrastructure using a unique combination of public and private investment dollars. Its national expressway development focuses on connectivity between the three key areas of Beijing, Shanghai and the Pearl River Delta. According to the FHDOT study, "China is building a transportation network in 10 years comparable to what the United States did in 50 years, and it is doing so by learning lessons from more developed countries."[3]

The majority of freight in China today moves by truck and barge; however, the trucking industry is extremely fragmented. It is estimated that there are over two million registered trucking companies in China today, with an average of 2.4 trucks for each company. These are family-owned, owner-operator businesses, with very little tracking technology (many simply use cell phones), and no reliable roadside support. This represents a major area of opportunity for LSPs willing to make the investment.

China's rail infrastructure is also developing at a vigorous pace.[4] The country's last five-year plan (2006–10) called for 17,000 kilometers of new rail lines. The plan also called for six new transportation hubs, 18 intermodal yards, 40 container-handling stations, 150 intermodal substations, and one million kilometers of rural roadway. China's goal is to have "all cities with more than one million people and 90 percent of cities with more than 200,000 people connected to the national road network."[5]

China's Ministry of Transport and Communication (responsible for highways, ports and inland waterways) estimates that by 2025 the expressway network in China will be 85,000 kilometers long, with seven expressways out of Beijing, nine north-to-south expressways and 18 east-to-west expressways, which the government refers to as the 7-9-18 plan.

China's port infrastructure also continues to grow at a breakneck pace. Of the 30 top container ports in the world today, nine are located in China (including Hong Kong as shown in Figures 2.2 and 2.3). Three of the top four

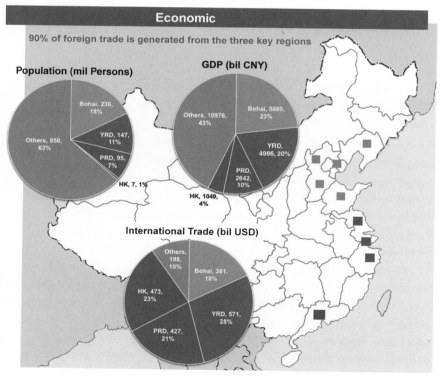

Source: Recreated by Margaret Li from original slide provided courtesy of GHK

Figure 2.2　Key China Economic Regions

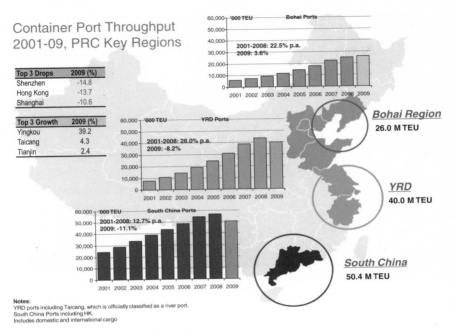

Source: Dr. Jonathan Beard—GHK Consulting

Figure 2.3   China Container Throughput

container ports globally are located in China and in 2010 Shanghai surpassed Singapore as the world's number one container port in terms of throughput.

In addition to ocean port development, China plans to build 97 new airports over the next 12 years according to the General Administration of Civil Aviation of China. That will bring the total number of airports in China from 192 in 2010, up to 244 airports by 2020.[6] By far the crown jewel of mainland airports is China's new Beijing Capital International Airport, which opened Terminal 3 just prior to the 2008 Beijing Olympic Games. Terminal 3 is the largest building in the world at 14 million square feet, and cost over US$3 billion to build.[7]

China's airport infrastructure development plan will cost US$64 billion and will put a vast amount of the population within a 90-minute drive to an airport by 2020. North China will have 54 airports, East China 49, South and Central China 39, Southwest China will have 52, and Northwest China will have 50 airports. This is in line with China's population development.

Source: Angelo Cavalli, Getty Images

Beijing's New Capital International Airport

China is intent on developing the country's infrastructure in a big way, and in a relatively short period of time. Thus far China has not been shy about spending the money to do it. As a comparison, the first U.S. stimulus package set aside US$48 billion for U.S. infrastructure projects, and US$27 billion of that was earmarked specifically for roads. China on the other hand, spent over US$84 billion on highway infrastructure in 2006 alone.[8] China is now setting the example for infrastructure development around the world and other countries are taking notice. After studying China the FHDOT report concluded that, "For the United States to remain competitive globally it needs to invest in transportation infrastructure, apply new systems and technologies, and consider institutional change in how it identifies, funds, operates and makes infrastructure improvements to key elements of the national transportation system."[9] In short, China's infrastructure is developing at an incredible pace, and the West is taking notice, China's infrastructure and development will facilitate the creation of more sophisticated logistics and transportation networks in the years ahead.

WHY HONG KONG IS SO IMPORTANT

Hong Kong has long been considered the gateway to China. Historically, Hong Kong was the place to go if a company wanted to do business with the mainland, but lacked the direct relationships and local expertise to get it done. Hong Kong was the ultimate middleman, facilitating product sourcing, manufacturing and transportation from the mainland on behalf of international customers. Hong Kong-owned factories and trading companies based in China generated incredible wealth for many Hong Kong businessmen. With all the attention surrounding the liberalization and development of mainland China, and the disintermediation of Hong Kong's middleman function, some have questioned whether or not the SAR will continue to play such a crucial role in the transportation industry in the years ahead. The educated answer to this question is that it most certainly will.

For all the improvements in China's infrastructure, work force and skill level over the years, many challenges remain. Hong Kong is still the best gateway to China for those who do not have direct access or expertise in dealing with the mainland. Twelve hundred and fifty two companies have their regional headquarters in the Hong Kong Special Administrative Region (SAR) and 2,328 companies have regional offices based in the city. Hong Kong's proximity to China's manufacturing base in the Pearl River Delta makes it an attractive alternative for companies wishing to avoid having to navigate the complexity of the mainland environment alone. In addition, Hong Kong offers the third lowest tax rate in the world, with a 16.5-percent corporate tax level and a maximum 15-percent personal income tax rate. In addition Hong Kong has no sales tax and no capital gains tax, making the SAR a very attractive place to live and work.

Hong Kong's ocean cargo terminals and airport facility infrastructure are state of the art. In 2008, Hong Kong's Chek Lap Kok Airport handled 3.7 million tons of airfreight and 47 million passengers. Ninety airlines operate over 5,700 flights a week to more than 150 destinations. Forty of those destinations are in China.[10] Hong Kong's ocean cargo terminals handled approximately 24.5 million TEUs (20-foot equivalent units) in 2008 and its cargo terminals remain among the most efficient port operations in the world.

For its part, the Hong Kong government considers transportation and logistics to be one of the four economic pillars of the SAR, placing a high level of priority on policies and initiatives that promote the industry.

Source: Allan Baxter, Getty Images

Hong Kong's Skyline at Night

Several facets of Hong Kong's logistics infrastructure make it particularly attractive for international business. Hong Kong is a free port, which enables maximum international freight operations with minimal customs intervention. Products can be imported from China and combined with products from other countries for re-export without the process complexity associated with China's bonded logistics parks. Value added services such as kitting and light assembly can also be performed without bureaucratic interference. Because of these attributes, Hong Kong is a perfect location for regional and international distribution centers, especially for the onward distribution of products into China.

There are numerous areas of opportunity for Hong Kong in the years ahead with regard to transportation and logistics in China. Hong Kong's logistics talent and industry best practice expertise will be in greater demand to assist China in the development of its own domestic network. The ability for Hong Kong-based logistics and transportation companies to partner with Chinese industry players creates the potential for service expansion and business growth beyond the SAR.

Source: Modern Terminals Limited

Modern Terminals Limited Hong Kong

The Closer Economic Partnership Arrangement (CEPA) between Hong Kong and China is a free trade agreement that was signed in June of 2003 and designed to help facilitate business between the SAR and the mainland. CEPA provides qualified Hong Kong companies with preferential access to the Chinese market. The areas of focus for CEPA include trade in goods, trade in services, and investment facilitation. In 2006, CEPA III was launched. This upgrade to the original agreement effectively allows approved products that originate in Hong Kong to be imported into China at zero tariff. Under CEPA, Hong Kong-registered freight forwarders that meet CEPA requirements are allowed to operate in China on a wholly owned basis (as opposed to a joint venture with a Chinese firm) with the same registered capital requirements as that of mainland freight forwarders.[11]

Besides its world class infrastructure, Hong Kong offers international companies a business environment that includes the rule of law, the free flow of capital, a preferential tax structure, open global connectivity, and an English-speaking, business-friendly community that prides itself on efficiency.

Hong Kong has a long and distinguished history in transportation and logistics and with the rise of China its future role in the industry will continue to evolve, not disappear. Hong Kong will differentiate itself in new ways,

Source: HKIA

Hong Kong's Chek Lap Kok Airport

focusing on supply chain innovation, logistics talent development, IT systems development, and new product distribution models in cooperation with mainland firms. In the years ahead, Hong Kong will remain not only relevant; it will be formidable as a center for supply chain innovation and thought leadership in the Asia Pacific region.

NOTES

1   "Freight Mobility and Intermodal Connectivity in China," US Department of Transportation and Federal Highway Administration (USDTFHA), (May 2008).
2   "China's Macroeconomic Development, Exchange Rate Policy and Global Imbalances," *Asahi Shimbun*, October 2005, 2-3.
3   USDTFHA, 11.
4   "Technical Assistance to the People's Republic of China for Preparing the Railway Development Project," Asian Development Bank, (September 2005).

5   Ibid., 14.
6   Dingding Xin, "China to Add 97 Airports in 12 Years," *China Daily*, August 2009.
7   Matt Vella, "China's Staggering New Airport," *BusinessWeek*, February 2008.
8   USDTFHA.
9   Ibid., 5.
10 "Hong Kong Industry Profiles: Air Transport, and Sea Transport," Hong Kong Trade
    Development Council, http://www.hktdc.com/info/mi/a/hkip/en/1X0018JT/1/Hong-
    Kong-Industry-Profiles/Air-Transport.htm.
11 "Invest HK, Gateway to Mainland China, Closer Economic Partnership Arrange-
    ment," The Government of the Hong Kong Special Administrative Region, http://
    www.investhk.gov.hk/default_bodies/whyhk/en_gateway.html.

CHAPTER THREE

THE DEVELOPMENT OF CHINA'S HUMAN CAPITAL

PETER LEVESQUE

The Chinese workforce has undergone considerable change over the past several years. As the country's urban areas continue to prosper, attracting rural migrant workers, the government's efforts to maintain "social harmony" have become more challenging. Whereas 85 percent of China's population worked in agriculture in 1950, that number has fallen to approximately 50 percent today.[1] A mass migration of farmers from China's hinterland continues to move east into the mega cities, in search of higher wages.

Just prior to the onset of the global financial crisis the Chinese government imposed new labor laws that had a significant impact on South China factory costs. There is now a maximum 36-hour a month overtime law, which equates to 1.8 hours per person of overtime per day. This, coupled with a mandatory five-day workweek, adds a great deal of cost pressure to factories already struggling to deliver products on razor thin margins. In addition, a new open-term worker contract clause has been established, which mandates that employees who have worked for a factory for 10 consecutive years, or two consecutive contract periods, are entitled to lifetime employment with that factory. This has resulted in cases where employers, looking for ways to circumvent the new law, are letting people go after nine years and then hiring them back on a new contract.

In 2008, just prior to the global recession, the Pearl River Delta factory employees saw a minimum wage increase of approximately 17 percent as factory owners attempted to provide incentives to migrant workers, who are typically from northwestern provinces, from moving to other job markets. The combination of labor law changes and factory cost increases, together with the global economic downturn, created a perfect storm in South China towards the end of 2008 resulting in an unprecedented number of factory closings. The resulting backlash from migrant workers has been equally unprecedented. According to Xinhua News Agency, China accepted 693,000 labor disputes in 2008 involving more than 1.2 million workers, a 98-percent increase in worker claims over 2007.[2]

As the global economy now recovers, factory owners find themselves paying migrant workers incentive bonuses and providing other benefits to attract workers back to South China for production jobs. Recently, migrant labor strikes have developed in major manufacturing plants such as Honda. In a more serious situation, migrant workers began committing suicide at the Foxconn factory in South China, which manufactures for brands such as Apple. These labor protests are now forcing factory owners in China to either implement large percentage pay increases for staff, or move manufacturing altogether to lower wage areas.

Migrant labor is just part of China's human capital dilemma today as the country's educated work force also struggles to find meaningful employment. The *Financial Times* reported that of China's 6.1 million recent graduates 50 percent cannot find work and over 1.5 million graduates from last year are still looking.[3] The sheer size of the annual graduating population is impressive given the fact that there were only 850,000 graduates being produced just a decade ago.[4] China realizes that it will need a higher educated work force to compete, but the competition for good jobs after graduation is intense. Family relationships and *guanxi* (personal connections) still play an important role in landing a good job.

Chinese statistics on education can be difficult to substantiate and often require additional clarification. It has been reported, for example, that China is graduating 600,000 engineers every year while the United States is only graduating 70,000 per year. When these numbers are examined more closely, however, it is discovered that in China graduates of automobile mechanic schools and appliance repair schools, for example, fall under the Chinese definition of an engineer. Without getting into a numbers debate on engineering graduates, suffice it to say that China will continue to focus on higher education as part of its national strategy and the traditional Chinese classroom that emphasizes memorization and discourages independent thought, will eventually shift toward embracing debate, inquiry, and personal creativity.

To a certain extent this shift is already taking place via the reverse brain drain phenomena. Chinese students, who used to go overseas to study in a Western style educational setting used to then remain in the West after graduation for their working career. Today many Chinese still travel overseas to receive a western-style education but they are now returning home after graduation to help build their country.

One of the key human resource issues for international companies doing business in China will be convincing managers and engineers to move away from the mega cities and into the hinterland. Because social security and pension payments are managed by each municipality in China, those benefits do not transfer with workers when they relocate. Hiring good managers and engineers who are already living in the hinterland can be a major challenge.[5] Resolving this talent location dilemma is where the concept of business process outsourcing (BPO) in China will play such a critical role.

BUSINESS PROCESS OUTSOURCING (BPO) IN CHINA

Daniel Pink, author of *A Whole New Mind—Why Right Brainers Will Rule the Future,* observes that business process outsourcing (BPO) is now expanding into the realm of the white-collar worker. For many years the trend was for companies to outsource basic data entry and call center support services to places like India. A Forrester Research study concluded that at least 3.3 million white-collar jobs and US$136 billion in wages will shift from the United States to low-cost countries like India, Russia and China by 2015.[6]

As an example, an increasing number of U.S. tax returns are being completed by outsourced accountants in India. One estimate is that by 2011 approximately 1.6 million U.S. tax returns will be completed overseas.[7] In fact, during the recent financial crisis Morgan Stanley completed a loan-by-loan analysis of Fannie Mae and Freddie Mac's mortgage portfolios using 1,300 people based in Morgan Stanley's Analytic Center in India.[8] In addition,

U.S. legal research is now being done by overseas paralegals, and some hospitals in the United States are even having their CAT scans read by radiologists in lower cost countries. Given the availability of a young college-educated workforce, China is fertile ground for the development of the BPO service industry.

Tom Reilly is Chief Executive Officer of Next Horizon, a pioneering business process outsourcing company based in Guangzhou, China. Next Horizon's leadership team is on the forefront of building work force solutions for international firms in China.

Reilly says that the term "outsourcing" generates many different connotations depending on the perspective of the listener. In fact, there are several variations of outsourcing beyond traditional manufacturing applications. The "Enterprise Services Outsourcing Tree" in Figure 3.1 breaks down the various components of the generic term.

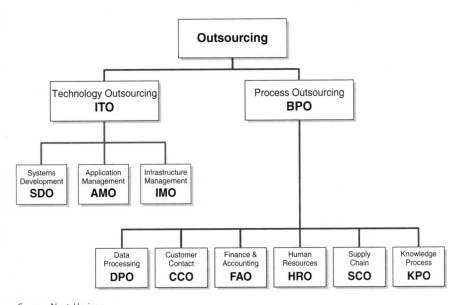

Source: Next Horizon

Figure 3.1   The Enterprise Services Outsourcing Tree

For many corporations the first experience with outsourcing came during the Y2K crisis, when highly trained computer programmers in India became an attractive alternative for preventing worldwide systems failure. This trend for BPO in India exploded, and eventually expanded to software development, technical support centers and customer service call centers. People buying computers in the United States were suddenly calling help desks in Bangalore for technical advice and software installation.

Next Horizon has been able to capitalize on the excess capacity of higher skill sets in the newly trained Chinese work force, as shown in Figure 3.2, to build BPO outsourcing capability in China. In addition, Next Horizon has been able to broaden the scope of traditional BPO offerings into areas such as human resources, finance, equity research, and supply chain management services. China's focus on education and its backlog of newly trained graduates provides Next Horizon with access to an enormous talent pool. For companies that utilize these types of services, the issues of high turnover in China, talent recruiting, and staff training are alleviated, allowing an organization to focus on its core business while achieving measurable savings.

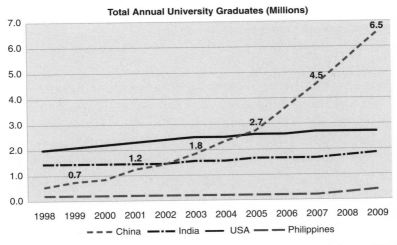

Source: Created by Margaret Li, based on data from UNESCO, BBC, and National Bureau of Statistics of China[9]

Figure 3.2   Comparison of Annual Graduates by Country

Source: Next Horizon

A Data Management Center in Guangzhou China

As is often the case, when China focuses its resources and attention on a particular area, things happen quickly. Over the last 18 months China has turned its attention to dominating the world's services market as announced by Hu Jin Tao during a series of meetings leading up to the recent annual congress of the CPPCC. China's goal is to generate one hundred million service sector jobs by creating 10 outsourcing cities that will provide support for one thousand world class outsourcing firms. While 60 percent of all offshore call center business is in the Philipines today due to its cost advantage and English speaking capability, China will surely become a formidable competitor in this space with the Government's focus and support.

A.T. Kearney collects data on the relative attractiveness of outsourcing locations around the world. Figures 3.3 and 3.4 show the world's most popular offshore destinations by workforce quality and availability in both 2004 and

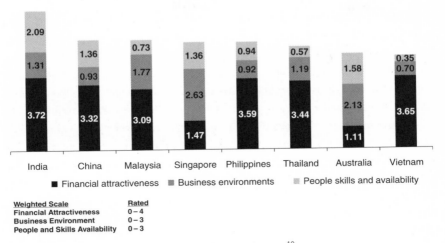

Weighted Scale   Rated
Financial Attractiveness   0 – 4
Business Environment   0 – 3
People and Skills Availability   0 – 3

Source: Created by Margaret Li, based on data from A.T. Kearney[10]

Figure 3.3   Attractiveness of Outsourcing Destinations 2004

2009. Other factors in the attractiveness ranking include stability of the business environment, and the overall cost base of the country. Looking at the data from 2004 it is clear that India held a wide margin in the attractiveness rankings, well ahead of China and Malaysia, particularly in the category of people, skills and availability.

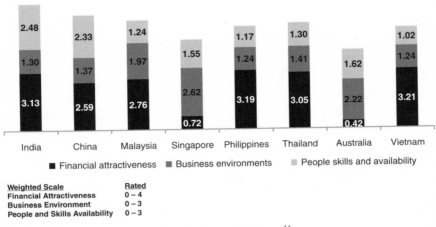

Weighted Scale   Rated
Financial Attractiveness   0 – 4
Business Environment   0 – 3
People and Skills Availability   0 – 3

Source: Created by Margaret Li, based on data from A.T. Kearney[11]

Figure 3.4   Attractiveness of Outsourcing Destinations 2009

Looking at these same data points five years later in 2009, we can see China gaining ground with regard to its attractiveness as an outsourcing destination. China also improved in the categories of people and skills availability as well as in the business environment category. The Chinese Government understands the potential value of the offshoring industry in China, which will most likely lead to greater support and significant growth for this industry in the years to come.

More important than the physical location of BPO solutions is the quality of the BPO company providing the services. The adaptability of the BPO service provider plays an important role in the overall success of an outsourced solution, particularly in China. Understanding the cultural nuances of doing business in the mainland and tailoring services around the specific needs of the client are important factors that need to be considered when choosing a BPO service provider. As international entrepreneurs like Tom Reilly bring their BPO expertise into the Chinese market, global clients will be able to achieve Western business standards from their outsourced solution providers at reasonable salary levels, as shown in Figure 3.5.

In the area of supply chain management, the opportunity for BPO solutions in China is widespread, mainly due to the availability of a well-trained pool of logistics expertise. Tom Reilly notes "as we ramped up operations for a leading logistics company we were inundated with over one thousand resumes of candidates trained in ocean freight, airfreight and supply chain management

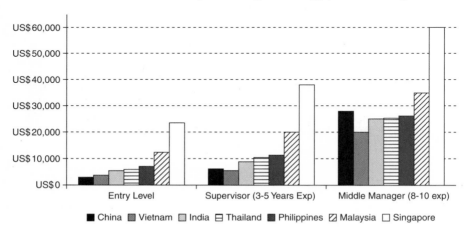

Source: Next Horizon

Figure 3.5   Average Base Salary for Outsourcing Staff

support services. Our entry-level positions were filled with multi-lingual candidates trained in logistics and foreign trade by local universities." It is this access to qualified, outsourced talent that has driven many international firms such as Johnson & Johnson, Motorola, Deutsche Bank and LG Philips to sign deals for Chinese BPO solutions.

The development of China's national infrastructure and human capital will create new opportunities and new challenges for both international companies and LSPs. A strategy of selling products back into China will be more easily facilitated as the hinterland becomes more accessible and the education level and purchasing power of the Chinese population increases.

The upside potential for innovative logistics companies willing to invest in the development of Chinese national networks is significant. Both retailers and LSPs, however, will need to deal with the downside risk of a population on the move. Changes in labor laws, customs regulations, and the inevitable cost increases that accompany a rapidly growing economy, need to be factored into any reasonable Chinese strategy. The utilization BPO companies in China can help mitigate risk associated with high turnover, labor migration, and cost containment, while maintaining a level of performance that exceeds the customer's expectations.

NOTES

1   Martin Jacques, *When China Rules the World*, 104.
2   Xinhua News Agency, "China's Labor Dispute Cases Double in 2008", May 9, 2009, http:www.China.org.cn.
3   Jamil Anderlini, "Rule of the Iron Rooster," *Financial Times*, August 25, 2009, 5.
4   Cong Cao, China's College Graduate Employment Statistics (July 28, 2009): http:www.Globilization101.org.
5   Guo Xin, "The Changing Demographics of the Workforce in China" (October 26, 2006): http:www.mercer.com.
6   John C. McCarthy, with Amy Dash, Heather Liddell, Christine Ferusi Ross, and Bruce D. Temkin, "3.3 Million U.S. Jobs to Go Offshore," Forrester Research Brief (November 11, 2002).
7   "Offshoring Tax Returns Preparation to India," Value Notes Sourcing Practice (November 2006): http://www.sourcingnotes.com/content/view/197/54/.
8   Andrew R. Sorkin, *Too Big To Fail: The Inside Story of How Wall Street and Washington Fought to Save the Financial System—and Themselves,* (New York: Viking Penguin 2009), 222.

9 UNESCO: http://www.unesco.org/new/en/unesco/ BBC: http://www.bbc.com National Bureau of Statistics of China: http://www.stats.gov.cn/english/.

10 "A.T. Kearny's 2004 Offshore Location Attractiveness Index, Making Offshore Decisions." A.T. Kearney (2004): http://kdi.mscmalaysia.my/static/reports/AT%20Kearney%202004%20Report.pdf.

11 Norbert Jorek, Johan Gott, Michelle Battat, "The Shifting Geography of Offshoring, The 2009 A.T. Kearney Global Services Location Index," A.T. Kearney (2009): http://www.atkearney.com/images/global/pdf/Global_Services_Location_Index_2009.pdf.

THE CHANGING FACE OF CONSUMER RETAIL

CHAPTER FOUR

THE AGE OF CONSUMER PARTICIPATION

PETER LEVESQUE

Daniel Pink's insightful book, *A Whole New Mind, Why Right Brainers Will Rule the Future,* explains that after years of extraordinary prosperity, the United States has in many ways become a society of overabundance, in what has been termed America's "affluenza."[1] Simply put, many people just have too much stuff. Pink cites the explosive growth of the self-storage industry as evidence of this over-

> **Shipping Point:**
> "Consumer participation and social networking are becoming embedded in the consumer retail experience."

abundance. The self-storage business in the United States is a US$23 billion industry today, with over 52,000 storage locations across the country.[2] This entire industry was created to support a society that has too much stuff, and no place to put it all.

Pink argues that in this society of overabundance, people have now become bored with having more than enough. As a result, people now search for meaning in their lives, in their work, and in what they purchase. Pink says that for today's consumer, "it is no longer enough to create a product that is reasonably priced and adequately functional. It must also be beautiful, unique and meaningful."[3]

Along with people's search for meaning in the things they buy, there is now increasing demand by consumers to be part of the design and functionality of the products they purchase. We call this activity "consumer-enabled design." As consumer participation and social networking become imbedded in the retail experience, the global supply chain will need to fundamentally change in order to support a more dynamic, modular menu of services, tailored to international markets of one.

Eric von Hippel of MIT has written extensively on the subject of "democratizing innovation." He explains how traditional manufacturer-centric innovation and design is being turned on its ear by end users, who create products that they want, rather than letting manufacturers make that decision for them. Von Hippel acknowledges that the switch to an open innovation process is in many ways disruptive and that "many firms and industries must make fundamental changes to long-held business models in order to adapt."[4] Significant enhancements to the traditional retail supply chain process will be required in order to meet this shift in consumer purchasing behavior.

THE RIGHT-BRAIN SUPPLY CHAIN

For all the left-brain analysis and computation that surrounds SCM today, it will be right-brain-based creativity and collaboration skills that will be critical in supporting the retail supply chain of the future. Consumer-enabled design and the democratization of innovation will require more flexible, complex and modular supply chain processes that can not only react, but also anticipate market nuances and demand fluctuations. In their book, *Competing in a Flat World,* Victor and William Fung explain that in the future "the best supply chain for each given order will be created individually, based on the order itself."[5] Clearly, this will have an impact on how LSPs and their customers build supply chain competency, and how they structure and staff their businesses in the years ahead.

Logistics and transportation companies will need to focus on hiring and retaining more right-brain logisticians that can recognize patterns, and anticipate the changing needs of the customer at every point along the chain. As Daniel Pink notes, "what is in greatest demand today isn't analysis, but synthesis—seeing the big picture, crossing boundaries, and being able to combine disparate pieces into an arresting new whole."[6] Interaction between participants in the new supply chain will need to progress beyond the transactional work model, toward a more comprehensive and empowered level of engagement. Let's look at some examples of where consumer-enabled design and social networking have manifested themselves in consumer retail today, and how the traditional supply chain model has been enhanced to meet the requirements of these new retail strategies.

ZARA

Founded by Amancio Ortega in 1975, Zara is part of the Inditex group of companies and one of the most successful retailers in the international marketplace today. Zara's business is built around a dynamic supply chain model capable of applying fast, flexible manufacturing and distribution to meet rapidly changing consumer preferences in fashion design. Zara calls this concept "continuous design" and their strategy is to have clothes with short shelf lives, with 75 percent of store merchandise turning over in a three- to four-week time frame.[7]

Zara customers know that the store styles will constantly change, which creates increased store traffic and a sense of urgency with regard to Zara purchases. Customers know that if they like something they see in a Zara store they had better purchase it soon, because it will probably not remain in the store for long. In addition, Zara clothes have a built-in obsolescence with regard to quality, as garments are designed to be worn approximately 10 times.

Source: Peter Levesque

Zara Store During Chinese New Year

Zara spends comparatively little money on advertising and instead uses the store as its primary advertising mechanism. Zara's marketing expenditures average 0.3 percent of revenue compared with competitors who typically spend 3–4 percent of revenues on marketing. In addition, Zara is able to limit its discounting to 15–20 percent of sales with an average discount of 15 percent. This, compared with their European competitors who typically sell 30–40 percent of clothes during sale events, with an average discount of 30 percent.[8]

While many fashion retailers focus on setting the trend, Zara focuses on quickly replicating the trend. New merchandise typically hits Zara stores 15 days after being designed, compared to the typical seasonal retailer whose design-to-store process can take several months. Zara's supply chain is able to take advantage of rapid changes in design to gain market share. Shorter lead times from idea generation to the store shelf, along with smaller quantities per style (intentional scarcity of supply) and more styles per year (11,000–12,000 styles per year), are unique factors that require a very dynamic and flexible supply chain model.

Zara can run this type of operation because they are vertically integrated with a majority of their cutting and dying processes being done in Europe, close to their head office in La Cauruna, Spain and inside Zara-owned or -controlled facilities. By sourcing greige material (fabric not yet colored), Zara has the flexibility to create the color for a garment that best fits with real-time customer preferences. The more labor-intensive stitching is typically done by a network of smaller factories in Galicia and Portugal.[9] The end result is that Zara has very little inventory in its supply chain as garments are made to meet immediate demand and shipped through Zara's DC to their retail stores as soon as possible.[10] The social networking aspect of Zara includes the ability of sales people and store managers to talk directly with customers about what the latest trends are, and then communicate that information to Zara product managers in the field for immediate consideration. Zara's innovative supply chain has been successfully designed to meet the high-speed, demand-driven requirements of their unique retail fashion business model.

RYZ FOOTWEAR MODEL

RYZ Footwear of Portland, Oregon was launched in June of 2008. The company was founded by Robert Flagstaff, formerly president of Adidas in the Americas. RYZ originally provided its online subscriber community with downloadable desktop design software, which allowed them to create their own sneaker designs. RYZ then held periodic design contests with its subscriber community who would vote on the best design. This encouraged what Flagstaff calls "viral marketing" since there was built-in incentive for designers to get friends and family to vote for their design, and to hopefully create sales demand for their particular shoe in the process.

The winning designer was awarded US$1,000 and a US$1 royalty on shoes sold online. Each pair of shoes came with a biography of the designer. RYZ's website explained that, "Unlike the fashionista elite who dictate the latest style, RYZ gives power to the people." CEVA Logistics helped RYZ to develop a unique supply chain program that would allow small lots of sneaker runs to be manufactured in China and rapidly shipped to RYZ's online consumers, based on actual sales demand. The immediacy of consumer design participation and the tailor-made aspect of the business model required a more flexible and dynamic supply chain solution compared with the traditional retail footwear sales channel.

A key feature of RYZ's unique business model was the social networking and design contest features of their consumer-enabled design business. The company was tapping into a new retail trend called "crowdsourcing," where online clusters of consumers come together online to design products and then

Source: RYZ Footwear

RYZ Footwear's Interactive Design Website

determine which ones will sell in the market. This model creates several new cost benefits to retailers since a by-product of the design process is that it eliminates the need for expensive research and development as well as marketing research dollars.[11]

Behind the scenes RYZ needed to be able to go from design to production to shipping in a very short period of time. The supply chain timeline from production to shipping was condensed to a fraction of what a new style launch would look like for a traditional footwear company (approximately five months for RYZ compared to 11-18 months for traditional brands). Rethinking any retail business model involves rethinking the supply chain that supports it. RYZ's customers may have been physically located in the United States, but the material for production and the location of the factory doing the manufacturing were 10,000 miles away in China. Getting the finished shoe into the hands of the end consumer had to be both feasible, and cost efficient in order for the consumer-enabled design model to be successful. RYZ has since modified its original business model to focus on design-driven men's footwear, and as the company has evolved so have its

Source: Threadless.com

Threadless.com Interactive Website

designs and product offerings. The original RYZ business model was similar to the wildly successful Chicago-based t-shirt design company called Threadless .com, which was started by two college drop-outs in 2000.

The community-based Threadless.com is still privately held and in 2007 sales were estimated at US$30 million. The company has contests that offer US$2,000 to a winning design, US$500 for each design reprint, and up to US$22,500 if the design wins a "Bestee" during the Threadless Awards, a contest the company conducts to reward the most popular design submissions.

GILT.COM AND GROUPON.COM

Two more excellent examples of where consumer retail is going can be found at Gilt.com and Groupon.com. Gilt.com is a members-only luxury and fashion accessory site that offers advance samples for sale to its membership online at 50 percent to 70 percent off. Sale items are posted by Gilt to its membership daily and sales last 36 hours. Once purchased the member can choose UPS next-day delivery (if ordered before 1 pm) or regular UPS ground service. Gilt strives to process and ship all orders within 2–5 business days if the inventory is in stock and 2–3 weeks if the product is on back order. Members know that purchasing from Gilt is on a first-come first-served basis and items will only remain in a member's shopping cart for 10 minutes before being returned to inventory. The incentive for Gilt members is to log onto the site early and buy quickly to avoid missing the deal. The Gilt site includes speciality sections for men (Gilt Man), women, children, home decor, entertainment and travel (Jetsetter). The company, which is based in New York City, was founded by Alexis Maybank, Alexandra Wilkis Wilson and Kevin Ryan in November of 2007.

Groupon.com is another interesting concept. Founded by Andrew Mason, the site uses collective buying power to generate volume discounts for its membership. Members receive the deal of the day by email and then they have the option whether or not to participate. Each deal has a tipping point which requires a certain number of members to participate or buy in to trigger the discount. Groupon, for example, might offer a $50.00 dollar pair of shoes from a retailer for a $25.00 discount. The deal may require that 100 members agree to buy the offer in order to activate the discount. Once the deal is triggered the member's credit cards are charged and members receive a redemption coupon that they bring to the retailer in order to collect the shoes. Groupon is able to offer retailers guaranteed customers in return for an attractive discount for its members.

Online retailing has many attributes and advantages for those who can adapt to the speed and service requirements that the customer demands. Today it's not just mass-market retailers that are taking their businesses online: luxury brands like Gucci, Chanel and Fendi are also testing the waters. British designer Henry Holland recently created a game-changing business model whereby he enabled his customers to purchase his new t-shirt line directly from the London Fashion Week catwalk using Blackberry technology. This idea reduced the lead time of product availability from six months to "immediately."[12]

Victor and William Fung explain this trend in consumer instant gratification, noting that "empowered end consumers now expect the mass customization

Source: V-Logic Limited

V-Logic's Marketing Campaign

and instantaneous response of the internet for products from customized computers to designer jeans. They know what they want, they want it exactly, and they want it now."[13] V-Logic Limited, a 3PL based in Hong Kong, highlighted the difficulty of servicing more demanding customers in one of its original ad campaigns shown on page 44.

BEST BUY

Some traditional retailers are having success in discovering innovative ways to improve store sales, increase employee satisfaction and retention, and generate new product offerings through social networking media applications. American retailer Best Buy is one such company on the forefront of connecting employees and consumer sentiment through this medium.

The Minnesota-based retailer has evolved from a product distribution and service company into a place where customers can find solutions. In 2003, Best Buy CEO Brad Anderson launched a "customer-centric strategy" that shifted attention from a one-size-fits-all service mentality to really understanding the unique requirements of each customer.[14] Anderson realized that customers were demanding more service and support and therefore focused employees on meeting customers' individual needs. In 2006, Best Buy also found an innovative way of putting both the voice of the customer and the employee into the DNA of the company. Blue Shirt Nation is a corporate-sponsored social networking site developed by Gary Koelling and Steve Bendt, two of Best Buy's advertising people. The site offers employees the opportunity to solve retail store issues by sharing ideas and experience. It enables the free flow of ideas from all levels of the organization right down to the sales floor, and provides keen insight into what Best Buy's customers are saying about product selection and store experience. The site has 25,000 regular users. Best Buy's retail employee turnover can be as high as 50 percent, however, the turnover for those employees using Blue Shirt Nation is reportedly by between 8–12 percent.[15]

CHINA AND THE INTERNET

The impact of the internet on design and social networking is taking off in China as well. The *Financial Times* quoted McKinsey's Yuval Atsmon as saying that "consumers are increasingly using blogs and other user-generated consumer reporting when deciding what to buy. In an environment where word of mouth is more trusted than advertising, internet marketing is moving from an opportunity to a critical necessity."[16] The importance of marketing toward people whose opinions are widely read online in China will be important says the *Financial Times*. What is important to understand is that China is not copying the West when it comes to the internet. Like the rest of China's development, the internet is growing in a uniquely Chinese way. There are approximately 384 million internet users in China (more than one fifth of internet users globally). Chinese sites such as internet-sourcing platform Alibaba.com (now owned by Yahoo) and Google competitor Baidu.com have drawn a loyal following in China where approximately 63 percent of users are under the age of 29.[17] Internet use is also spreading beyond the major port cities and into the hinterland where the poorest of China's population is located. Important to the development of Western internet retailing in China will be understanding the cultural nuances of doing business there. Chinese internet consumers, for example, prefer not to type using Latin-based keyboards because translating Chinese characters into Latin-based words during the online ordering process is slow and complicated.[18] Developing web-based retail models that utilize Chinese character data entry and easy-to-use drop-down boxes will make Western-based web retailers more competitive with popular Chinese online competitors.

The convergence of web-based, consumer-enabled design and internet social networking in the retail space creates a business platform for democratized innovation. Retailers, and the LSPs that support them, must be able to execute more sophisticated and flexible supply chain models in order to make the concept of co-creation and crowd-sourcing, together with the physical delivery of the finished product a reality.

There are many advantages to knowing what retail consumers and store employees are thinking and saying about the design and functionality of products being sold. Social networking and consumer-enabled design capability makes this possible. The success or failure of applying these online tools in the retail environment lies in the ability to execute them within a more complex and modular supply chain. Being able to use these tools to adjust product mix in order to meet demand and anticipate changes in consumer preferences will not be an easy task. Getting it done will require a much more collaborative environment between retailer, employee, consumer and LSP, and a more modular approach to SCM in general. LSPs will need to be staffed with more right-brain logistics talent. LSPs will also need to be empowered to monitor the real-time sales environment of their customers in order to make business decisions on the most cost-effective fulfillment process, transport mode, and delivery window to meet the specific requirements of each customer order. In summary, there will be numerous challenges ahead in developing and executing more dynamic and complex retail supply chain solutions, and significant upside potential for those companies which are willing to make it happen.

NOTES

1   John De Graaf, David Wann, Thomas Naylor, *Affluenza, The All Consuming Epidemic*, (San Francisco: Berrett-Koehler Publishers, 2001).

2   Daniel Pink, *A Whole New Mind, Why Right Brainers Will Rule the Future*, (New York: Penguin, 2006), 33; see also http://www.selfstorages.net/storage/guide/self-storage-industry.html and www.selfstorage.org.

3   Ibid., 33

4   Eric von Hippel, "Democratizing innovation: The evolving phenomenon of user innovation" *State-of-the-Art-Artikel* 55 (2005): 63-78; see also *Democratizing Innovation*, (MIT Press, 2005), http://www.MITPress.mit.edu.

5   Victor Fung, William K. Fung, Jerry Yoram, *Competing in a Flat World, Building Enterprises for a Borderless World*, (New Jersey: Wharton School Publishing, 2008), 8.

6   Pink, *A Whole New Mind*, 68.

7   Andrew McAfee, Vincent Dessain, Anders Sjoman, *Zara IT for Fast Fashion* (Boston: Harvard Business School Publishing, 2007), 4.

8   Ibid., 4.

9   Devangshu Dutta, "Retail @ the Speed of Fashion," *Third Eyesight*, (August 2003): http://www.3isite.com.

10 McAfee, *Zara: IT for Fast Fashion*, 6.

11 Jonathan Brinckman, "Portland Startup RYZ uses Consumers," *The Oregonian* June 27, 2007, http://oregonlive.com/business/index.ssf/2008/06/portland_startup_ryz_uses_cons.ht.

12 Fiona Mackay, "In The Palm of Your Hand," *International Herald Tribune* March 9, 2010, 11.

13 Fung et al, *Competing in a Flat World*, 121.

14 Rajiv Lal, Carin-Isabel Knoop, Irina Tarsis, "Best Buy Co., Inc.: Customer–Centricity" (Boston: Harvard Business School Publishing, October 16, 2006): 3, 4.

15 Patrick Thibodeau, "Best Buy Getting Results from Social Network," *IT World*, March 3, 2009, http://www.itworld.com/internet/63621/best-buy-getting-results-social-network.

16   Kathrin Hille, Richard Waters, "A Species Apart," *Financial Times* January 20, 2010, 7.

17   "Statistical Report On Internet Development in China," Ministry of Industry and Information Technology, China Internet Network Information Center (July 2009): 16, http://www.cnnic.net.cn.

18   Hille, "A Species Apart."

CHAPTER FIVE

THE DEVELOPMENT OF CHINA'S RETAIL SECTOR AND BRANDS

PETER LEVESQUE

Shopping malls, once the symbol of abundance and leisure time in America, have gone global. In fact, in the list of the 10 top malls in the world today, only one is located in the United States. The world's largest mall is actually located in Beijing.[1] Walk down any busy city street in China today, and you will see hordes of shoppers bustling in and out of

> **Shipping Point: "We used to build civilizations, now we build shopping malls."**
>
> *Bill Bryson*

stores, malls and retail brand outlets. Victor and William Fung in their book *Competing in a Flat World* note that, "between 1979 and 2006 per capita retail sales in China increased 2,685 percent. Between 2005 and 2010 the Chinese middle class with incomes between US$7,239 and US$60,240 is expected to expand from 5 percent of households today, to 45 percent. In addition, retail sales in China are expected to hit 20 trillion yuan by 2020."[2]

China has become both retail manufacturer and retail consumer, but there are still many issues to deal with as the country evolves. Up until the recent financial crisis, China focused on exports to fuel its economy, In fact China now exports more in a single day than it exported in all of 1978.[3] With the onset of the global financial crisis Beijing began focusing on ways to decrease China's dependency on exports, by growing domestic consumption. The issue for China's retail sector is that most of what China produces for global markets is still carefully regulated from entering its own markets. Cassian Cheung, the former head of Wal-Mart in China writes, "some of the world's best known brands have no distribution in China, in spite of the fact that their products are primarily manufactured there."[4] He notes that because many factories in China are set up in special economic zones, designed for export and commercially licensed for export operations, what those factories produce must be exported out of the country.

Because of these export regulations an entire logistics industry called U-Turn has been created to facilitate the re-importation of some products that are manufactured in, and initially exported from China. U-Turn products are shipped via truck or barge from China to Hong Kong, for example (Hong Kong is a Special Administrative Region and not considered to be mainland China), and then those products are turned around and imported back across the border from Hong Kong into China. Import taxes and duties are collected by China Customs as the products re-enter the mainland.

The U-Turn process is only a band-aid, and does not represent supply chain best practice by any stretch of the imagination, but it does resolve a unique regulatory problem in China by utilizing the supply chain and Hong Kong's status as a Special Administrative Region. The heritage regulatory inefficiencies that created the need for U-turn are slowly improving in China. This will have positive down-the-line implications for global retailers, global brands, and the logistics companies that support them. Selling to the source in China will become easier for Western businesses, brands and retailers in the years ahead.

Despite the ambiguity surrounding Chinese regulations, some international brand retailers and quick-serve restaurant chains have already been successful selling to the source in the Chinese market. Why have some retailers been so successful while others have crashed and burned? Some of the answer lies in understanding the business definition of the PRC. The acronym that PRC is most commonly associated with is the People's Republic of China. However, as successful foreigners doing business in China have discovered, the PRC also represents a kind of golden rule for prosperity in the mainland, whereby the PRC stands for "patience, relationship and cash." Foreign retailers who have been successful in China understand the cultural nuances of doing business there, and they share some key attributes, such as being notably patient in learning to deal with the complexity and ambiguity of China's rules and regulations. In addition, they have invested the time necessary to build local and national business relationships in China to create good will and *guanxi*. In addition these successful foreign retailers all viewed their investment in China as a long-term opportunity rather than as short-term gain. In many ways patience and relationship are the cornerstones of any successful business venture in China, and the foreign retailers who understood these cultural truths early on are now seeing their investments pay off.

Wal-Mart is an excellent example of a foreign retail success story in China. Wal-Mart is one of the largest purchasers of Chinese-made products destined for retail stores in the United States, but by selling to the source the company

Source: Getty Images

Wal-Mart Stores in China

Source: The Eng Koon, Getty Images

A Carrefour Store in China

has been able to significantly change the scale of their international business. Wal-Mart Stores, Inc. now has more than 189 stores in China with over 50,000 employees.[5] Ninety-five percent of products sold in these stores come from Wal-Mart's 20,000+ Chinese suppliers.[6] French retailer Carrefour also purchases a large amount of its products from China for their overseas business and at the same time they sell to the source through their extensive retail-store network in China. On July 9, 2010, Carrefour opened its 138th Chinese store in the city of Kunming.[7]

In January 2009, UK-based retailer Tesco opened its first freehold mall in Qingdao, China and 50,000 customers showed up to help get things started. Tesco plans to open 23 such freehold malls in China, which will add to their expected 82 hypermarkets already serving mainland customers. The freehold malls will include everything from movie theaters to wet markets that sell fresh turtle and stingray. Tesco was estimated to have spent US$801 million expanding their market and their scale in China in 2010.[8]

While China is notorious for copying luxury brand items like Louis Vuitton and Chanel the rapid economic rise of China's middle and upper classes has created an interesting reversal of high-fashion buying behavior. Where bargain shoppers used to cross the border from Hong Kong to Shenzhen China to purchase knock-off handbags on the cheap, today main-land Chinese are crossing the border from Shenzhen into Hong Kong to shop in authentic Louis Vuitton, Fendi and Chanel stores to avoid high China taxes on luxury goods and to make sure they are buying the real thing!

To meet this pent-up demand luxury goods makers are also changing the scale by expanding their presence in China. As an example, New York-based handbag company Coach originally opened a flagship store in Hong Kong and plans to acquire its retail outlets in China, which had previously been operated by regional distributors. The company plans to open 50 new stores in China over the next five years, including another flagship store in Shanghai.[9] But luxury brands are not just making their current line of products available in China; they are tailoring their product offering to meet the specific tastes of the Chinese consumer. French luxury brand Hermes, for example, recently opened a specialty store in Shanghai that features their new Chinese brand called Shang Xia. Instead of just selling Hermes scarves the store contains Chinese furniture and pottery. The French brand Chloe is introducing a Chinese version of its popular Marcie handbag in the color red, which is a color associated with good luck in Chinese culture. In addition, companies like Estée Lauder are developing cosmetic brands suited to the Chinese beauty market.[10]

Source: Peter Levesque

Coach's Flagship Store—Central Hong Kong

Source: Peter Levesque

A New McDonalds in China

Fashion retail and cosmetics are not the only examples of Western success in China. The fast-food retail industry has also made huge strides in the mainland. The industry was worth approximately US$200 billion in 2007, according to China's Ministry of Commerce.[11] McDonalds first opened in China in 1990 and today they have more than 950 restaurants across the mainland and over 60,000 employees.

KFC, which is part of Yum! Brands, opened its first restaurant in 1987 and expects to have more than 2,700 restaurants in China by the end of 2010 (see Figure 5.1). KFC opens new stores at a staggering rate of one per day in China.

Another successful retail restaurant example in China is Starbucks. For many years marketing groups were bearish on coffee brands in the Asia Pacific market because of the widespread cultural preference for tea. Starbucks changed all that. Over the past 12 years Starbucks has opened more than 1,700 stores in the Asia Pacific region, including China. Certainly, there have been bumps in the road. In 2003, Starbucks sued the Chinese brand Xingbake for using the same three Chinese characters as Starbucks (*Xing* meaning "Star" and *bake* similar to "buck"). Xingbake also used a logo that was very similar to the Starbuck's logo. Starbucks won the case in a Chinese court, and Xingbake was ordered to pay a 500,000-yuan fine (US$75,300) and forced to stop using the name and the logo.[12]

Aside from the legal battle associated with Xingbake, however, Starbucks has been an overwhelming success in China. Starbucks signs are ubiquitous

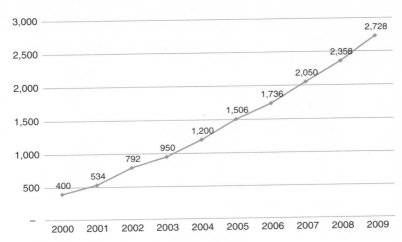

Source: Created by Margaret Li, with data from Yum! Brands

Figure 5.1   Growth Trend of KFC Outlets in China

across the Chinese landscape, an amazing feat inside a country and a culture that was raised on drinking tea.

All of these fast-food retailers require sophisticated domestic distribution networks in order to be successful in China. Restaurant building materials, kitchen equipment, foodstuffs, fresh meats and produce, as well as disposable paper products must all be shipped across a vast geographic footprint of store locations. This type of Western brand expansion creates opportunities for innovative LSPs who want to grow their mainland operational capability and expand their China domestic network.

The mainland's domestic retail brands are also skyrocketing with four of China's own domestic retailers gaining respectable rankings in Deloitte's 2008 Global Powers of Retailing Report:[13]

- Shanghai Bailian—Rank #101
- Gome Electrical Appliances—Rank #218
- Suning Appliance Ltd—Rank #216
- Dalian Dashang Group—Rank #224

Also of the 50 "fastest-growing" retailers from 2001 through 2006, Gome Electrical Appliances was ranked 3rd with a CAGR of 65.8 percent, Suning

Appliance was ranked 7th with a CAGR of 41.1 percent, and Dalian Dashang ranked 11th with a CAGR of 36 percent. Let's look at some examples of this growing domestic retail trend in China.

GOME STORES IN CHINA

Consumer electronics retailer Gome has been called the "Best Buy of China" and has rapidly expanded since its first store opened in Beijing in 1987. By 2005, the chain included 259 stores and four digital stores with revenues of RMB 18 billion (approximately US$2.5 billion). In 2007, the company merged with China Paradise to become the leading retailer in China for household appliances and consumer electronic equipment.

By the end of 2008, Gome's sales network covered 205 cities in China with 859 stores and revenues of RMB 45.9 billion (US$6.6 billion).

The company, which is listed on the Hong Kong stock exchange, hit a roadblock in 2008–09 when its chairman, Huang Guangyu, was forced to resign over corruption and securities violations. Trading was suspended for seven months but the stock soared 150 percent when trading resumed in June 2009 with news that Bain Capital had entered into a refinancing deal with Gome. In a bizarre twist, the former chairman, who was still in police custody, was able to remain active in trading his company shares, increasing his stake in the company from 33.7 percent to 34 percent while in prison.

The issue of corporate governance in China and specifically at Gome is beyond the scope of this book. What is relevant for this discussion is that Gome operates one of the largest domestic retail distribution networks in China with 151 distribution centers throughout the mainland. The retailer offers a customer loyalty program and claims to have 22,000,000 customers in the program. Gome has also constructed numerous call centers to increase customer satisfaction and established 2,376 repair service centers around China. Gome represents a successful domestic sales and distribution model that will surely be an example for other Chinese firms to emulate in the future (the CEO's plight not withstanding). The Gome model offers potential partnership opportunities for Western brands looking for China distribution capability rather than building it from scratch. The Gome model also offers LSPs with a potential blueprint for establishing China distribution networks in the future.

CHINA'S RETAIL AUTOMOBILE MARKET

Well-known brands such as Ford, General Motors, Volkswagen and Toyota all manufacture automobiles in China, but so do China domestic companies such as BYD Changfeng Motor, and Geely—all Chinese domestic brands that you may not have heard of that are doing extremely well. According to the China Association of Automobile Manufacturers (CAAM), in 2008 Chinese automakers manufactured 9.34 million units, up 5.21 percent over 2007, and sales reached 6.76 million units, up 7.27 percent year-on-year. In 2009, as the U.S. automobile industry resorted to the "cash for clunkers" program to sell units, General Motors' sales in China were up 78 percent. As China's expertise in auto manufacturing continues to improve so does their desire to expand their brands into international markets like the United States.

BYD and Changfeng Motors have both expressed interest in the U.S. market, though many experts believe quality and safety standards are still critical issues that will need to be overcome before they are able to gain traction in the United States. BYD (also a leading battery manufacturer) wants to introduce its new F6DM hybrid plug-in car into the U.S. market in three to five years according to BYD chairman, Wang Chuanfu.[14] BYD made global headlines in September 2009 when Warren Buffett took a 10 percent stake in the company for US$230 million. Chinese companies know that every little marketing advantage helps, which might explain the striking resemblance in color and design between BYD's original logo and the more famous BMW logo. BYD has since revamped its logo to a more original design. BYD's tag line is now "Build Your Dreams." The company, recognizing potential confusion with the global brand of Formula One Racing, also rebranded its F1 passenger car model to the F0.[15]

Automobile distribution has several supply chain components beyond the basic delivery of the car, which can be both complex and lucrative. These components include raw material distribution, vendor-managed inventory, parts distribution, reverse logistics, and repair-service logistics. A "Made in China" auto industry that begins exporting units globally, will present a major opportunity for international logistics, companies that can provide integrated Chinese domestic distribution capability, international supply chain expertise, and business access to foreign markets.

For all the retail growth in China, whether its luxury goods, fast food or automobiles, the mainland remains a cash society, with savings rates of approximately 40 percent. Future growth in retail will surely be enhanced by the Chinese government's liberalization of credit to promote consumer spending and to make consumer demand a bigger part of China's economic development.[16] While retailers continue to focus on China's 200 million middle class consumers based in the major coastal cities, the real opportunity to create growth and brand loyalty lies in the hinterland, where the emerging middle class still resides.

While estimates vary on how fast China's rural consumer base will emerge, hinterland development is a priority for the government, and where there is priority in China there is usually opportunity. Initiatives are included for rural market development in China's centralized planning structure. These initiatives seek to build a "new socialist countryside." Also in motion is the government's "Market Project of Thousands of Villages and Townships," which seeks to create a domestic retail network that covers 70 percent of China's villages.[17]

McKinsey & Company estimates that "since 1985 extreme poverty in China has been cut in half and that 62 million, mostly rural, citizens have been lifted above the US$1 per day income threshold."[18] The Chinese government understands full well the growing economic disparity between its rural and urban populations, and gives top priority to maintaining social harmony. As these rural populations evolve into retail markets, the need for transportation and logistics networks to supply retail stores in the hinterland will grow exponentially, creating new markets and new opportunities for logistics service providers willing to make the investment.

There is of course the issue of low personal income levels in China. There will need to be a financial mechanism in place that will allow people in the hinterland to buy products from all the new stores being built around them. The retail financing model that might work in China can actually be found today in Brazil. Brazilian retailer Casas Bahias created the retail-financing model as highlighted in C.K. Prahalad's popular book *The Fortune at the Bottom of the Pyramid*. Prahalad describes how this Brazilian-based retailer has been able to thrive where global retailers have failed.

The key to Casas Bahias' retail success is in its innovative financing model, which specifically caters to Brazil's lower income consumer. Casas Bahias has created a systematic approach to determining a customer's creditworthiness that also includes evaluating the human elements of honesty and sincerity. The company employs 800 credit analysts to handle the 750,000 financing applications that are generated each month. Ninety percent of the store's overall sales are financed. Salespeople at the store provide counseling on how to spend within a budget, and how to improve a low credit score.

Casas Bahias issues creditworthy customers a passbook that allows for an installment payment plan for store purchases. Customers must come back to the store to make their payments, and when they do they become opportunities for the store to cross-sell new products through expanded financing.[19]

What is unique about the Casa Bahias finance model is that it is based on relationship building. This makes it a perfect fit for China, where relationships are paramount and where the culture emphasizes the importance of paying one's debts. The Casa Bahias business model could help unlock China's rural retail market and once unlocked, the need for logistics and distribution capability deeper into the hinterland will create additional opportunities for logistics and transportation service providers.

Wal-Mart is already taking steps to enter the consumer-financing space in China as a complementary service to retailing. Wal-Mart announced a strategic cooperation agreement with Chinese offline payment provider Lakala to "provide financial services to people in 80 cities across China."[20] Wal-Mart will offer daily payment services to its Chinese customers via payment terminals. Since the program started in May 2009, more than 90 stores are already participating in the program with transactions totaling RMB 18 million so far.[21]

The growth of retail in China is a big topic to cover, and the subject matter could easily fill several books on its own. There are a few key points from the chapter, however, that are most critical for our discussion here as it relates to supply chain management. The first key point is that we can expect rapid expansion by Western retailers into the Chinese market over the next 10 years. Some retailers will be patient and build a strong foundation of relationships for long-term success in China; others will crash and burn. The second key point is that as Western retailers expand into China they will require innovative LSPs to provide domestic distribution network capability across the mainland. That will mean new business opportunities for those Western LSPs that are prepared to make the investment. The final take away is that China is creating its own branded retail industry and has its own loyal following of Chinese consumers. These Chinese retail brands will eventually seek international markets outside the mainland, and that will require Western logistics and transportation expertise to bridge the supply chain gap, and to assist Chinese companies with distribution into foreign markets. The next decade will be full of new and exciting opportunities.

China's Consumer Brand Development

Over the years there have been very few internationally recognized Asia Pacific brands. Acer computer from Taiwan, Tiger Balm ointment from Singapore, and Mao-Tai, the strong white liquor from China, are a few of Asia's more notable products. But China has now come full circle, reigniting the creativity and innovation that went dormant with the rise of the West after the 18th century. The Chinese are now actively developing their own popular domestic brands, as they expand their traditional role of original equipment manufacturer (OEM) to include technical innovation, product design and retail brand development.

Some of the most successful domestic Chinese brands are now gaining popularity and market share in the international marketplace. This trend of Chinese product and brand development creates an opportunity for LSPs to engage domestic Chinese manufacturers and provide them with something they desperately need—access and distribution capability into foreign markets. For LSPs, being able to identify these China domestic opportunities in their early stages is critical for building solid business relationships that prosper over time. A quick win approach will not build the cultural foundation necessary for long-term success with these Chinese firms. As in most examples when it comes to business in China, failure of LSPs to invest time and resources in relationship building will likely lead to disappointment. Understanding the cultural nuances of China, and having the patience to invest in relationship building with these firms, could produce lucrative new long-term business opportunities for Western 3PLs and transportation companies. The time to begin identifying these opportunities is right now.

The power of domestic brand building in China cannot be underestimated. The mainland population's pride in all things Chinese means that once loyalty is established for a local brand in China it will be very difficult for a foreign entrant to overcome that loyalty. Let's look at some examples of today's emerging Chinese brands.

Li-Ning logo

LI-NING

You might not be familiar with the logo above but most Chinese consumers know it very well. If it bears a striking resemblance to the Nike swoosh it's probably not an accident. The Li-Ning company was founded in 1990 by

Source: Xinhua News Agency

Li-Ning Lighting the Olympic Flame

China's famous gymnast Li-Ning who won three gold medals, two silver medals and a bronze medal in the 1984 Olympic games in Los Angeles.

If the name Li-Ning still does not sound familiar, you might remember him as the man who flew atop the Birds Nest Stadium at the 2008 Beijing Olympics opening ceremonies to light the Olympic flame. One thing is for sure; the people at Adidas will never forget him. After paying millions of dollars to be an official sponsor for the Olympic games in Beijing, Adidas could only watch in disbelief as Li-Ning, their largest competitor in China, flew his marketing sortie in front of four billion viewers when he lit the famous flame.

Li-Ning the company sells athletic footwear and equipment including its "Flying Armor" basketball shoe and its "Flying Feather" running shoe. The company has 6245 retail stores in China today, and revenues of over US$980 million.[22] Li-Ning also has an additional 672 retail store outlets in China that support their joint venture with French sporting brand Aigle and the Italian sporting brand Lotto.

The company focuses on brand marketing, research and development, design, manufacturing, distribution and retail. Li-Ning competes head-to-head with Nike and Adidas in China, but it has an element of national pride behind its name that foreign brands such as Nike and Adidas find difficult to trump. This Chinese association with the brand helps explain Li-Ning's phenomenal growth over the last several years.[23]

Instead of manufacturing for a major global footwear brand, Li-Ning has become a global brand. Rather than producing to meet another brand's design specifications for export, they are creating their own designs, engineering their own products, and distributing product through their own marketing network. Rather than testing their products in the Chinese market, Li-Ning is itself part of the Chinese culture, and from this position of strength they can aggressively grow and begin to reach beyond China to capture market share globally.

In 2005, Li-Ning signed a strategic partnership with NBA Properties, Inc., the marketing arm of the National Basketball Association,

> Shipping Point:
> "It will be difficult for foreign countries to dislodge Chinese brand loyalty once it has been established."
>
> *Peter Levesque*

and in 2006 Li-Ning signed a five-year deal with Shaquille O'Neal to market the Li-Ning Shaq line of basketball shoes in China (Yao Ming signed with Reebok/Adidas).

Companies like Li-Ning represent a convergence of international supply chain opportunity for LSPs. They are a manufacturer in China, whose primary market is domestic but whose growth potential is international. They require a comprehensive domestic distribution network to maintain their 6,000+ retail stores, but they will eventually require an international distribution model to support global growth. They will likely offer consumer-enabled design capability through their website to supply the Chinese market with "made-to-order" sneakers, which will increase the company's supply chain complexity further and require more sophisticated support services.

HAIER

Many people know the Haier brand but because of the name think it's a German company; similar to the way many people believe Nokia is a Japanese brand (it's Finnish). Haier, which began in 1984, was originally a Chinese collective called the Qingdao Refrigerator Factory. The company partnered with the German-based Liebherr Group to manufacture refrigerators under the brand name Qingdao–Liebherr. The Liebherr Group provided technology and equipment to the new venture, and the refrigerator business took off. In 1993, under the direction of Zhang Ruimin, the factory was re-named Haier after the Chinese pinyin character pronunciation for Liebherr, which is pronounced "libo-haier."

Today, Haier is China's largest home appliance manufacturer and the fourth largest in the world. The company has an annual turnover of US$16 billion and employs more than 50,000 people worldwide. Haier is involved in all aspects of manufacturing, technology research, product design, trade, and finance. Haier has 29 manufacturing facilities making refrigerators, air-conditioners, washing machines, as well as TVs, phones, and computers. They have 64 trading companies, eight design centers, and 15 industrial manufacturing complexes. In addition, the company has a sales network that stretches across 160 countries.

In 2007, Haier obtained 502 invention patents. The company's Client Solution Business specializes in "intelligent appliances, interior design, and medical equipment." In 2008, Haier received Wal-Mart's "Vendor of the Year" award, and later the company became the official HDTV brand of the National Basketball Association.[24] Mr. Ruimin, who spearheaded the rise of Haier, now serves as the company's chairman.

LENOVO

In 1984, Liu Chuanzhi received US$25,000 in funding from The Chinese Academy of Sciences and started New Technology Developer Inc.,[25] which was eventually spun off to become Legend Computer Products and Services. Legend began as an agent and contract manufacturer for computer products that were imported by foreign companies and sold in China. In 1990, the company shifted direction, becoming a manufacturer rather than a reseller, launching its own branded PC in the Chinese market.

In 1995, it began making Legend servers, and in 1996 became the market share leader in China. In 1999, Legend became the top PC vendor in the Asia Pacific region and in 2003 in preparation for global expansion Legend changed its name to Lenovo, which in Chinese characters loosely translates to "connected thinking."[26] In 2004, the company launched the "Yuanmeng" PC series for sale in China's rural markets. In 2005, Lenovo acquired IBM's Personal Computing Division for US$1.25 billion, giving it the rights to the IBM ThinkPad brand and making Lenovo the third largest personal computer brand in the world. In 2006, the first Lenovo-branded products were introduced to consumers worldwide.

Today, Lenovo has an annual turnover of US$16 billion in sales, 23,900 employees and a market capitalization of US$1.7 billion. The company is truly global with manufacturing locations in China, India, Mexico, and Poland and a global call center that supports customers in 25 languages. Lenovo also runs research and development centers in Japan, China, and the United States. They support their customers with 25,000 certified field technicians, 2,500 technical support agents, and 18 service delivery centers.[27]

Lenovo is a powerful example of a former Chinese domestic contract manufacturer and global brand reseller that rapidly re-invented itself to become its own globally recognized brand. Legend originally required only Chinese domestic distribution capability, but today under the Lenovo brand the company requires a sophisticated global supply chain distribution model capable of shipping millions of units to customers around the globe.

TINGYI

Look at most packets of instant noodles in China, and you are likely to see the famous chef caricature of Master Kong from Tingyi, a company that originally started as a cooking oil venture in Taiwan. Targeting the demand for quick-serve instant food in China's factories and construction sites, Tingyi's chairman, Wei Ingchou, established his processing facility in Tianjin in 1992, creating what would become the world's largest brand of instant noodles, Kang Shifu. The growth of Kang Shifu across China is due in large part to the company's extensive distribution network that supplies not only large food retailers but also street corner grocery shops. Despite the economic crisis Tingyi's business grew by 20 percent in the first nine months of 2009 to over US$4 billion. The company is now expanding into bottled water, snacks and various teas.[28]

SEPTWOLVES

Zhou Shaoxiong had been manufacturing garments for export out of his Fujian factory for many years before deciding that there was a Chinese domestic market for clothing made with the Chinese consumer in mind. Septwolves markets clothing to Chinese professionals ranging in age from 25–45 years old and his clothing is tailored toward a unique Chinese look, and detailed fit. Today Septwolves has more than 3,000 stores in mainland China. In a unique designer business model, Septwolves still employs foreign designers for its creations, and they market their clothing using both Chinese and Western fashion models.[29]

Both Tingyi and Septwolves are examples of companies that have been wildly successful in China and are now well positioned to take their brands global.

China's re-emergence post-18th century as a global force in innovation and product development is just beginning. Between 2000 and 2008 U.S. patent applications by the Chinese increased 12-fold according to the U.S. Patent and Trademark Office: In 2008, China's residents had submitted approximately 5,129 U.S. patent applications.[30] The sheer size of China's population together with the ability to share their new ideas and conduct research via the internet creates the potential for new markets, new products, and new thinking. Transportation and SCM in the years ahead will be as much about providing logistics services into and around the Chinese market, as it is about exporting China-made products out of it.

NOTES

1   Fareed Zakaria, *The Post American World*, (New York: W.W. Norton, 2008).

2   Ibid., 159.

3   Steven DeKrey, David Messick, Cassian Cheung, *Leadership, Experiences in Asia*, (Singapore: Wiley & Sons, 2007), 46-49.

4   Ibid.

5   Wal-Mart China Fact Sheet, http://wal-martchina.com/english/walmart/index .htm#china.

6   Fung et al, *Competing in a Flat World*, 158.

7   Carrefour Latest Store Openings, http://www.carrefour.com/cdc/group/our-business/ latest-store-openings/china-opening-of-the-138th-carrefour-hypermarket.html see also www.Carrefour.com.

8   Patti Waldmeir, "China Push Gives Tesco the Edge," *Financial Times* January 12, 2010.

9   Frederik Balfour, "Coach Builds its Brand in China," *BusinessWeek* June 4, 2008, http://www.businessweek.com/globalbiz/content/jun2008/gb2008064_054209.htm.

10   Sonia Kolesnikov-Jessop and Rana Foroohar, "Made for China," *Newsweek*, October 18, 2010, 26-29.

11   Liu Jie, "McDonalds Growing in China" *China Daily*, August 8, 2008, http://www .chinadaily.net/bizchina/2008-09/08/content_7007412.htm.

12   "Starbucks Sues China Competitor Over Name," Associated Press February 6, 2004, http://www.msnbc.msn.com/id/4192116/ -http://www.ccpit-patent.com.cn/News/ 2006012602.htm.

13   "2008 Global Powers in Retailing," Deloitte, http://www.deloitte.com/assets/Dcom-UnitedStates/Local%20Assets/Documents/us_cb_2008GlobalPowersRetailing_011 708.pdf.

14   Mike Milliken, "BYD Auto Introduces Plug-in Hybrid Electric Vehicle in Detroit; On Sale This Year in China," Green Car Congress (January 14, 2008): http://www .greencarcongress.com/2008/01/byd-auto-introd.html.

15   BYD company history and business information can be found at: http://www.byd .com/press.php?index=0.

16   Peter Ford, "Consumer Tidal Wave on the Way: China's Middle Class," *Christian Science Monitor* January 2, 2007, http://www.csmonitor.com/2007/0102/p01s02-woap.html.

17   Fung et al, *Competing in a Flat World*, 163.

18   Diana Farrel, Eric Beinhocker, Ulrich Gersch, Ezra Greenberg, Elizabeth Stephenson, Jonathan Ablett, Mingyu Guan, Janamitra Divan, "From Made in China to Sold in China—The Rise of the Chinese Urban Consumer," (McKinsey Global Institute, November 2006): 12 http://www.mckinsey.com/mgi/reports/pdfs/china_consumer/ MGI_china_consumer_demand_fullreport.pdf.

19   Coimbatore K. Prahalad, *The Fortune at the Bottom of the Pyramid, Eradicating Poverty Through Profits*, (New Jersey: Wharton School Publishing, 2009), 159-67.

20 "Wal-Mart to Provide Financial Services in 80 Chinese Cities," *China Retail News,* July 9, 2009, http://www.chinaretailnews.com/2009/07/09/2815-wal-mart-to-provide-financial-services-in-80-chinese-cities/print/.

21 Ibid.

22 Li-Ning 2008 revenue information can be found at www.lining.com/EN/home/index.html.

23 See www.haieramerica.com/en/aboutus/?sessid=5c656a7cb18d65372d164223c5d60606.

24 Haier history, http://www.haier.com/AboutHaier/CorporateProfile/index.asp.

25 Lenovo information can be found at www.pc.ibm.com/ww/lenovo/investor_factsheet.html.

26 www.csmonitor.com/2005/0630/p13s02stct.html.

27 "Lenovo-Investor Relations Fact Sheet," http://www.lenovo.com.

28 Austin Ramzy, "Follow the Leaders", *Time* March 8, 2010, 37, www.time.com/time/magazine/article/0,9171,1967941,00.html.

29 Ibid., 37.

30 "Best Buy, Wal-Mart named in patent dispute," *China Daily*, July 27, 2009, www.chinadaily.com.cn/bizchina/2009-07-27/content_8963200.htm.

RETAIL SUPPLY CHAIN INNOVATION

CHAPTER SIX

UNLOCKING SUPPLY CHAIN INNOVATION

PETER LEVESQUE

Cliff Conneighton in his book, *The Venture Management Handbook,* argues that, "there are (almost) no new ideas, only opportunities to execute an old idea better, faster, or cheaper."[1] In many ways we have become desensitized to the advances in science and technology that occur so often these days, believing that all the "big things" have already been invented. Below is a quote from a famous historical figure who seems to have been caught up in a similar mindset early in life, before making his game-changing breakthrough in aviation:

> By the time I was old enough and became a pilot, things had changed. The record-setting flights across oceans, over the poles, and to the corners of the earth had all been accomplished. I was disappointed by a wrinkle in history that had put me here, one generation too late. I had missed all the great times and adventure in flight.[2]
>
> —Neil Armstrong

There have been tremendous gains in logistics and supply chain efficiency over the last decade with the development of more powerful logistics technology and software. But breakthrough innovation has not always been the result of sophisticated technology. There are also examples of game-changing innovation that were the result of simple ideas and basic process improvements.

Source: Getty Images

Malcolm McClean

In April 1956, Malcolm McLean first put trucking containers on board his ship the *Ideal X* in Newark, New Jersey, and the age of containerized shipping had begun. The concept was simple but the idea changed international supply chain economics forever.

Later in 1984, American President Lines developed the North America stack train operation, which exponentially improved cargo rail efficiency across the United States by simply stacking one container on top of another using specially designed rail cars.

As sophisticated as supply chain technology has become over the years, it was basic process improvements and ideas such as inter-modalism that dramatically changed the transportation industry. Are there any new ideas

Source: APL.com

APL Stack Train Innovation

left to be discovered in the area of SCM? The answer is most assuredly yes. The question is how to identify these ideas to explore them further.

Oftentimes, innovation lies dormant within an organization because no framework or structure exists for getting new ideas into the light of day. Successful ideas are more likely to come from companies that have an internal process for identifying and rewarding innovative thinking within their organization. These types of organizations are able to share and develop new ideas with their customers, and expand traditional business cooperation by identifying mutually beneficial improvement opportunities. The transportation industry has been around for a very long time, and old ways of thinking about the business are still very hard to change. The challenge and the opportunity lies in creating logistics organizations that break down traditional paradigms and allow innovation to occur, so that we can better understand what is possible.

A WIN-WIN APPROACH TO SUPPLY CHAIN PRICING

Professor Keith Murnighan at Northwestern University's Kellogg School of Management teaches a fascinating class on game theory. On its most basic level game theory attempts to analyze strategic situations, and to mathematically capture people's behavior, when successful decision making is dependent upon the actions of others. The application of game theory can be found in areas such as economics and military strategy.

To illustrate game theory concepts Murnighan has his class play "The Gas Station Game." The class is divided up into an equal number of teams, and each team represents an owner-operated gas station. The teams are paired off so that each station is competing against another station, theoretically located directly across the street from one another. Students are told that the object of the game is to maximize profits. The competing stations are able to see each other's price per gallon of gasoline, and all prices at the start of the game are equal. The gas stations then have the ability over several rounds (weeks), to either cut their price, or keep their price constant. Stations are not allowed to speak to one another while making their pricing decision, and the results of each round are gathered and announced to the entire class by Murnighan.

If one gas station cuts its price, and the competing gas station holds its price, the price-cutting station will gain more customers for that week, and they will make more money than their competitor. But taking a rate cutting strategy inevitably means that there will be retaliation from the competitor when it comes time to decide on pricing for the following week (a tit-for-tat strategy). If both stations cooperate, however, and hold their prices constant, both stations can continue making the same money, week after week without fluctuation in profit.

After several rounds of pricing Murnighan allows the competing gas stations to talk to one another before making their next round decision on whether to cut rates or stay the same. These face-to-face meetings between competitors can be spirited if the opposing teams have been involved in a tit-for-tat rate-cutting scenario. Trust, integrity and reputation figure into the game dynamics based on the results and actions of previous rounds. The Gas Station Game can become intense and emotionally draining, as teams try to work out how best to maximize profits. The ultimate lesson from The Gas Station Game is not surprising—the only way for both gas stations to maximize their earnings, and avoid the bad feelings that develop in a rate war, is for both teams to hold their rates steady from round to round, to create a long-term win/win gain. Some teams figure this out from the very first round, and those teams often win the game by profiting the most.

In the real world, price discussions between competing transportation providers would be illegal and The Gas Station Game example is not meant to advocate pricing cooperation between service providers. Where cooperation could use some improvement is between transportation providers and their customers. It is remarkable how closely The Gas Station Game resembles the actual tit-for-tat interaction between many customers and transportation

service providers in the market today. Historically, customers will have the market leverage to
drive transportation prices down over a period
of time, eventually followed by a market reversal, where the transportation companies suddenly have the market leverage to raise prices
dramatically. The magnitude of price fluctuation in these market cycles is usually dramatic,
and painful for the losing side to absorb.

> **Shipping Point:**
> **"Lack of flexibility**
> **can creat adversarial**
> **pricing relationships**
> **between the**
> **customer and the**
> **service provider."**
> *Peter Levesque*

There is clear evidence of this tit-for-tat
pricing strategy playing out right now in
many trade lanes. The global recession forced ocean carriers to take vessel
capacity out of the market, as ocean freight prices in some trade lanes fell to
zero. This created a temporary windfall for many shippers while creating a
potentially catastrophic financial burden for many ocean carriers. However,
as the peak Christmas shipping season heated up in China (August,
September, October) the market leverage was reversed and ocean carriers
began implementing substantial price increases, trying to recoup past losses.
Shippers who refused to pay the rate increases risked having their cargo left
behind on the dock in China. While no one is debating the principal of
supply and demand, or the very real plight of carriers who are trying to
achieve profitability, the crux of the issue is the industry's refusal to take a
more flexible, longer-term approach in creating win/win pricing models.

Ocean rate contracts negotiated by asset-based carriers, for example,
attempt to lock in freight rates for 12 months at a time, and do not allow
for significant market corrections (other than fuel surcharges) in either
direction. This lack of flexibility creates an adversarial relationship between
carrier and customer, as leverage rotates from customer to service provider and
back again. Traffic managers face an impossible situation in terms of setting
budgets, because uncertainty and a lack of flexibility for handling movements
in the market, force traffic managers to either overshoot or undershoot their
costs estimates by unacceptable margins.

Innovative companies should be able to figure out a pricing mechanism
that keeps both the customer and the carrier in the market with regard to
rates, while preventing either side from being caught too far out of the
market. Carriers need to be profitable and customers need dependable and

stable pricing to manage against budgeted landed costs. A flexible pricing model which helps keep customer rates at market levels and carrier rates at profitable levels, using some form of agreed upon industry pricing index would seem like a reasonable solution.

MITIGATING RATE VOLATILITY IN CHINA TRADE

A key reason for the development of the tit-for-tat pricing environment that exists today has been the absence of sound financial instruments that would allow companies to mitigate pricing risk. Once an ocean contract is signed between a carrier and a beneficial cargo owner (BCO) those rates have traditionally been locked in for the period of one year. The BCO can be fairly certain that their rates will remain constant for the period of 12 months (aside from fuel and currency adjustments) and the ocean carrier can be fairly certain as to what the expected revenue streams will look like over the same 12-month period, using basic volume assumptions.

The problem, of course, is that a lot can change over the course of a year. Oil prices can rise and fall, economies can grow and contract, and geopolitical unrest can impact key manufacturing bases overseas. Container shortages due to global trade imbalances, and space constraints on vessels due to reduced capacity or significant increases in cargo flows can also create market uncertainty and increased risk.

While the bulk shipping industry that transports commodities such as grain, iron ore, and other raw materials has long had a mechanism for hedging risk through dry bulk derivative instruments such as freight forward agreements (FFAs), the container freight industry has lagged behind. To be fair, bulk shipping has been around for hundreds of years, whereas container shipping only made its debut in 1956, but there has been more than enough time for new innovative solutions to be introduced.

Bulk commodity shipping FFAs are basically financial contracts placed in the market where one side of the contract (counterparty) believes that rates will rise above a certain agreed upon contract level within a specified time period, and the other counterparty believes rates will fall below the contract level. The contract price is settled against one of the Baltic Exchange Indices. A typical FFA lists the counterparties to the agreement (buyer and seller) where the buyer opines that rates will rise while the seller's view is that rates will fall. A specific contract route or trade lane is specified as well as the agreed contract rate, contract quantity and contract duration. Critical to the agreement is the settlement date and the settlement rate which is typically an average of a specified Baltic Dry Index rate level over the month leading up to the settlement date, for a particular trade route. If the settlement rate is higher than the contract rate, the contract buyer receives the difference, which is the settlement sum. Likewise, if the settlement rate is below the contract rate, the contract seller is paid the difference.

The Baltic Exchange produces the Baltic Dry Indices, which provide a comprehensive indicator of market movement. The Baltic Exchange inquires with brokers around the world to provide market freight rates of various commodities by voyage and by ship cost per day in US dollars. Parties who secure these contracts are either shippers with freight to move, or shipping companies with ships to fill. The indices measure the demand for ship capacity, which indirectly measures the supply and demand of the commodities being shipped. A low rate per day for a bulk freighter from Africa to China, for example, might indicate excess ship capacity in that trade lane which could indirectly indicate decreased demand for commodities moving into China.

Extrapolating further, decreased raw material into China may mean reduced production, which could be an indicator of reduced demand from markets that purchase products from China. Some of the routes within the indices are tailored toward certain commodity trades, and rates are shown (per/ton). These indices can be used to gauge future commodity activity, which some view as a leading economic indicator. Other more generalized trade routes are shown in vessel charter rates per day. This type of market visibility and transparency has eluded the container shipping industry where ocean contracts between asset-based container shipping lines are signed directly with BCOs and non-vessel operating common carriers (NVOCCs) with a typical duration of one year.

THE SHANGHAI SHIPPING EXCHANGE

The Shanghai Shipping Exchange was established in 1996 as a joint venture between what was China's Ministry of Communications (MOC)[3] and local

Shanghai government authorities to provide data, agency support services, and to facilitate effective communication between industry and government. Membership on the Shanghai Shipping Exchange consists of Chinese shipping companies and foreign shipping companies in local representative offices.

The Shanghai Shipping Exchange publishes both the China Coastal Bulk Freight Index (CBFI) and the China Container Freight Index (CCFI). In March of 2009, the Exchange launched the Shanghai Containerized Freight Index (SCFI), for testing followed by the index going live in October 2009. The SCFI is comprised of 30 panelists who submit their spot weekly freight rate assessment to the index. The panel takes into account both supply and demand data, using 15 carriers (supply) as well as 15 forwarders and logistics companies (demand) to provide a neutral assessment of the container freight market. The index is published at 3pm every Friday and reports rates in either US dollars per 20-foot equivalent unit (TEU) or US dollars per 40-foot equivalent unit (FEU) for 15 major trade lanes out of Shanghai. Figures 6.1 and 6.2 are two examples of index reports.

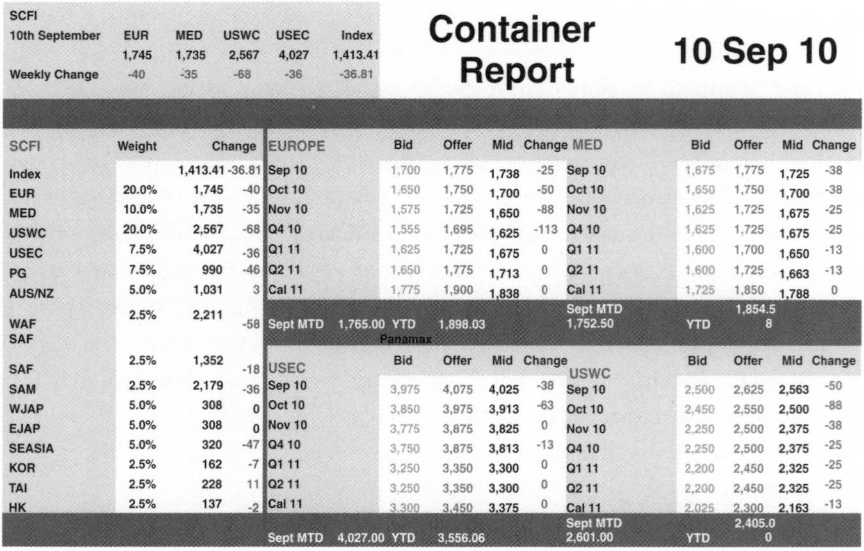

Container Report 10 Sep 10

SCFI 10th September	EUR	MED	USWC	USEC	Index
	1,745	1,735	2,567	4,027	1,413.41
Weekly Change	-40	-35	-68	-36	-36.81

SCFI	Weight		Change
Index		1,413.41	-36.81
EUR	20.0%	1,745	-40
MED	10.0%	1,735	-35
USWC	20.0%	2,567	-68
USEC	7.5%	4,027	-36
PG	7.5%	990	-46
AUS/NZ	5.0%	1,031	3
WAF SAF	2.5%	2,211	-58
SAF	2.5%	1,352	-18
SAM	2.5%	2,179	-36
WJAP	5.0%	308	0
EJAP	5.0%	308	0
SEASIA	5.0%	320	-47
KOR	2.5%	162	-7
TAI	2.5%	228	11
HK	2.5%	137	-2

EUROPE	Bid	Offer	Mid	Change	MED	Bid	Offer	Mid	Change
Sep 10	1,700	1,775	1,738	-25	Sep 10	1,675	1,775	1,725	-38
Oct 10	1,650	1,750	1,700	-50	Oct 10	1,650	1,750	1,700	-38
Nov 10	1,575	1,725	1,650	-88	Nov 10	1,625	1,725	1,675	-25
Q4 10	1,555	1,695	1,625	-113	Q4 10	1,625	1,725	1,675	-25
Q1 11	1,625	1,725	1,675	0	Q1 11	1,600	1,700	1,650	-13
Q2 11	1,650	1,775	1,713	0	Q2 11	1,600	1,725	1,663	-13
Cal 11	1,775	1,900	1,838	0	Cal 11	1,725	1,850	1,788	0
Sept MTD 1,765.00	YTD 1,898.03				Sept MTD 1,752.50	YTD 1,854.58			

Panamax

USEC	Bid	Offer	Mid	Change	USWC	Bid	Offer	Mid	Change
Sep 10	3,975	4,075	4,025	-38	Sep 10	2,500	2,625	2,563	-50
Oct 10	3,850	3,975	3,913	-63	Oct 10	2,450	2,550	2,500	-88
Nov 10	3,775	3,875	3,825	0	Nov 10	2,250	2,500	2,375	-38
Q4 10	3,750	3,875	3,813	-13	Q4 10	2,250	2,500	2,375	-25
Q1 11	3,250	3,350	3,300	0	Q1 11	2,200	2,450	2,325	-25
Q2 11	3,250	3,350	3,300	0	Q2 11	2,200	2,450	2,325	-25
Cal 11	3,300	3,450	3,375	0	Cal 11	2,025	2,300	2,163	-13
Sept MTD 4,027.00	YTD 3,556.06				Sept MTD 2,601.00	YTD 2,405.00			

Source: Clarksons, London

Figure 6.1 Container Freight Indexed Market Trends—Example 1

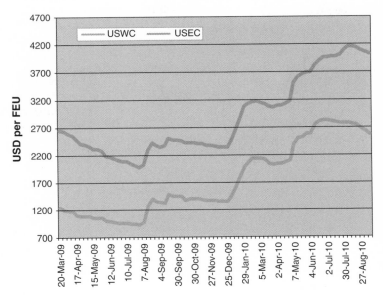

Source: Clarksons, London

Figure 6.2 Container Freight Indexed Market Trends—Example 2

The Shanghai Shipping Exchange's president, Zhang Ye, announced in December 2009 that the exchange would begin offering a container-rate-based financial derivative. In January 2010, London-based Clarkson's Securities announced that it had facilitated its first derivative contract on the SCFI.

As this container rate derivative market develops, ocean carriers, freight forwarders and beneficial cargo owners will be able to hedge the inherent risk associated with volatile freight rate environments. For example, an ocean carrier who locks in an ocean rate with a customer for a one-year period has an advantage in a declining rate environment and has a disadvantage in a rising rate environment. Likewise, a beneficial cargo owner who negotiates a one-year rate with a carrier within a specific trade lane has the advantage in a rising rate environment leaving the carrier with the downside. But what if forwarders, carriers and cargo owners could hedge their rate agreements by purchasing or selling futures contracts that could help mitigate their exposure to volatile market movements? That's what the future of container freight derivatives will be able to offer, as shown in Figures 6.3, 6.4, 6.5.[4]

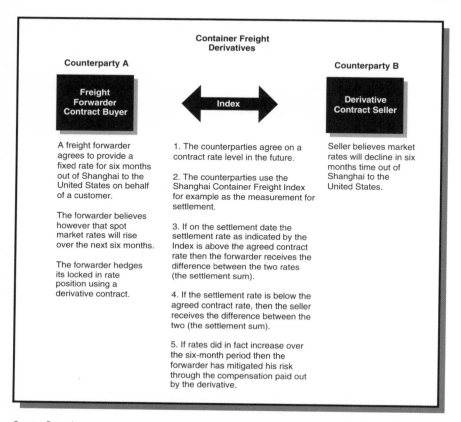

Source: Peter Levesque

Figure 6.3   Possible Freight Forwarder Hedging Scenario

In order to be a viable financial hedging tool there needs to be regulation, transparency and oversight. These key ingredients have proven challenging within China in the past and could effectively hinder the development of a viable container derivative market in the future. The Shanghai Shipping Exchange has expressed its commitment to producing an index product that is robust and transparent enough for derivatives trading. The Shanghai Shipping Exchange just completed an independent audit of the SCFI product, which showed positive results possibly opening the way for index-based contract pricing in the near future.

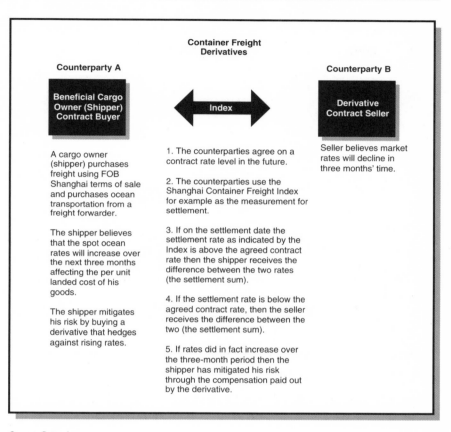

Source: Peter Levesque

Figure 6.4 Possible Beneficial Cargo Owner Hedging Scenario

UNLOCKING INNOVATION

Unlocking innovation in large organizations is not easy, and is largely dependent upon a firm's senior leadership and corporate culture. This can be especially difficult to achieve in China. Fortunately, there are tools available that can help provide a framework for unlocking creativity and innovation within the organization. Keith Murnighan and John Mowen call these tools "creativity heuristics" in their book *The Art of High-Stakes Decision-Making.*[5] Heuristics by definition involves breaking from the normal path to discover innovative new strategies. The following are some key creativity heuristics,

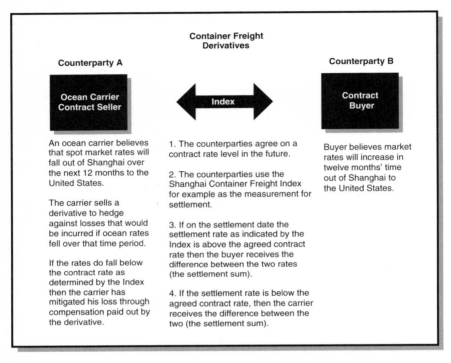

Source: Peter Levesque

Figure 6.5   Possible Ocean Carrier Hedging Against Rate Decreases

along with examples of how they have been applied in the area of SCM in identifying breakthrough ideas.

Heuristic 1: Identify the Inverse

Crocs was founded by three friends from Boulder, Colorado, during a sailing holiday in the Caribbean. Lyndon "Duke" Hanson, Scott Seamans, and George Boedecker began selling the original shoe made by a Canadian company called Finproject NA out of a warehouse in Florida. They wanted a brand name that would associate the product with water, and since "Alligator" was already taken, they chose Crocs. In 2004, as the company grew, they hired a former Flextronics executive named Ronald Snyder to run the business after he had served a brief time as a Crocs consultant.

Crocs did several things with regard to their supply chain that were the inverse of the conventional wisdom at the time. Rather than focus on large big box retailers, Crocs focused on boutique markets, promoting their shoes at boat shows, garden shows, sporting events, and concerts around the world. By focusing on smaller retailers, Crocs was able to build their brand quickly and gain important market leverage, which they were then able to use later when selling to larger retailers. Identifying the inverse for Crocs meant having to deal with a much more complex supply chain that was capable of filling smaller order quantities across a wider customer base, but their early strategy paid off.

Crocs also reversed the traditional retail distributor model, by offering their retail customers the ability to order more product during a selling season, as opposed to having to pre-buy everything in bulk, which was normal industry practice at the time. They reversed yet another industry standard by allowing custom configuration of shipping packs to include multiple styles and colors based on specific customer requirements. By enabling their retailers with a more dynamic ordering model Crocs was able to help their customers avoid both overstocks and shortages.[6]

The Crocs shoe is a marketing phenomena and a business sensation. A portion of the company's original success came from identifying the inverse. Targeting small retailers instead of big box retailers, and reversing industry supply chain standards on how product could be purchased and packed, helped Crocs differentiate itself on their process as well as on their product.

Heuristic 2: Add or Combine Features (Combine Networks & Services)

Successful logistics service providers (LSPs) today are creating a new menu of value-added solutions by combining functions from outside the traditional scope of LSP services. Some LSPs are now tasked with coordinating networks of ancillary service providers on behalf of the client, in order to provide more coordinated and comprehensive visibility across a broader spectrum of the supply chain.

As supply chains become more modular and network-based, there is an opportunity for additional value creation. Those who can connect the dots to access and leverage combined networks will see the biggest advantages.

In Victor and William Fung's book, *Competing in a Flat World*, the authors explain that, "whereas competitive advantage once was defined largely by the capabilities the company directly developed or owned, now it depends on the capabilities inside as well as those capabilities outside that the company can connect to."[7]

Combining networks and services such as packaging design, quality inspection, remote back room services and trade financing within a traditional 4PL-managed solution, for example, increases the ability to aggregate a greater amount of data across a larger area of the supply chain. The end result is a more comprehensive view of what is actually happening.

Combining value added services in China is a rapidly growing trend that allows retailers to lower costs by doing at origin what has been traditionally done at destination. Barcode label printing and scanning, piece sorting, component kitting, and store-ready display construction are just a few of the services that have been successfully migrated to China.

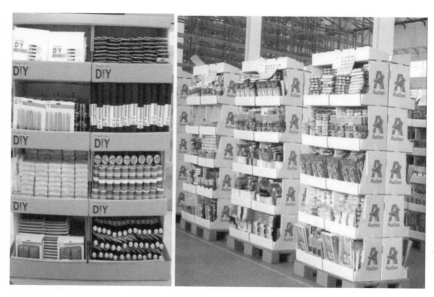

Source: Elee Corporation

Store Displays Combine Value Added Services in China

Heuristic 3: Change the Scale

We discussed the success that companies like Wal-Mart and Carrefour are having with selling to the source which effectively changes (increases) the scale of what is possible. But changing the scale can also be achieved by changing the sales channel. International internet sales offer retailers the ability to expand their brand presence without the cost and financial risk of opening physical storefronts. There are more internet users in China today than in the United States.[8] The percentage of users per capita is still higher in the United States, but the actual number of users in China is higher, and this creates a tremendous opportunity for both retailers and LSPs to expand what is possible by increasing the scale.

V-Logic Ltd is a company that was founded in 2000 specifically to enable global brands to change the scale by providing access to the Chinese market via the internet, using a direct distribution model from the manufacturing point of origin.

As an example, let's say a person living in Shenzhen, South China, wants to buy an inexpensive microwave oven from Wal-Mart.com. The shopper in China has no problem accessing the Wal-Mart.com website, or filling in purchasing information such as credit card, and mailing address. When the shopper goes to the final checkout, however, they discover that Wal-Mart.com will not ship products purchased online to countries outside the United States.

Wal-Mart's International Shipping Policy

"The Walmart.com website only ships orders to addresses within the 50 states, APO/FPO military addresses, American Samoa, Guam, Northern Mariana Islands, Puerto Rico and the U.S. Virgin Islands."

Source: Wal-Mart.com

The order then needs to be cancelled, and an opportunity for Wal-Mart to build international brand loyalty through the internet is lost.

Intuitively it makes sense that Wal-Mart would not want the cost and hassle of shipping products from the United States across the Pacific to customers in South China. But, most of the products Wal-Mart is selling online are in fact made. . . . in South China.

Using Hong Kong's free port status for its distribution center V-Logic's model was to allow retailers to fill their international orders directly from the manufacturing point of origin, at lower cost, with faster shipping time, and overall better value. The logistics design also allowed for a product returns process, whereby return labels could be inserted within the product shipment packaging, and if a customer was not satisfied with the product they could affix the return label and return it using the courier company that delivered it.

While V-Logic's idea was a bit ahead of its time in 2000, the basic international fulfillment model is as valid today as it was 10 years ago. If executed properly this type of model could provide a low-risk option for domestic retailers in the United States and Europe to significantly change the scale. In our chapter on innovative supply chain flows we provide more details on this type of fulfillment model.

Heuristic 4: Control the Variance

Traditionally, U.S. importers from China have used FOB (freight on board) or FCA (free carrier alongside) terms of sale when buying from Chinese suppliers. Under these terms of sale, as shown in Figure 6.6, the responsibility for transportation of freight from the warehouse to either the ocean port or the 3PL's warehouse facility is for the account of the supplier.

Over the last several years, with the implementation of the Customs and Trade Partnership Against Terrorism (C-TPAT) and the Container Security Initiative (CSI), the transit of goods between the factory in China and the ocean

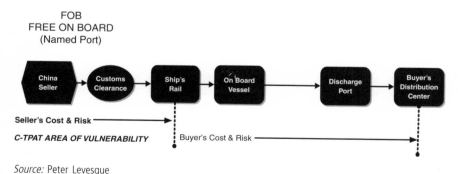

Source: Peter Levesque

Figure 6.6   FOB Transfer of Risk Analysis

port of vessel departure has been identified as a security risk or black hole. The reason is that there is no visibility of the container's status during this portion of the transit. A trucker in China, for example, could pull over en route to the port, and tamper with the integrity of the container, and no one would ever know. Many global retailers have begun to explore the financial and security benefits of controlling the variance in the trucking process, using FCA terms of sale.

There is often confusion over the difference between FCA terms of sale and Ex Works' terms of sale. The fundamental difference is in who is responsible for customs clearance. In Ex Works' terms of sale the buyer is responsible for Chinese export customs clearance, whereas under FCA terms of sale, as shown in Figure 6.7, the seller is responsible for Chinese export customs clearance.

Under FCA terms of sale, shippers can utilize LSP's trucking fleets in China to pick up product that is ready for shipment from the factory's dock. The switch to FCA accomplishes two things. First, it provides an opportunity to lower the first cost of goods sold, by negotiating the original trucking cost out of the factory's unit price. The total factory cost for trucking can usually include both the dray-to-port as well as the back-haul cost component for bringing raw material into the factory location. So there are usually some dollars on the table that can be negotiated with the vendor though in many cases getting to these savings can be difficult.

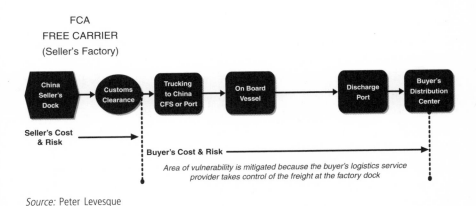

Source: Peter Levesque

Figure 6.7   FCA Seller's Factory—Transfer of Risk Analysis

The second advantage to FCA terms of sale is that it allows the shipper's LSP to take control of the container earlier in the supply chain, thereby providing immediate visibility on the container's status, and closing the cargo security black hole described earlier.

The heuristics we've described here can help provide a basic framework for brainstorming new ideas and initiating thought leadership. Unlocking innovation is not always easy. There needs to be a mechanism that allows ideas to be expressed and considered within organizations, and this is dependent upon a corporate culture that rewards innovation. As we have shown, supply chain innovation need not be overly complicated in order to make a difference. As one SCM executive jokingly expressed, "cargo transportation is not rocket surgery." Sometimes executing an old idea better and faster is the best way to achieve game-changing results.

WHAT KILLS INNOVATION?

More often than not, what kills business innovation is corporate culture. Specifically, a corporate culture that fails to embrace continuous employee development and fails to create an environment that encourages calculated risk taking. It can be difficult to foster innovation inside the traditional Chinese company for example, where managers are seen as the keepers of the information, and employees are briefed on a need-to-know basis.

Sometimes innovation can be made more difficult because of the tools and criteria corporations use in evaluating an investment in a new idea. The net present value of future cash flows is a common financial tool that may not offer the best measurement analysis when evaluating an investment in innovation.[9] Because money can earn interest and grow in value over time, the discounted cash flow (DCF) analysis assumes that the value of a dollar today is less than the value would be if the dollar was received in the future (the time value of money). A company may evaluate an investment in innovation based on the net present value of the investment's future cash flows over some period of time. But Christensen, Kaufman and Shih in their *Harvard Business Review* article, "Innovation Killers—How Financial Tools Destroy Your Capacity to do New Things," argue that there is an "anti-innovation bias" built into the DCF formula, because the analysis is based on the assumption that there are no negative financial consequences for doing nothing.

In the real world, however, things are in a constant state of change, especially in China. Deciding not to make an investment in innovation may save money in the short term, however the competition might be making decisions that will significantly change the current competitive landscape in their favor. The competition, for example, could be investing in new information technology, upgraded trucking fleets, network infrastructure or human capital, all of which have the potential to put downward pressure on pricing, margins, and market share. Not making an investment in innovation can therefore have negative financial consequences that are not reflected in the DCF model. Eileen Rudden at Boston Consulting Group notes that, "the most likely stream of cash for the company in the do nothing scenario is not a continuation of the status quo. It is a nonlinear decline in performance."[10]

> **Shipping Point:**
> **"You can be imaginative all day long without anyone noticing—to be creative you actually have to do something."**
> *Ken Robinson—*
> *The Element*

Christensen, Kaufman, and Shih go on to explain that better analysis can be achieved by "assessing the projected value of the innovation against a range of scenarios, the most realistic of which is often a deteriorating competitive and financial future."[11] Phil Bobbitt calls this flaw in DCF evaluation the "Parmenides Fallacy," after the Greek logician who claimed to have proven that conditions in the world must be unchanging.[12] Evidence of the Parmenides Fallacy can be found when dealing with companies who are deciding whether or not to invest in an outsourced supply chain solution. Because logistics departments are often organized as cost centers within the corporation, decisons that involve an initial investment and potentially higher upfront logistics costs are difficult to make even though there are clear long-term benefits to the organization by making the investment. Under cost pressure the transportation department may come to the conclusion that the worst-case scenario for doing nothing is simply a continuation of the status quo.

The reality, however, could be that the competition is making supply chain investment decisions that will significantly alter the status quo, by investing in projects and programs that will change the competitive landscape entirely. The worst-case scenario, as shown in Figure 6.8, may actually be that the

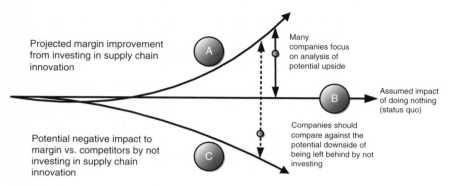

Projected margin improvement from investing in supply chain innovation

Many companies focus on analysis of potential upside

Assumed impact of doing nothing (status quo)

Potential negative impact to margin vs. competitors by not investing in supply chain innovation

Companies should compare against the potential downside of being left behind by not investing

Source: Chart created by Peter Levesque, based on an idea presented in the *Harvard Business Review,* and modified with permission[13]

Figure 6.8   The SCM Investment Dilemma

transportation department finds itself reacting to competitive investment, when it may be too late and end up costing much more.

Knowing the true impact of not taking action is important in the retail SCM arena, where companies are increasingly competing on supply chain capability and process. Asking questions about what could possibly change in the marketplace is critical to making intelligent investment decisions and to avoid killing innovation. Christensen, Kaufman, and Shih explain that, "more often than not, failure in innovation is rooted in not having asked an important question, rather than in having arrived at an incorrect answer."[14]

NOTES

1   Cliff Conneighton, *The Venture Handbook: An Entrepreneur's Practical Guide to Stock, Finance, and Contracts,* (Hollis N.H.: Venturebooks, 2002).

2   James Hansen, *First Man: The Life of Neil Armstrong,* (New York: Simon & Shuster, 2005).

3   China's Ministry of Communications changed its name to the Ministry of Communications and Transport in 2008.

4   Ben Gibson, "Container Freight Swap Agreements, A SCFI settled Container Derivative," PowerPoint presentation to American Chamber of Commerce, AmCham Offices, Hong Kong (May 2010); see also www.clarksons.com.

5   Keith Murnighan and John C. Mowen, *The Art of High-Stakes Decision-Making, Tough Calls in a Speed-Driven World,* (New York: John Wiley & Sons, Inc., 2002), 78–81.

6   David Hoyt and Amanda Silverman, "Crocs: Revolutionizing an Industry's Supply Chain," Case No. GS-57, Stanford Graduate School of Business (2007), 78–81.

7   Fung et al, *Competing in a Flat World*, 17.

8   Randeep Ramash, "China Soon to Be the World's Biggest Internet User," *The Guardian*, January 1, 2007.

9   Clayton Christensen, Stephen P. Kaufman, Willy Shih, "Innovation Killers—How Financial Tools Destroy Your Capacity to do New Things," *Harvard Business Review* (January 2008).

10 Ibid., 2.

11 Ibid., 2.

12 Ibid., 2.

13 Ibid., 8.

14 Ibid., 8.

CHAPTER SEVEN

THE INNOVATIVE RETAIL SUPPLY CHAIN

CHRIS ROBESON

Bringing products to market invariably presents challenges and trade-offs in support of satisfying consumer demand. Key among these are decisions related to inventory and timing of commitments. Speculation (anticipated demand) and postponement (delayed differentiation) are concepts that derive from where and when to add value to products within the supply chain. Postponement is based on the principle that changes, in form and identity, occur at the latest possible point in the supply chain. Postponement serves to reduce marketing risk, since every differentiation that makes a product more suitable for a specified segment of the market makes it less suitable for other segments.[1] Postponement can also reduce risk to obsolete product and minimize inventory risks associated with variability in demand. However, the use of postponement is not without risk and it is not appropriate in all circumstances. Postponement is not the same thing as procrastination. The strategy only works when there is rigorous business discipline around its use as a tool. It can, however, be a powerful SCM tool.

> **Shipping Point:**
> **"We must understand variation."**
> *W. Edwards Deming*

The underlying factor in considering an approach to inventory models is the degree of variability inherent in the demand for the product. The further out the decision is made to commit to inventory (differentiated product), the less accurate forecasts related to product attributes will be. For example, in the fashion apparel industry, decisions related to color, style, volumes, and price made too far in advance of market introduction increase the risk of low acceptance and reduced margins, due to price markdowns and other highly promotional activities used to liquidate slower moving inventories.

In a make-to-stock environment, businesses make product to hold in inventory until customers make a purchasing decision that draws upon this inventory. This is inherently a more speculative model since it requires committing to manufactured quantities to be placed into stock prior to confirmed demand signals. A full speculation model can benefit from economies of scale related to production costs with discounts received for raw material purchases and long production runs at manufacturing sites. However, the model must evaluate these gains against the risk of obsolete inventory and cost associated with inventory carrying. This approach to inventory is better suited to products that can be forecasted with high consistency.

At the opposite end of the continuum is a make-to-order model that manufacturers item in response to the consumer's decision to purchase an item. This is a strategy aimed at postponing the decision to manufacture (or to differentiate with final processing) until a demand signal is known. This approach minimizes risk associated with product obsolescence and provides the opportunity for customization to customer preferences. In his speech at TED, writer and consultant Joseph Pine speaks of a progression from commoditized products and services toward experiential-based consumer models. He describes the future as one in which consumers will increasingly be spending time and money satisfying the desire for authenticity. Authenticity includes both the experiential effect of the buying experience and the ability to have products customized to consumers' expectations. Under this theory, the postponement model offers an opportunity to operate successfully in the face of changing consumer expectations and facilitates what he refers to as mass customization. Apple computer offers an example of the possibilities for mass customization using this model. Users can utilize the web or Apple store locations to order iPod music players in desired colors and capacity. At the point of payment an engraved message can be added to the units.

Source: Peter Levesque

Personalizing the Technology We Use

Engraving is done at factories in China and expedited to consumers within three to five days of the order. Engraving is simply the last step in an integrated manufacturing model that dynamically allocates production to colors, device capacity, and other consumer preferences providing for a "customized" purchasing experience. In-between these two models is a continuum of options that balance trade-offs that exist between various market and product attributes. Various considerations for determining the appropriate balance are addressed throughout the balance of this chapter.

MANUFACTURING POSTPONEMENT

Manufacturing postponement in its purest form would have as its aim to hold a zero inventory of component parts and manufacture only upon receipt of an actual order. As a practical matter, economies of scale associated with manufacturing in efficient batch sizes are compelling. The objective therefore is to find the appropriate compromise between economies of manufacturing (which may vary at the component level) and the benefits of minimizing inventory in order to meet with a customer's desired configuration. Therefore, manufacturing postponement achieves its value through maintaining products in a non-differentiated state until the latest possible moment within the supply chain.

A good example of this approach can be seen in actions taken by Hewlett Packard (HP) to address its distribution of DeskJet© printers in the European market.

In the 1990s, printers manufactured in Canada were distributed to worldwide markets with lead times to European markets via ocean transportation approximating one month. The lead time required that significant safety stock be held in the supply chain to ensure service levels by market. HP redesigned the supply chain to manufacture the base printer in its generic form and shipped aggregate volumes to centralized European distribution locations. Late-stage differentiation was then done in-region by adding market-specific power supply and instruction manuals. The approach allowed HP to reduce printer inventories by an estimated 18 percent while simultaneously maintaining customer service levels with rapid late-stage differentiation.

The scope and diversity of today's supply chain can make manufacturing postponement challenging in some instances. However, with the increasingly vertically integrated markets in China and other manufacturing centers, opportunities to use this approach are growing.

LOGISTICS POSTPONEMENT

Another approach to postponement uses time-utility associated with the location of goods to drive value to the supply chain. Using this approach, economies of production are realized since production volumes are done at an aggregate level; however, instead of forward deploying inventory to multiple at-rest locations, inventory is held in central or regional facilities and distributed using fast and highly reliable transportation to fulfill customer orders. This approach is particularly well suited to parts fulfillment due to variability of demand. A distributed model of inventories creates significant carrying costs—particularly if high in-stock positions are associated with customer service objectives. Although expedited transportation associated with logistics postponement may be high, the cost must be viewed in the context of overall end-to-end costs and desired customer service objectives.

Volkswagen provides an example of the strategy in question when in the mid-1990s it consolidated its European parts network into a coordinated response model. The design required that distribution information of parts for factory, wholesale, and retail channels be aggregated for coordinated delivery. Carrying inventory at an aggregate level in the European region reduced distribution costs through lower inventory requirements, shorter average inventory carrying periods, and closer-to-market production processes.

USING PRODUCT ATTRIBUTES TO DRIVE DECISIONS REGARDING MODEL SELECTION

In determining which model best supports an organization's business model, organizations should be guided by product and market attributes. It is doubtful that all products will necessarily group under a given model—not all products are equal. Therefore, care should be taken to stratify an organization's products into characteristics and either a) make knowing compromises that balance out across products, or b) build flexible supply chains that can accommodate different needs for different products. Too often decisions are made within silos where solutions are suboptimal, based on too limited a view of the issues facing the supply chain on an end-to-end basis. The opportunity to flow products through the supply chain in a manner that matches the characteristics of the product is therefore not fully realized.

The objective is not to optimize purely the manufacturing process, operations within a four-walls environment, or the transportation network required to move product through the supply chain. The best solution is one that considers a balance of these objectives on an end-to-end basis. Processes and systems exist to make this a reality by providing supply chain managers with visibility to costs, lead times, and key-decision points from initial concept to consumer presentation.

PRODUCT LIFECYCLE

Much has been written about product lifecycle management (PLM) and how products at various stages of the lifecycle present differing challenges to the supply chain. Product lifecycle is a significant input to decision making about inventory levels and differentiation. For example, consumer product goods (CPG) often have long lifecycles exhibited by brand names that may evolve in formulation, but typically have much greater predictability of demand. Focusing on this characteristic leads solutions to emphasize accurate forecasting of demand to minimize dwell time of product in the supply chain while using demand signals to pull inventory through the chain. This reflects a largely pull (or demand chain) model as sales information, seasonality, and promotional activity can be used to drive highly reliable demand forecasts. Sufficient critical mass of volume exists to ensure efficient manufacturing sizes are achieved while simultaneously minimizing inventory dwell times.

NEW PRODUCT LAUNCHES

Forecasting sales for innovative products introduced to the market is an inherently more risky proposition. For example, in a highly variable industry like fashion apparel, new product launches begin with a highly speculative set of assumptions about how products will be accepted into the marketplace, since there is, by definition, no sales history upon which to draw for modeling purposes.

Source: Peter Levesque

Chanel in Hong Kong—Fashion and Luxury Brand Logistics Can Be Complex

Whereas fashion basics (denim, t-shirts, accessories, etc.) may exhibit more predictable demand patterns and lend these products to a replenishment model, products with highly fashion-oriented attributes are less likely to exhibit predictability of demand. In this highly variable environment, a multi-tiered approach to product introduction and management, as shown in Figure 7.1, often makes more sense. At product launch, a speculative model where the product is pushed into the marketplace based on best estimates of market receptiveness can be used as the basis of planning initial flows. No history for the product exists so products are introduced based on merchant's ability to read market trends and possibly model an entrance strategy based on previously introduced products with similar characteristics.

Using this approach can benefit supply chain planning since initial flows are established in advance of finished product being ready for shipment. Initial presentation quantities can be modeled based on store profiles and communicated to the factory so that manufactured items are packaged in store-ready cartons.

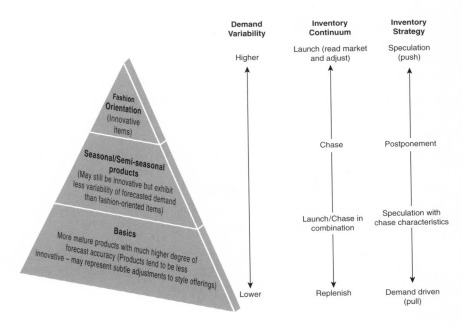

Source: Chris Robeson

Figure 7.1   The Dynamics of Inventory Strategy

This step eliminates the need to process the goods further in a distribution center following departure from the factory.

This approach differs to a pure speculation strategy, as is often described. The primary differentiation is in reference to the amount of risk assumed in initial production quantities. Taking a large speculative position on inventory for an item exhibiting a high degree of demand uncertainty presents a high degree of risk of product obsolescence and exposure to margin-eroding actions. The strategy, as described, differs by focusing on smaller batch sizes, thus reducing this risk while simultaneously increasing the iterations of innovative product offerings to the market. Successful offerings are pursued aggressively and less favorable offerings are phased out quickly.

The speed at which products are introduced to market can often determine success of the product's lifecycle. For example, the ability to bring fashion items to market quickly and before the items are "knocked off" (copied) by competition can determine how uniquely the items are perceived in the market and consequently how much of a margin the items can command. Market launch is often accomplished in conjunction with store profiles that note differences in sizes or regional preferences for colors or other product attributes based on historical observations in sales patterns. For example, stores designated as being located in top-tier mall locations or with specified amounts of foot traffic may be designated as A-profile stores. These stores would get a broader assortment of colors, sizes, and styles than other profiles. The objective is to keep the store profile count to a manageable number so that the factory can pack across the store profile and reflect carton designations on the packing list for processing at subsequent points in the distribution process.

Lifecycle of fashion-oriented product is often measured in days and weeks, so an approach that provides for a market read on early introduction followed by adjustments can support a product introduction strategy effectively and ensure overall margins during the product lifecycle.

FROM LAUNCH TO RESPONSE

Once initial reads of the market are available on a new product launch, the focus shifts to a pull approach where product attributes provide a pull signal to the supply chain. This model is well suited to postponement or a late differentiation approach. In the fashion apparel industry this is accomplished

Source: Peter Levesque

In-Store Fashion Changes Rapidly, Creating the Need for Dynamic Supply Chain Management

with various manufacturing techniques. One approach makes use of positioning un-dyed, or greige, fabric. Since fabric can be one of the longer lead time raw materials, positioning greige fabric compresses lead time on raw materials when raw materials and manufacturing processes are planned in a sequential manner. As a result, it is often practical to take a position on greige fabric and carry this at the factory for response to market acceptance of colors.

The late differentiating characteristics of color and silhouette (style based on the cut of fabric) can then be postponed until more certain demand is established from market tests and other customer feedback mechanisms. Using this approach, fashion product can chase market trends instead of forcing speculative decisions on style and color. While the approach may not result in the most efficient manufacturing process, margin realization on product that suits market demand more than compensates for additional manufacturing costs.

When products enter a more mature phase, supply chain solutions must evolve to meet the shift in market treatment. Mature products are generally better established and reflect only minor changes when offered in the market. For example, many fashion companies have core programs built around standard pants that involve only mild changes to styling over time.

Accordingly, speed-to-market of these types of products is less critical than more innovative market-entry products. Only a detailed assessment of each product can determine which approach is likely to yield the best result.

MANUFACTURING CAPACITY

The discussion of postponement strategies is often undertaken in a theoretical manner without the practical consideration of real-world constraints on capacity. If capacity is unconstrained it may be possible to delay differentiation on an entire production quantity until the latest possible moment; however, it is more likely that capacity to make late-stage differentiation within required lead times will be constrained, forcing some degree of inventory commitment in conjunction with product differentiation strategies.

The key theme is that it is not an all or none proposition. In the personal care market, production quantities of multiple SKUs are often based on the same underlying formulation of product. The only differentiating character-istics are fragrance and labeling that makes the product acceptable for a market (or perhaps several markets if a multilingual label can be used in conjunction with desired product aesthetics). If labeling were done entirely in advance, each market (or market grouping) would have a discrete inventory. Creating an ability to label the base product in response to market demands relieves the issue of discrete inventories; however, capacity for late-stage differentiation of product in a high-volume category is often impractical.

Consequently, a two-tiered approach can be applied whereby a base amount of the total forecast is manufactured to stock and the variability above the base is responded to with late-stage differentiation. This accom-plishes the objective of reducing reliance upon multiple inventories while simultaneously supporting postponement of final differentiation with a pool of shared inventory that ensures adequate capacity available at the time of differentiation. This approach has the added benefit of reducing risk of forecasting error through aggregation of demand. Disaggregated demand is inherently more risky since it incorporates forecasting error at the product or market level. At the product differentiation stage commitments must be made to the lower level of detail; however, this occurs at a later stage in the end-to-end process when information about actual demand is closer to market.

INFORMATION TECHNOLOGY—A KEY ENABLER

The focus of this chapter is not on information technology and yet no discussion of market strategies such as those under review would be complete without some mention of the importance of information technology as a key enabler of decision support in the pursuit of implementing these approaches. Many of the strategies involve significant coordination between multiple disciplines with internal and external supply chain partners. The use of systems to assimilate data from multiple sources and perform analysis in support of end-to-end decision making is a critical support structure for managers.

Substantial progress has been made incorporating sophisticated planning algorithms into today's enterprise planning systems. Many of the trade-offs surrounding inventory positioning, product lifecycle management, market testing, store profiling, and so on, benefit from system functionality now well established in today's software solutions. The systems provide the capability to pursue the strategies; it is the responsibility of managers to lead organizations to embrace the capabilities. Too often systems are underutilized because organizations are structured, measured, and managed in parts rather than as an interdependent organization and process.

Sales and operations planning (S&OP) is gaining momentum in many industries as a guiding methodology to ensure coordination across enterprise objectives. S&OP is the collection of processes and systems that provide an organization with visibility to manage supply and demand variability in its supply chain. A robust S&OP process provides managers with real-time data to evaluate trade-offs in pursuing different market responses. Multiple scenarios can be evaluated and reviewed across the organization to evaluate deployment decisions and ensure maximum effectiveness in the pursuit of enterprise objectives.

QUALITY CONTROL/ASSURANCE MANAGEMENT

Many organizations have pushed quality control/assurance activities up the supply chain in order to benefit from lower-origin labor costs. It is now relatively common to find quality control rooms within the operational space of 3PL logistics providers. The spaces are co-located where freight is being consolidated and processed so that inspections can be done in-line with processing and not slow the flow of freight. This represents an opportunity for those organizations that have not yet embraced the idea. However, the next step in the evolution of quality is moving further back in the supply chain to individual factories. Anyone who believes that quality management is beyond the capability of Chinese factories has not visited the territory recently enough to gain an appreciation for progress.

Levels of competency in quality management still vary between factories, but competition for customers on a global scale is fierce and factories are responding with increasing investment in middle managers with a focus on quality management. Expectations for suppliers of raw materials are increasing as well. Where factories once inspected inward flow of raw materials to ensure that suppliers were meeting specifications, competition across the supply base is setting the expectations that each member of the supply chain execute to accepted levels of product specifications so that cost and time are not wasted in redundant oversight of the process (get it right the first time). Companies unable to operate under this model will find it increasingly difficult to remain viable suppliers to markets with compression of lead times that force quality as a requirement.

BACK-ORDER MANAGEMENT IN THE FULFILLMENT INDUSTRY

Leveraging the aforementioned improvement in the flow of information visibility presents an interesting opportunity for company's interested in improving back-order management. Traditionally, when an order is received for a product that is not in stock, a demand signal registers with procurement that aggregates the incremental volume request to pending order activity. A subsequent order is placed with the factory and upon completion of the production run units are shipped through to a destination distribution center (DC) and expedited through the facility for customer fulfillment. The unit satisfying the customer's order may have been made days before the final bulk order completed for shipment, but additional lead time is incurred while the unit waits for the balance of the order to be finalized and shipped.

Today's improvement in order management systems and connectivity with manufacturing facilities means that factory systems can now be made aware of the pending order and process the unit for direct shipment upon completion of unit level within a broader production run. The immediate concern may be one of the transportation cost associated with courier shipments to a direct customer from overseas manufacturing locations. This can be mitigated to some extent by consolidating customer-level packages into larger "gaylord containers" that aggregate customer packages into geographic zones. Doing so leverages the initial international shipment into a single higher density point-to-point freight shipment. Upon arrival at destination the bulk shipment can be inducted into a courier network at the package level for distribution to customer, as shown in Figure 7.2.

This is undoubtedly a higher cost model than the traditional flow model that benefits from economies of scale throughout the transportation network. Nonetheless, in the fulfillment industry, customers have come to expect availability of product. Fulfillment companies track initial order fill rate as a key metric, because the ability to deliver on customer expectations has a material effect on profitability. Reports put the cost of backordered items in excess of US$15 per item. In many cases, this can represent a loss against the sale. More importantly perhaps is the damage to goodwill and associated future sales. Taking all of this into consideration showcases the opportunity to rethink the traditional approach to addressing backordered merchandise.

DIRECT-TO-STORE SHIPMENTS

A variation on the back-order model is worth considering in reference to store-based product introductions. As described earlier, effectiveness of product introductions is highly dependent on the ability to read and react to market demand signals. Traditionally, most product launches move through established supply chain processes by shipping product in bulk and utilizing distribution centers for processing. More recently, there has been increasing use of DC by-pass programs that distribute via regional facilities or through outsourced 3PL companies. These programs successfully bring product to market more quickly than traditional processes and can reduce costs by reducing the number of touches in processing goods for market. Global transportation companies have now developed and are marketing solutions that provide the ability to bring goods to market directly from the point of manufacture. This solution can deliver products to retail store in as little as

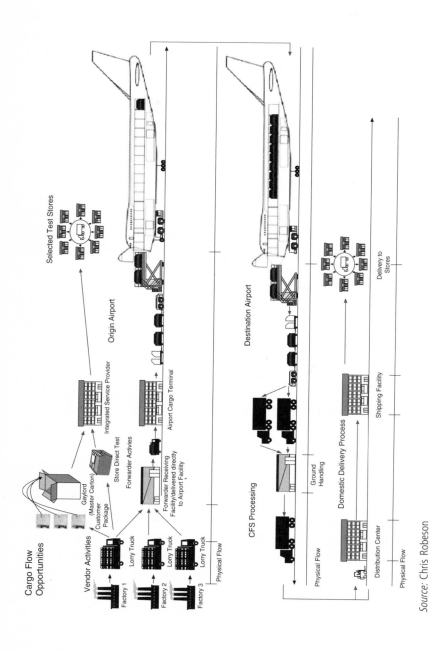

Source: Chris Robeson

Figure 7.2 Cargo Flow Opportunities

three to five days. Although this represents a higher cost solution, the value of having early customer acceptance information can mitigate costly mistakes in subsequent manufacturing cycles.

RECONSTRUCTING THE BASIS OF PRODUCT COST

Recent history is filled with examples of negotiations that focus on freight rates as a means of addressing cost pressures on product margins. Freight costs are a highly visible and often significant portion of a product's total landed cost. Additionally, market dynamics such as competition for shipyard capacity during periods of relative prosperity in global trade create an environment where carriers are forced to commit to ship orders well in advance of delivery (three to five years in many cases) creating tremendous volatility in supply and demand.

Changes in market demand for capacity force aggressive pricing environments for shippers and carriers alike. As shippers have become adept at negotiating within this environment, opportunities for competitive pricing have been realized. The traditional view of transportation rates as a cost center that requires aggressive management continues to be a prime focus for many organizations involved in international trade. These are costs that indeed require attention; however, this is not the only area of opportunity to manage costs associated with landing product.

An area of greater opportunity now exists in many industries in the ability to reconstruct the cost of product and determine where costs are addressed within the supply chain. For example, in many industry verticals, fees associated with logistics services performed at origin are paid by vendors and recovered in the cost of the product. In some ways this makes transactions for buyers more streamlined since differences in fees and exchange rates between origins makes the process of calculating landed costs more complex. However, the convenience of a simpler model has the potential of creating significant cost exposure.

Typical Hong Kong rates for consolidation of less-than-container-load size shipments approximate US$25 per cubic meter of cargo. Figure 7.3 shows a selection of component logistics costs as an example of the cost build-up for a product category with 25-percent duty rate exposure (there may be other variable and fixed costs for consideration in a more detailed analysis).

Stated assumptions	Value	Unit of measure
D40 standard CBMs	55	per cubic meter (CBM)
Average duty rate	25%	
CFS rate per CBM	$ 25.00	
Trucking cost per CBM factory to port	$ 4.00	

Annual CFS volume	50,000	CBMs
Annual container (Std)	909	FEU

Supplier-borne cost to ship D40 through consolidator (included in first cost)

	Paid By	Dutiable (Y/N)	Duty Incurred On Logistics Costs	Annual Cost Exposure
CFS receiving (stuffing)	$ 1,375.00 Factory	Y	$ 343.75	$ 312,500
THC	$ 184.00 Factory	Y	$ 46.00	$ 41,818
BL fee from carrier	$ 20.00 Factory	Y	$ 5.00	$ 4,545
Trucking factory to port	$ 220.00 Factory	Y	$ 55.00	$ 50,000
Total impact on first cost	$ 1,799.00		$ 449.75	$ 408,864

Importer-borne cost for origin services

	Paid By	Dutiable (Y/N)	Duty Incurred On Logistics Costs	Annual Cost Avoided
CFS receiving (stuffing)	$ 1,375.00 Importer	N	$ -	$ (312,500)
THC	$ 184.00 Importer	N	$ -	$ (41,818)
BL fee from carrier	$ 20.00 Importer	N	$ -	$ (4,545)
Trucking factory to port	$ 220.00 Importer	N	$ -	$ (50,000)
Total impact on first cost	$ 1,799.00		$ -	$ (408,864)

Source: Chris Robeson

Figure 7.3   Duty Matrix

Since duty cost is predicated on the cost paid or payable at the time goods are sold for exportation to the buyer (FOB price), as shown in Figure 7.3, any costs that suppliers are required to pay will increase the commercial invoice price and consequently increase the duty exposure to importers. The example portrays an importer with an annual import volume of approximately 900 containers. This discussion should be a cost-neutral discussion since it is simply a matter of shifting where the cost is treated within the supply chain. In industries with a tradition of bill of materials-based pricing, this can be a reasonably straightforward exercise of shifting costs from prepaid to collect terms (FOB to EXW for example) with associated costs being realized as a result of the change.

However, in some cases industry practice has traditionally treated these costs as insignificant in the overall cost structure. Under these circumstances, change management is the key to a successful transition from current state to proposed state. Concern with the ability for importers to engage in the management of product from factory to port has been a source of resistance to exploring these options in the past. Indeed, in the 1990s it was not uncommon to hear mainland China referred to as the "hinterland."

A lot has changed in the past decade to support a renewed interest in exploring origin-based logistics operations. Infrastructure within China has developed significantly and third party logistics providers have been steadily building out origin-based capabilities for warehousing, distribution and regulatory oversight. The building blocks are in place to support a fresh look at the opportunity. An added advantage of shifting buying terms in support of earlier supply chain involvement addresses ongoing review and changing regulations of supply chain security threats. Changing regulations and security expectations may drive shippers to take greater control of upstream logistics processes than previously held necessary. Shippers can get ahead of this by working with 3PL companies to define and manage factory-to-port services.

Discussions with vendors should be focused on the generation of value relative to the overall transaction. That is, by paying for these charges is the vendor generating value in the overall movement of product? If the answer is no, then a forum exists to engage in a dialogue around a better solution. Make no mistake; in many industries the costs in question relative to total product costs seem trivial. The measure of opportunity only becomes apparent in the context of overall volumes since the impact on any given order may not generate attention to the opportunity relative to the perceived degree of change required to realize the benefits of a new model.

SIZE AND SCALE CONSIDERATIONS

Importers familiar with industry practices are likely to identify with this chapter's references to processes and terms. Small- and medium-size organizations may not have the critical mass or in-house expertise to have as much exposure and experience to topics referenced. Nonetheless, the principles and practices can just as easily be applied to these organizations. Whereas traditional 3PL organizations focused on more specific tasks within the supply chain, like consolidation, customs processing, and local distribution, these services have now become largely commoditized. As a result, companies like APL Logistics, CEVA, DHL (Excel), Hellmann Worldwide Logistics, Maersk Logistics, to name but a few, are now engaged in developing customer solutions that bridge across a multitude of services. What these organizations offer is an opportunity to leverage their in-house expertise that runs deep within functional and industry verticals so that small- and medium-size companies can benefit from industry best-practice approaches that scale effectively as business expands and adapts to changing market demands.

The Fashion Industry's Progression Toward Postponement

In the late 1960s and well into the 1970s it was common to find major department stores making biannual buying trips to suppliers in Asia and elsewhere to place orders for spring and fall seasons. Due to lead time on fabric and commitments to production, this model resulted in highly speculative procurement of styles as buyers anticipated, and attempted to exert aspirational influence upon, fashion trends and associated customer demand. Factories and mills enjoyed the consistency that these extended time frames represented for secure production schedules. Buyers who found success with particular styles realized healthy margins; unfortunately, unsuccessful styles caused buyers to give back much of the profitability of the popular styles in terms of net results. In the midst of this environment a model of "speed sourcing" emerged, which is often considered a given in today's environment. Merchants began a process of purchasing in smaller order quantities and bringing product to market quickly (often utilizing airfreight) to expedite a read of market receptiveness to the styles. Successful styles were reordered and expedited to market while laggards were exited quickly through markdowns and resulting funds were channeled back to styles with encouraging results.

The approach developed and improved in execution with the introduction of technology to communicate in a more seamless fashion. Sales data recorded at retail store locations could be polled daily and run through algorithms to generate sales forecasts. This model resulted in a natural cadence of store sales and order management developed as an operating model that proved highly successful for two decades.

However, the success of the model was not overlooked by the industry and increasingly the approach of staying close to market and defining more frequent changes of product offering became the industry norm. This situation created new challenges for suppliers and manufacturers in the supply chain, but the customer came to demand the approach and demonstrated their evaluation of retailers with purchases as their voting mechanism. The transition is in some cases a higher cost model since it can require more disruptive manufacturing processes (for example, shorter production runs, smaller batches of raw materials, etc.). However, the value created by keeping supply closer to the demands of customers can vastly overshadow the increase in costs. The cost of mark-downs, sell-offs, and other margin-eroding activities is frequently underestimated in the decision-making process. Many organizations have failed to adapt to the reality and will likely suffer as a result of resistance to change.

A more competitive model was required to respond to shorter product lifecycles and increasing global competition. European retailers H&M and Zara have developed a method of sourcing that embodies the speed of previous models while introducing new approaches to further respond to customer preferences in an agile manner. Zara, with its vertical integration has tremendous control over the supply chain it uses to bring products to market. However, key to its success is the decision-making environment created to act swiftly on information from the market. Zara shop employees are

(continued)

intimately familiar with their customer base and take action to adjust products in the development pipeline. Their organizational structure is the key to this success by viewing designers as the creative input to a process that subsequently is acted upon by a "commercial team." The team comprises all functional areas of the organization that are physically co-located to act as a team in evaluating market opportunities on an end-to-end basis of costs and margins in reaching a rapid decision on styles.

CONCLUSION

Global competition, compressed product margins, and increasing consumer expectations for unique and customized purchasing experiences are increasing at an unprecedented rate. This reality requires supply chain professionals to deliver supply chains that provide responsiveness and flexibility in support of evolving market expectations. Responsive products are increasingly an imperative rather than a differentiating strategy as markets continue to evolve toward ever-increasing levels of change. The new environment requires that supply chain professionals rethink traditional methods of operating in order to ensure solutions are keeping pace with the new consumer model.

Information technology has become a key enabling mechanism in linking together strategies and planning tools to support decision making in an increasingly complex environment. However, systems and strategies can only be effective when implemented by leaders with the ability to build out processes and organizational structures that manage and measure effectiveness across all functional areas of the business. Successful dynamic supply chains in the years ahead will need to take all these factors into careful consideration.

NOTE

1   James F. Robeson and William C. Copacino (eds), *The Logistics Handbook*, (New York: The Free Press, 1994), 453.

CHAPTER EIGHT

THE ROLE OF PEOPLE AND TECHNOLOGY IN DYNAMIC SUPPLY CHAINS

PETER LEVESQUE

Anyone who has ever sat inside an airplane cockpit has seen the myriad of complex flight instruments, computer technology and communications equipment, designed to help a pilot fly safely from one point to another. For a student pilot, the cockpit can seem like information overload, particularly in the early phases of flight training. It can be difficult to strike a balance between the need to know what the instruments are indicating and the more fundamental requirements of simply flying the airplane.

It varies by individual, but at some point during flight training a student pilot becomes comfortable with the cockpit environment. All the training comes together and the student pilot actually begins to fly the airplane, building confidence along the way. Once a pilot is comfortable in the cockpit, however, an airplane's advanced technologies such as autopilot can sometimes create a false sense of security. One flight instructor's story warns of the dangers that can result:

> *On a sunny day over North Texas two airplanes were involved in a mid-air collision, killing both pilots. At the ensuing press conference the NTSB crash investigator was asked how two state-of-the-art airplanes, each containing the latest in radar and crash-avoidance technology could possibly collide, on a day without a cloud in the sky. And the NTSB investigator replied: "Because every so often you still need to look out the window."*[1]

Source: Gary Ombler, Getty Images

Airplane Cockpit Information Can Appear Overwhelming

Most mid-air plane collisions in fact happen in daytime, in good weather conditions and clear visibility.[2] The NTSB reports that the most probable cause of these mid-air collisions is that the pilots failed to see and avoid the other aircraft (pilots not looking out the window).[3] The moral of the story is that the best information technology in the world cannot replace the human attributes of situational awareness and common sense.

As IT systems become more complex and integrated into our daily work, there is a growing tendency to focus too much on what the computer system is saying while ignoring common sense factors that lie beyond the computer screen. Too much reliance on any system can lead to problems. If you have ever tried to change an airline ticket reservation at the service counter, then you know the anxiety and frustration of a computer system designed to prevent common sense all together. The airline agent enters an endless series of keystrokes (with a few phone calls added in), only to advise at the end of the process that the ticket change is

> **Shipping Point:**
> **"People are not your most important asset . . . The right people are."**
>
> *Jim Collins,*
> Good to Great

not possible. When asked why not, the answer from the customer service agent is usually, "because that's what the system is telling me." Airline reservation systems offer a perfect example of where the human element, that is so critical to problem resolution and customer satisfaction, has been lost. Preventing the same thing from happening in supply chain management by focusing on the human aspect of problem resolution is a worthy endeavor.

While logistics computer systems will continue to play a critical role in executing more flexible and dynamic supply chain models in the future, having the right people on board will be even more important. LSPs need to begin focusing on the recruitment of people who have the analytical skills to interpret systems data, as well as the creative and artistic capability necessary to recognize patterns, anticipate trends, and create solutions on the spot.

In the hyper-competitive landscape that lies ahead, LSPs will differentiate themselves more on the talent they employ than on the technology they use. Daniel Pink describes the need for people who can create "symphony" in their daily work, which is "the ability to put together the pieces. It is the capacity to synthesize rather than to analyze; to see relationships between seemingly un-related fields; to detect broad patterns rather than to deliver specific answers; and to invent something new by combining elements nobody else thought to pair."[4]

The need for new talent in SCM becomes more pronounced when dealing with China. Because there are so many opportunities for young Chinese people with solid skill sets, employee turnover rates are very high. Because of this high turnover, managers in China have been hesitant to spend the time and money training staff on IT systems and higher-level business processes. A manager in China may ask, "what if we train our staff and they leave?" when the important question for the future of SCM is "what if we don't train our people and they stay?" Successful SCM will require well-trained staff, enabled with the best logistics technology available. Short cuts and quick fixes in the area of human capital will not be sustainable.

An article on IndustryWeek.com said that, "Despite the numerous advances in ERP systems, dynamic demand planning tools and supply chain modeling software over the past decade, most major supply chain decisions are still ultimately made by people."[5]

In their book, *Competing in a Flat World*, Victor and William Fung describe their experience with IT this way: "Although information technology has transformed business organizations, the heart of any network and enterprise consists of human judgment, trust, human relationships, and business processes. What is most remarkable about Li & Fung technology is not the technology itself but how important human judgment and experience continues to be."[6]

In order to successfully execute flexible and dynamic supply chain models moving forward, having the right people will be as important as having the right system. Finding, training and retaining the right people in China will continue to be a major challenge, and advances in IT will need to be more closely linked with advances in HR.

Another issue that will need attention in order to support demand-driven supply chains is the area of corporate structure. How information is shared, analyzed and acted upon depends in large part on the organizational structure of the firm. To be effective in the demand-driven marketplace companies will need to break down functional silos to create an environment that enables rapid processing of vast amounts of information into actionable intelligence. Retailers in the years ahead will need to quickly understand and anticipate individual consumer patterns and trends as they develop. To do this, companies will need to re-evaluate how they gather, analyze, and disseminate key market and supply chain data across the organization.

Many corporations today face the same issue that the United States intelligence agencies faced prior to September 11, 2001. The 9/11 Commission Report highlighted the fact that the FBI and the CIA had a significant amount of data that pointed toward an impending attack. What they lacked was the ability to aggregate and analyze all the data across agencies making it impossible for anyone to connect the dots before it was too late. Former CIA director, George Tenet, wrote "From my perspective, the single biggest obstacle we needed to overcome was that there was no single place where foreign intelligence and domestic information could be put together and analyzed quickly to empower those who could do something about it."[7]

Likewise within many corporations, functional departments can have tremendous amounts of information, but lack the corporate culture and organizational structure that would allow all the data to be analyzed together. The result is that management receives chapters of information rather than getting the full story.

Prahalad and Krishnan in their book, *Innovation*, describe the convergence of the social architecture of a firm (organizational structure, performance metrics, career management, skills, beliefs, values) with the firm's technical architecture (database systems, application, and analytics) in the execution of business processes. The social architecture of an organization, say the authors, needs to support the "co-creation" of knowledge across business units by providing a corporate culture and incentive structure that supports and rewards information sharing. A good example of simplicity in social architecture and information sharing for successful SCM, can be found inside the *dabbawallah* daily lunch program in Mumbai, India.

Source: Getty Images

A *Dabbawallah* Lunch Cart

In 1890, Mahadeo Havaji Bachche started this lunch delivery network after he found that people who were moving to Mumbai could not get home-cooked food for lunch.[8] Today, over 175,000 home-cooked lunches (tiffins) are delivered by more than 5,000 *dabbawallahs*, working in teams of four, to lunch customers at their place of work every day by 12:30pm, covering a total transport area of over 75 kilometers. In actuality, the total number of deliveries per day equals 350,000 because between 1:15 p.m. and 2:00 p.m. each tiffin is picked up after lunch and dropped back at the customer's home.[9]

The *dabbawallahs* do not prepare the lunches; they only deliver them. The lunches are prepared by the customers themselves, reflecting Mumbai's preference for home-cooked food. What is of particular interest in the

Dabbawallah Coding System

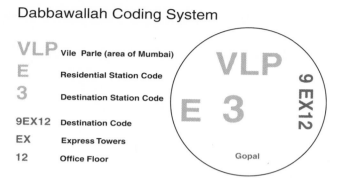

VLP	Vile Parle (area of Mumbai)
E	Residential Station Code
3	Destination Station Code
9EX12	Destination Code
EX	Express Towers
12	Office Floor

Source: Created by Peter Levesque with data from Chandra Sekhar Ramasastry[11]

Figure 8.1   The *Dabbawallah* Delivery Code Information Sheet

dabbawallah model is that the service failure rate for all these pick-ups and deliveries is reported to be one in every 15 million deliveries. This is equivalent to a 99.9999-percent degree of accuracy earning the *dabbawallahs* six sigma recognition by *Forbes Magazine* in 1998.[10] Each new *dabbawallah* recruit goes through a two-year apprenticeship to learn the trade and the codes as shown in Figure 8.1, before purchasing a route and becoming a fully-fledged *dabbawallah*. After training, the recruit basically has a job for life.

Visibility of accurate, consistent and timely data across the enterprise allows businesses to configure the best solution for each customer based on availability, capacity, cost, quality, and timeliness. Getting the social and technical architecture right will enable businesses to anticipate consumer demand in real time, while understanding the resources needed to support the changing business.[12] Well-trained people, that can quickly analyze consumer preferences as well as supply chain data and turn that information into actionable intelligence, will be critical to the success of the demand-driven supply chain of the future.

THE ROLE OF TECHNOLOGY IN DYNAMIC SUPPLY CHAINS

The extraordinary improvements made in the area of SCM over the last several years can be attributed in large part to the development of more powerful logistics information systems. Transportation management systems help optimize routing and delivery schedules, while warehouse management systems help increase inventory turns and support pick and pack distribution models.

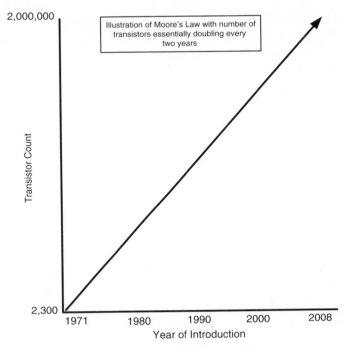

Source: Created by Peter Levesque; based on data from Jon Stokes[13]

Figure 8.2   Moore's Law in Chart Format

Purchase order management systems calculate landed cost per unit and provide milestone event tracking from origin to destination. These systems will continue to become more powerful and complex in the years ahead.

Intel co-founder Gordon E. Moore recognized a technology trend back in 1965 with regard to computing power. Moore's law, as shown in Figure 8.2, says that the number of transistors that can be placed on an integrated circuit doubles every two years. This essentially means that computing power doubles every two years. If Moore's law holds true, we can expect more powerful and capable systems to be developed for years to come. But system-computing power has never really been the issue in SCM. The roadblock with logistics systems continues to be their inability to integrate with each other in order to present a single view of what is happening across the entire supply chain.

Wal-Mart has been on the forefront of aggregating business data and linking market demand with real-time SCM. In the early 1980s, Wal-Mart had already invested in a satellite network in outer space that could enable the transmission of point-of-sale data information (POS) and even video conferencing to its entire retail store network. In 1991, Wal-Mart developed a private extranet called Retail Link, which has since become the largest civilian database in the world. The key to the system is that they share it with their suppliers who can then plan for their own stock replenishment and production runs on behalf of Wal-Mart.

These powerful systems give Wal-Mart the ability to merge weather data with store demand. In one example, Wal-Mart's historical data showed that prior to a hurricane beer was the top selling item and strawberry pop-tarts sold at seven times their normal rate.[14] Consumer data like this helps to explain how Wal-Mart achieved US$401 billion of revenue in 2009. That's approximately US$46 million of revenue an hour, 24 hours a day, 365 days a year.

As advanced as Wal-Mart's systems are, many U.S. and European companies are still trying to solve the most basic of product visibility requirements. Those requirements include purchase order management, vendor and milestone reporting, inventory and carrier management, along with the ability to calculate landed cost. While there are numerous software solutions available today that can support some of these requirements, it is difficult to find a single system that can offer a complete solution. This creates what has been called the "IT Expectation/Performance Gap," where customers place a great deal of value on an LSP's system capabilities, but in general feel a lot more work is needed to achieve better, more integrated supply chain visibility.[15]

The primary reason for the expectation/performance gap has to do with the historical development of IT in the supply chain industry. LSPs and other multi-modal transportation companies came to view the development of proprietary visibility systems as a competitive advantage in the marketplace. The development of proprietary systems was seen as a way to increase customer retention, by embedding LSP-owned technology into the client's business process. This resulted in a wave of systems development as LSPs and transportation companies rushed to build their own in-house systems in the hope of gaining competitive advantage.

The systems that were developed during this flurry of activity were one-dimensional and mode-specific. Ocean carriers, for example, developed container-tracking capability, but only for cargo riding on their own vessels. Domestic distribution companies developed proprietary warehouse management systems

(WMS) and route optimization software for use in their own network. International logistics companies developed purchase order management systems with varying levels of industry connectivity. At the end of the day, millions of dollars were spent across the transportation industry developing IT systems that were designed to protect information rather than to share it.

The end result of all this activity was a hodgepodge of proprietary supply chain systems in the market that could provide customers with pieces of the story, but could not tell the whole story. Recognizing this as a business opportunity, several pure IT companies (companies not affiliated with any transportation providers) entered the market with the goal of aggregating supply chain data across the broad spectrum of service providers and delivering that information through web-based visibility platforms.

While this approach was a step in the right direction, it was quickly discovered that these neutral web-based hubs were only as good as the willingness of service providers to populate them with information. Carriers and LSPs who had developed their own proprietary systems were not willing to give up the value and control of their data by sharing it with customers through an independent data-service platform. This is essentially what delayed the aggregation and integration of multi-modal data in the global supply chain.

One example of progress in SCM data visibility can be found at GTNexus, as shown in Figure 8.3. This web-based IT platform provides LSPs and their clients with a global trade and logistics portal, enabling supply chain visibility

	Visibility Into...	Process Automation
"Upstream"	Purchase Orders	Order Management
	Supplier Activities	Supplier Scorecards
	Inventory	Inventory Financing
"Where's my Stuff?"	Shipments	Shipment Tracking
"Downstream"	Trade Documents	Document Automation
	Costs	Actual Landed Cost
	Payments	Transaction Processing

Advanced platforms like GT Nexus enable customers to extend supply chain visibility beyond basic shipment tracking which opens up a range of strategic opportunities across the enterprise.

Source: Courtesy of GTNexus

Figure 8.3   Visibility and Automation

that begins with the purchase order and ends with cargo delivery at the final destination. Companies such as GTNexus are replacing the one-dimensional logistics software model of the past with neutral IT platforms capable of telling a more complete story as cargo moves from point A to point B. These platforms act as a data hub, connecting electronically with multiple service providers including ocean, air, brokerage, and financial institutions to provide the customer with a single view of what is happening across the supply chain.[16]

Milestone tracking within the GTNexus solution includes an early warning system when the estimated time of arrival for cargo goes beyond the scheduled arrival date. Exceptions that occur within the supply chain are communicated to customers and their LSPs via a dashboard function for immediate visibility and resolution. Other benefits of this neutral platform as shown in Figure 8.4 include the electronic storage and transmission of shipping documents such as purchase orders, packing lists, commercial invoices, bills of lading, customs documentation, and container manifests. Most recently, the addition of ISF 10+2 compliance has been added to the GTNexus platform, helping clients meet U.S. government cargo security requirements.

The GTNexus platform has the added feature of being able to calculate transportation costs on a per unit basis. Clients can establish a target shipping cost per unit, and then accurately measure the target against the actual cost per unit. Being able see this data helps clients make adjustments to freight transportation that can bring the actual cost per unit back toward the target

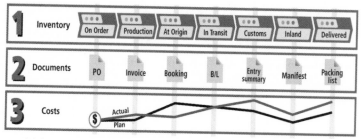

Global inventory-in-motion-related documents and costs can all be tracked and managed over a single on-demand platform, like GT Nexus.

Source: Courtesy of GTNexus

Figure 8.4   Inventory in Motion

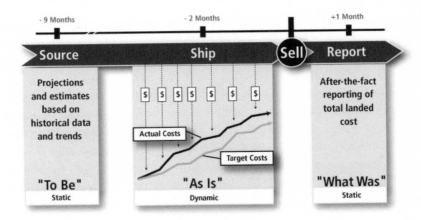

Actual landed cost helps shippers augment estimated landed costs with actual landed costs, that are captured as inventory moves from order to final delivery.

Source: Courtesy of GTNexus

Figure 8.5   Dynamic vs Static Landed Cost Visibility

cost in situations where it may be over the budgeted level. The GTNexus solution can also retain and manage multiple carrier contracts and rate filings, reducing transportation contract complexity and providing a built-in rate audit function. Systems such as GTNexus provide customers with a clearer picture, as shown in Figure 8.5, on the gaps between what is supposed to happen and what is actually happening, giving the customer and the LSP the ability to make real-time decisions to address exceptions in the system.

In addition to visibility tools like GTNexus, the development of neutral finance platforms such as TradeCard, are helping customers improve working capital by managing the financial flows that impact the supply chain, and enabling real-time decision making that can positively impact the bottom line. The TradeCard platform provides financial supply chain services by managing transactions between companies and their suppliers. Because the platform represents an open, service-neutral network, multiple trading partners can connect and transact from anywhere in the world.

Areas of automation within the finance function can include electronic invoicing, access to third party inventory and receivables financing, as well as reverse factoring. Facilitating the international buying and selling process using an open account finance model allows clients to move away from costly letters of credit and banking fees. Reverse factoring enables a supplier in China to utilize their customer's credit rating and beneficial interest rates to purchase raw materials used in product manufacturing. The savings generated are then passed on to the customer through a lower first cost of goods.[17]

An integrated approach to supply chain visibility that includes both the physical and financial flows associated with international trade can be advantageous. An integrated approach can help companies identify performance levers within the global supply chain, and reduce working capital through better inventory management and reduced cycle times. The key, however, is having visibility to the complete picture rather than attempting to draw conclusions based on any single component of the supply chain process.[18]

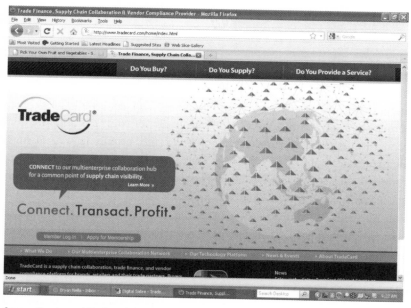

Source: Courtesy of Tradecard.com

The TradeCard Web Portal

Supply chain visibility software has come a long way over the last several years. The historical roadblocks caused by the rush to create proprietary software solutions have been replaced with service-neutral, web-based IT platforms. It is now possible for clients and LSPs to aggregate multi-modal transportation data into a single front-end application, and at the same time support the documentation and financial flows associated with international supply chain. These neutral platforms will help bridge the expectation/ performance gap between clients and their LSPs by providing a more robust solution for the collection and transmission of a broader range of supply chain information.

RADIO FREQUENCY IDENTIFICATION TECHNOLOGY

Over the last several years the SCM community has been paying a great deal of attention to radio frequency identification technology (RFID). But the questions still remain: Can RFID be implemented in a cost-effective manner? What problems will an RFID tag solve that an inexpensive barcode label cannot? Is RFID killing an ant with a sledgehammer?

In 1999, the Auto ID Center was developed at MIT as a non-profit collaboration between research academia and the private sector to develop a global product-tracking infrastructure using RFID technology. This infrastructure used the standardized electronic product code (EPC) numbering scheme. The EPC contained a global trade item number (GTIN), which kept barcode-level information as well as a serial number that could identify each individual item.

The center was phased out in September of 2003. In its place, the Uniform Code Council (UCC) and European Article Number (EAN) International established a non-profit organization called EPCglobal, to further commercialize EPC technology as a global standard. Auto-ID labs at universities around the world carry on the RFID research that started with the MIT Auto ID Center. To many, EPCglobal has become the supply chain standard for RFID tags Class 1 Gen 2, also known as ISO-180006-c.

There are two specific kinds of RFID tags. The first is called a "passive" tag in that it does not contain its own power supply. Energy from radio waves converts to electricity when hitting the tag, which powers a microchip that reflects information back to the reader. These tags can range between US$0.10 cents and US$0.17 cents per tag and higher, which could be cost prohibitive in large volumes. The second type of tag is called an "active" tag. This tag contains a small battery that powers a transmitter, which sends signals to the reader. These tags can be read from as far away as 300 feet, but they cost more.

Source: Steve Taylor, Getty Images

Sample RFID Tag

One example of where RFID is being applied successfully is the micro supply chain between the retailer's supply room and the store shelf. A case study on Wal-Mart's supply chain notes that, "according to researchers about 25 percent of out-of-stock inventory in the United States was not really out of stock: the items were misplaced on the store floor or mis-shelved in the backroom." The Wal-Mart case study also highlights the benefits of RFID usage in the micro supply chain, noting that, "in a study by the University of Arkansas, Wal-Mart stores with RFID tags showed a net improvement of 16 percent fewer out-of-stocks on the RFID tagged products that were tested."[19] Let's look at some other examples of successful RFID usage.

METRO GROUP & RFID

German retailer Metro Group began testing RFID technology in 2003, and in 2004 the retailer opened the Metro Group RFID Innovation Center. By 2005, pallet-level RFID tagging was taking place from 33 selected suppliers to nine Metro DCs and 13 Metro stores. Metro Group had several goals in mind with its phased RFID initiative, including a reduction in the amount of shrinkage (theft) in the supply chain, reducing incidents of stock-outs, improving on-shelf availability, and improving promotional compliance. Improving labor productivity by eliminating human data entry and barcode scanning was also on the list of RFID goals.[20] These issues that Metro sought to address with RFID certainly warranted management's attention. Reducing the shrinkage issue alone would have a major impact on the business. The National Retail Security Survey Final Report in 2003 estimated that incidents of shrinkage cost the retail industry 1.3 percent of sales, or US$26 billion.[21]

In the Metro case study analysis, the largest potential benefits of RFID technology came from automating manual processes and making current processes more efficient. Reducing the number of inventory stock takes (inventory counts) and improving product availability were also desired outcomes.

Metro was able to improve its truck loading efficiency by using pallet RFID tags. This eliminated the need for barcode scanning of pallets prior to loading and required less warehouse supervision for the loading process. Case level RFID tags helped improve warehouse order pick accuracy and reduced incidents of wrong picks using a specific signal, which indicated that the wrong item had been chosen. Improvements were also made using RFID in knowing what items were actually available in the retailer's storage room in order to match that data with point-of-sale information. This allowed Metro to get replenishment items to the store shelf faster while reducing the number of stock-outs.

In many cases, however, the theory behind RFID has been difficult to transform into reality. Some of the issues have to do with the technology itself. RFID tags can operate low frequency (135khz) or high frequency (13.56 mhz). The higher frequency tags can transmit data faster, but they use more power than lower frequency tags. The problem with radio frequency waves is that they are less reliable around surfaces containing liquid or metals, because liquid absorbs radio waves and metal objects reflect them. This can prevent radio signals from getting to and from the RFID tag and the RFID scanning equipment as these types of surfaces interfere with the typical RFID tag antenna.[22] Considering the amount of metals, foils, and liquids contained in a typical grocery store shipment (even the high iron content in rice can be an issue for RFID), one can begin to see the hurdles that need to be overcome before this technology can ever become as ubiquitous as the traditional barcode label.

While some companies claim to have developed tags that resolve these problems the fundamental issue of RFID's cost per tag continues to make the solution prohibitive. More research and development is still needed to make RFID technology both cost effective and easy to use. A 2007 Capgemini report surveyed 1,568 logistics executives across 61 countries and noted that respondents felt RFID use was still questionable and that RFID cost was prohibitive.[23]

Many view the absence of RFID global standards as a major obstacle that must be overcome before a more aggressive adoption of the technology can take place. The same 2007 Capgemini survey noted that only about 3–5 percent of customers were inquiring about 3PL RFID capability in their requests for proposal, compared with approximately 10 percent just three years earlier. The 2008 Capgemini survey noted that only 13 percent of customers reported any use of RFID by their 3PL service providers; however, 61 percent of customers said they expected to be using RFID sometime in the future. By contrast, 80 percent of survey participants in 2008 said they were using barcode label printing and scanning technology, or planned to use it in the future.[24]

On the technology horizon is a new form of shipping label currently being developed at MIT's Media Lab. The label is called Bokode, named after the Japanese photography term "*bokeh*," which is the blob-like image produced by a camera when photographing an out-of-focus light source. The data in this tiny tag can be read by a normal camera with its focus set to infinity and can also be read by the naked eye when viewed up close. If the development of the Bokode tag is successful, it could potentially complement or replace traditional barcode label technology.

While the commercial applications of Bokode are still being explored, Ankit Mohan from MIT's Media Lab notes, "As a replacement for conventional barcodes, the Bokode system could have several advantages. It could provide far more information (such as the complete nutrition label from a food product). The tag can also be read from a distance by a shopper scanning the supermarket shelves allowing for easy product comparisons, because several items near each other on the shelves could all be scanned at once."[25] Media Lab's David Chandler also explains that the tags do not require laser scanners and can potentially be read by digital camera technology contained

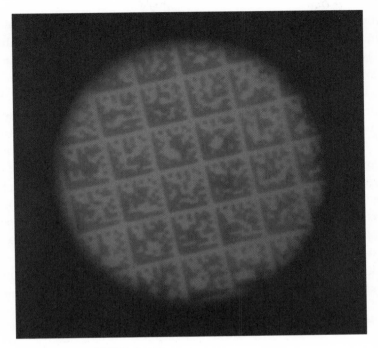

Source: Courtesy of MIT Media Lab

Bodoke Tag

in everyday cell phones. The current tags being tested cost about US$5.00 each; however, the Media Lab predicts that the price could fall to US$0.05 each once they are produced in volume, giving the Bokode tag a cost advantage over RFID. Whether it's Bokode, RFID, or some other form of data tag technology, it appears likely that SCM visibility tools will continue to improve in the years ahead. Better visibility will drive greater efficiency and enable more dynamic and innovative logistics programs to be developed over the next decade.

SUPPLY CHAIN SECURITY & TRACKING TECHNOLOGY

While purchase order visibility and milestone tracking have improved significantly over the last several years, the integration of international and domestic last-mile delivery and road management solutions into supply chain IT solutions has been slow. The next wave of systems integration in SCM tools will include more robust transportation management and security platforms such as GEARS, a web-based tracking solution developed by GeoDecisions, a division of Gannett Fleming based in Harrisburg, Pennsylvania.

GeoDecisions focuses on geographical information systems (GIS), which include mapping and geospatial technology that allows clients to better visualize what is happening across the supply chain. GeoDecisions recognized early on the value of integrating this type of mapping technology within larger corporate- and government-based enterprise systems. The technology provides supply chain managers with a more comprehensive picture of what is actually happening on the ground, anywhere in the world. The solution enables multiple parties across different organizations or entities to simultaneously view the same information.

GEARS supports transportation and supply chain security initiatives and provides early warning emergency management capability to logistics teams and distribution networks. GEARS is able to track multi-modal shipments around the world, whether by rail, road or sea. The system is able to provide

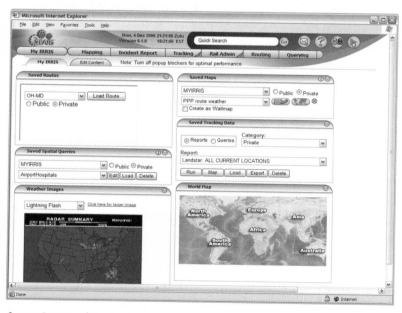

Source: Courtesy of GeoDecisions

GEAR's Comprehensive Tracking Portal

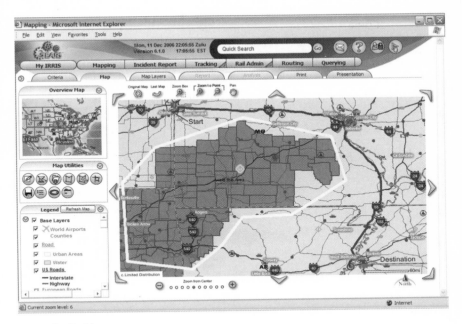

Source: GeoDecisions

GEARS GeoFence Area is Highlighted in White

up-to-the-minute directions to truck drivers, and enables route optimization using available information on traffic speed, weather conditions and accident delays. Milestones are implemented using "GeoFences," which creates pre-determined areas of concern that clients wish to be notified about.

GEARS provides what GeoDecisions calls a "common operating picture" (COP) that incorporates all the relevant information on cargo movements into an easy-to-read map format allowing for more dynamic decision-making capability. Tracking can be achieved via simple GPS-enabled cell phone technology or by other more sophisticated signals. From a security perspective, clients can receive notification of vehicles that have deviated from their assigned routes. Of particular interest to logistics management teams is the ability to quickly implement contingency plans around incidents that may occur across the supply chain. GEARS incident reporting capability enables transport management teams to activate contingency plans more rapidly and with greater confidence.

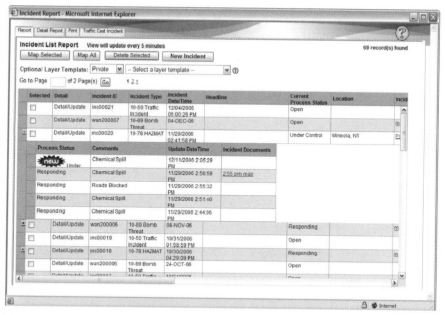

Source: Courtesy of GeoDecisions

GEARS Web-Based Incident Reporting Capability

There are exciting opportunities for advanced tracking technology such as GEARS in places like China. There is also the possibility, however, that the Chinese government might perceive these types of mapping technologies as a potential threat to national security. The mapping of roads, sea ports, and other key areas of China's infrastructure, would be extremely useful in the development of China's domestic logistics network. Government sensitivity around the technology would need to be addressed head-on in order to be successful. Once the sensitivity issues are resolved, the ability to provide greater transparency to cargo as it moves from the manufacturing point of origin in China all the way to its final destination will add a higher degree of safety, security and visibility to the supply chain network, both internationally and domestically.

While the development of these new tracking systems will offer greater visibility and functionality in the area of SCM, customers may not be as eager to adopt yet another stand-alone system into their supply chain technology suite if they can help it. A system that integrates tracking and tracing functionality with items such as vendor management, purchase order management, landed cost analysis, trade finance, and documentation would be an attractive offering in the market. The good news is that we can expect to see more systems integration occur over the next several years as the demand for a more consolidated view of events across the supply chain intensifies.

NOTES

1   As recounted by Brian Carter, CFI McKinney, Texas, 1994.
2   On August 8, 2009, a small plane and a helicopter collided over the Hudson River in New York killing nine people. The accident happened at 11:56 a.m. There wasn't a cloud in the sky. See Rich Schapiro, Wil Cruz, Alison Gendar and Larry Mcshane, "Helicopter, Small Plane Collide, Crash in Hudson River; Mayor Bloomberg: All 9 Onboard Presumed Dead," *NY Daily News*, Sunday, August 9, 2009, www .nydailynews.com/ny_local/2009/08/08/2009-08-08_helicopter_crash_near_new_ jersey_.html.
3   "Mid-Air Collision Avoidance," Dover Air Force Base Flight Safety Office 436 AW (October, 2008).
4   Pink, *A Whole New Mind*, 130.
5   *IndustryWeek*, http://www.idustryweek.com/printarticle.aspx?articleID=18285& sectionID=14.
6   Fung et al, *Competing in a Flat World*, 63, 128.
7   George Tenet, *At The Center of the Storm, My Years at the CIA*, (New York: HarperCollins, 2007), 502.
8   Larry Menor and Chandra Sekhar Ramasastry, "Dabbawallahs of Mumbai (A)," (London, Ontario: Ivey Publishing, Ivey Management Services, 2004).
9   Ibid.
10 Ibid.
11 Ibid.
12 C. K. Prahalad and M.S. Krishnan, *The New Age of Innovation: Driving Cocreated Value Through Global Networks*, (New York: McGraw Hill, 2008), 96–99.
13 Jon Stokes, "Classic.Ars: Understanding Moore's Law," ARS Technica, September 27, 2008, see http://arstechnica.com/hardware/news/2008/09/moore.ars and a chart by W.G. Simon, which can be found at http://en.wikipedia.org/wiki/File:Transistor_ Count_and_Moore%27s_Law_-_2008.svg.
14 Constance L. Hays, "What Wal-Mart Knows About Customers' Habits," *New York Times*, November 14, 2004.
15 Ibid., 14.
16 All GTNexus system and company information can be found at http://www.gtnexus. com.
17 All Tradecard system and company information can be found at http://www .tradecard.com.

18   Thomas Krupp, Michael Krupp and Peter Klaus, "A Quantum Leap in Reducing Working Capital Commitment in a Global Supply Chain," CSCMP Supply Chain Innovation Award Paper (2006): http://cscmp.org/downloads/public/education/06 innovation/CEAG.pdf.

19   Fraser P. Johnson, "Supply Chain Management at Wal-Mart," Case 907D01, (London, Ontario: Ivey Publishing, Ivey Management Services, 2006), 10.

20   Zeynep Ton, Vincent Dessain, Monika Stachowiak-Joulaìn, "RFID at the Metro Group," (Boston: Harvard Business School Publishing, April 1, 2009).

21   Prahalad, *The New Age of Innovation*.

22   Peter Cole, Zhonghao Hu, "Solving the Water and Metal Problem," *RFID Journal*, April 6, 2009, http://www.rfidjournal.com/article/view/4755.

23   "The State of Logistics Outsourcing, 2007 Third-Party Logistics, Results and Findings of the 12th Annual Study," Capgemini, Georgia Institute of Technology, Oracle, DHL.

24   "The State of Logistics Outsourcing, 2008 Third-Party Logistics, Results and Findings of the 13th Annual Study," Capgemini, Georgia Institute of Technology, SAP, DHL.

25   David L. Chandler, "Barcodes for the rest of us, tiny labels could pack lots of information, enable new uses," *MIT News*, July 24, 2009, http://web.mit.edu/news office/2009/barcodes-0724.html.

CHAPTER NINE

BUILDING RESILIENCE AND SUSTAINABILITY INTO THE CHINESE SUPPLY CHAIN

PETER LEVESQUE

Webster's Dictionary defines "resilience" as the ability to recover quickly from illness, change or misfortune, and it defines "sustainability" as a business process capable of being continued with minimal long-term effect on the environment. These two areas of focus as applied to supply chain management may appear mutually exclusive. In practice, however, there are many advantages to blending the two when developing a comprehensive international supply chain strategy.

The importance of building a resilient strategy has been known to the military for centuries. The Prussian general and military strategist Karl von Clausewitz, in 1832 outlined the fundamentals for building a resilient strategy that are as relevant today as they were back then. Von Clausewitz said that:

1. Strategy is the evolution of a central idea through continuing changing circumstances.
2. Detailed planning often fails because of the inevitable frictions encountered.
3. Try to set broad objectives and be flexible enough to seize unforeseen opportunities.

Centuries earlier Sun Tzu in *The Art of War* said that the secret to winning is not so much in having a specific action plan, but to be flexible enough to put almost any plan into motion in order to meet changing conditions on the ground.[1] As we have discussed in previous chapters, the situation on the ground in China is always changing and companies doing business there need to be prepared to anticipate and react to unexpected events whatever they may be. From a strategic perspective a resilient supply chain should be sustainable, and a sustainable supply chain should also be resilient. The blending of resilient and sustainable initiatives through comprehensive contingency planning and environmental scenario testing should be an integral part of any corporate supply chain strategy.

In this chapter, we will examine the importance of supply chain resilience from an overseas operating perspective, in critical areas such as terrorism, pandemic outbreak, and product safety. We will look at vulnerability assessments and contingency planning and see how they may contribute to effective supply chain strategy. We will also look at examples of successful global supply chain sustainability initiatives as well as new eco-friendly innovations being made in container ship design.

SUPPLY CHAIN TERRORISM

Since the attacks on September 11, attention to the threat of supply chain terrorism has been welcomed and justified, however, the scope and scale of the problem is daunting and complex. Stephen Flynn, in his book *America the Vulnerable*, highlights just how complex the issue really is: "In 2002 over 400 million people, 122 million cars, 11 million trucks, approximately eight million maritime containers, and 59,995 vessels entered the United States at more than 3,700 terminals and 301 ports of entry."[2]

Given the number of moving parts in the global supply chain the West has been fortunate in avoiding a serious supply chain terrorist incident. The fear, however, is that this success will create a false sense of security and reduce the sense of urgency necessary for securing the supply chain against a future terrorist attack.

Most multinational corporations and importers in the United States are involved to some degree with the Customs & Trade Partnership Against Terrorism (C-TPAT) and the Container Security Initiative (CSI) programs, which were created to prevent an attack on America using the nation's supply chain as a delivery mechanism. These programs represent a conscientious first step in addressing the "Trojan horse" scenario, whereby a weapon of mass destruction is sent via an ocean container into the United States.

While there is value in these post-September 11th security initiatives, there are also shortcomings. One area of concern is the fact that these initiatives place a great deal of emphasis on preventing a terrorist attack and not enough attention on how to get the international supply chain up and running again after an attack occurs. A second shortcoming is that with the best of intentions these SCM safeguard initiatives place too much focus on security and prevention at the destination point (in the United States) rather than focusing on securing products at the manufacturing point of origin.

Unfortunately, the sheer number of potential opportunities to infiltrate the global supply chain gives the advantage to the bad guys, particularly if the focus of security lies mainly on prevention. Because of the size and complexity of today's international supply chain, terrorists have the advantage as far as being able to infiltrate and disrupt weak links in the system. Terrorists cannot, however, control the speed and efficiency at which the supply chain rebounds after a terrorist incident occurs. A resilient supply chain, then, represents a key defense against a terrorist attack, mainly because it focuses on an area that we can better influence and control.

Yossi Sheffi's definitive book on this subject, *The Resilient Enterprise,* describes various approaches for corporate risk assessment and contingency planning. In determining vulnerability Sheffi says companies should ask three questions:[3]

1. What can go wrong?
2. What is the likelihood that it will go wrong?
3. What would the business consequences be if it did go wrong?

Of particular importance is a company's ability to rebound from what Sheffi calls "high impact/low probability" events. These are events that have the potential to shut down business operations for an unacceptable length of time. For many companies doing business globally, the operating footprint of the supply chain is geographically extensive, making it difficult to build resiliency across vast networks without some kind of outside assistance. In many cases the most accessible and capable partners for developing and implementing contingency plans across supply chain networks are international logistics service providers. Larger LSPs typically have broad, geographic operating capability, advanced communication technology, and well-staffed local offices at the manufacturing points of origin. These LSPs have the potential and the ability to function as the client's first line of defense to activate and execute contingency plans at the earliest point in the supply chain.

The information available to LSPs as part of their daily work function also makes them a good partner for building contingency plans. LSPs usually know where customer's factories are located, what those factories are manufacturing and who they are manufacturing for. The ability for an LSP in China, for example, to pre-audit vendor compliance to C-TPAT security guidelines (i.e. perimeter fencing, CCTV cameras, employee ID cards) complements their overall service offering and creates a client solution that might otherwise be more expensive and time consuming. With a few exceptions, the potential benefits of expanding the LSP's role and responsibility into the area of security and contingency planning on behalf of beneficial cargo owners has not been adequately explored.

One example where the LSP is playing a larger role in supply chain security is the implementation and execution of the U.S. Customs and Border Protection's import security filing (ISF) procedures, which expand data elements beyond the former 24-hour manifest rule that was established in 2003. The ISF rule (otherwise known in the industry as "10+2") went into effect in January of 2009 and requires that importers provide CBP with the following data elements 24 hours prior to cargo being placed aboard a vessel overseas that is bound for the United States.

Importer's Responsibility

1. Manufacturer's name and address
2. Seller's name and address
3. Location where the container is actually loaded
4. Consolidator's name and address (if used)
5. Buyer's name and address
6. Address of where the cargo is ultimately being shipped
7. Importer of record
8. Consignee number

9. Country of origin
10. Commodity harmonized tariff code

Ocean Carrier's Responsibility

1. Vessel stowage plan
2. Container status

Many LSPs are now being asked to assist their clients with meeting these new ISF requirements because in many cases the LSP may have better access to the required information at the manufacturing point of origin than the client does back in the United States. Larger LSPs have the ability to aggregate and report on the required data from client's vendors as well as from the client's other service providers within the supply chain. The penalties for non-compliance to ISF once the program trial period is over are severe. Penalties may include a US$5,000 fine for each data violation and the potential to have cargo "flagged" for inspection at the U.S. port of entry. So it is critical that the 10+2 process be well implemented and executed, to avoid potential cargo delay and to avoid unnecessary cost in the supply chain.

Terrorism is only one type of threat to the international supply chain. As we have seen, global economic recessions like the one we just experienced can be a catastrophic business disruption and can be difficult to predict. Pandemic disease, ocean piracy, typhoons, and geopolitical conflict are a few more examples from a very long list of what can potentially go wrong. In one AMR research survey on supply chain risk management, the area that respondents chose as having the most potential threat to their organization was "supplier failure." Since supply chains now stretch around the world, the threat of supplier failure becomes more pronounced, and the ability to recover becomes more problematic as suppliers can be located thousands of miles away.

We can see a comprehensive list of potential business threats inside the concentric vulnerability map (Figure 9.1). This map accounts for threats across four areas of concern including financial, strategic, hazard, and operational risk.[4] The vulnerability map is a useful tool for taking into account a broader spectrum of possible failures in order to better evaluate their likelihood and the potential business impact should a failure occur. For the purpose of

Manufacturing and Supply Chain Risks

Source: Debra Elkins is credited with a version of the diagram in her presentation, on "Managing Uncertainty for High-Impact/Low-Probability Disruptions," given at The New Frontier for Managing Supply Network Uncertainty conference in December 2003[5]

Figure 9.1   Concentric Vulnerability Map

better global SCM, international corporations can benefit by evaluating potential vulnerabilities across geographies and then determining where their LSPs might be able to assist with contingency planning, implementation, and execution.

LSPs, for example, can assist their clients with contingency planning for excessive demand fluctuations by providing buffer-stock management, origin postponement, overseas supplier management, and back-up operations centers. Other areas of assistance can include product recall planning, and emergency direct-to-customer shipping programs. Figure 9.2 depicts Shef®'s Disruption Profile, which has been modified to include potential areas where LSP involvement with contingency plans could be implemented on behalf of clients at the manufacturing point of origin.

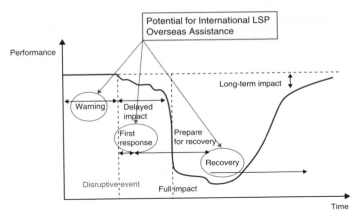

Source: Originally created by Professor Yossi Sheffi and modified with permission by Peter Levesque[6]

Figure 9.2   Where LSPs Add Value

BUILDING SCM RESILIENCY IN CHINA

The Chinese language uses two characters to form the word "crisis": the first character means danger, and the second character means opportunity. The Chinese written interpretation of the word crisis is useful in describing the potential advantages and opportunities that might be available during times of significant disruption, for those companies that take the time to prepare. Building resilient processes that can withstand times of crisis creates competitive advantage, and with competitive advantage comes the potential for greater gains.

Many infamous accidents and disasters such as the Challenger shuttle explosion in 1986 and the Union Carbide accident in Bhopal, India, in 1984 occurred because of what Yossi Sheffi calls a "confluence of causes." A confluence of causes is the coming together

> **Shipping Point:**
> **"In fair weather,**
> **prepare for foul."**
> *Thomas Fuller*

of a series of small mistakes, coincidences, and lapses in human judgment that by themselves might not be a serious problem, but when combined create the recipe for catastrophic failure. This confluence of causes can be magnified in the Asia-Pacific business arena, where the cultural aspects of doing business play such a critical and oftentimes unpredictable role in determining successful and unsuccessful outcomes. China is in a constant state of change where government regulations and basic rules of engagement can be ambiguous at best. Areas such as export customs regulations, for example, are not uniform across the country; they differ by province and by customs zone. Business licensing and registration requirements may also vary by province. The goal posts on the Chinese playing field are always moving and this adds another dimension of complexity to corporate contingency planning and building resilient supply chains. Being prepared to put almost any plan into action to deal with the situation on the ground in China is critical. Let's look at some examples of low probability/high impact situations that have occurred in china over the last several years.

In 2003, the SARS epidemic hit Hong Kong without warning. This example of a low probability/high impact disruption had the potential to shut down the supply chain of most major corporations doing business out of China for a very long time. The world feared that the China trade was exporting SARS around the world. Employees in many Asia-Pacific offices were sent home and many businesses closed altogether.

There were very few substantive corporate contingency plans in place for dealing with disease during the SARS crisis even though Hong Kong had experienced two incidents of deadly flu outbreak in the past: the Asian Flu of 1957–58, which was responsible for close to 70,000 deaths in the United States and the Hong Kong Flu of 1968–69 which killed approximately one million people worldwide.[7] If there was anything positive to come out of the SARS epidemic of 2003 it was that Hong Kong and China emerged better prepared for any future recurrence of an epidemic as proven by the way in which the H1N1 pandemic was recently handled across the region. But many international businesses still struggle to build corporate resiliency around these types of outbreaks.

As incidents of pandemic outbreak become more frequent and more virulent, corporations doing business globally will need better preparation and training to be able to implement a plan quickly. The Hong Kong International School (HKIS) provides a good example of contingency planning for pandemic outbreaks. Faced with the possibility of contagious flu running rampant through the student population, the HKIS contingency plan calls for students to work from home, by accessing lessons and homework assignments through the school's website, Dragon Net. Students log into the site using a personal security code and utilize FTP drop boxes for obtaining class material.

Some companies in Hong Kong and China are cross-training staff so they can handle a broader range of job functions and provide greater support in times

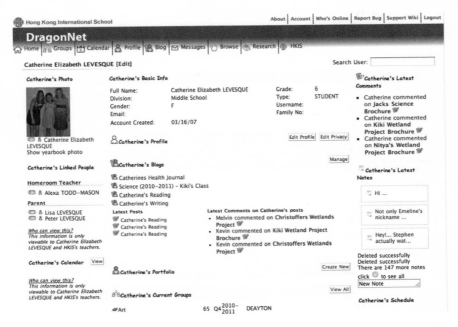

Source: HKIS

Hong Kong International School Home School Contingency Plan

of crisis. Cross-trained staff enables companies to flow resources to areas where the most critical work needs to be done. Having a contingency plan and technical support structure in place that allows cross-trained employees to work from home, for example, can pay huge dividends in crisis situations overseas.

Creating a command center concept that is capable of backing up the overseas main office with people and systems in the event of office contamination is also a prudent step for mission-critical operations in China.

Epidemics are one form of possible disruption. There are many more. Two famous companies from the United States shared a similar situation in 1998, highlighting the importance of being resilient. Avon Products, Inc. had been doing business in China since the late 1980s and had invested over US$90 million into its Chinese business, with annual sales topping US$75 million. The direct-marketing giant, Amway, had invested US$100 million in eight distribution centers and had a factory operating in Guangzhou. By the 1990s, it was estimated that over 20 million people were engaged in the direct-marketing business in China. Then without warning in April 1998 the government in Beijing suddenly declared that direct marketing was illegal.

The government's concern over the potential for criminal abuse of independent distributor networks, door-to-door sales campaigns, and motivational sales meetings were the main reasons for banning direct marketing. The government also feared that so-called closed organizations would have criminal tendencies and would seek excessive profits.[8] It is difficult for Westerners to envision the "Avon lady" as being a threat to national security, but for the Chinese government it's all about maintaining social harmony, and in their view, the threat of social unrest brewing inside organized marketing groups across China was very real.

The ban on direct marketing lasted for several years. It was not until April 2005 that the Chinese Ministry of Commerce officially approved Avon Products, Inc. (China) to test direct selling, after the establishment by the government of direct selling rules of engagement.[9] Amway, on the other hand, was able to quickly adapt its business model and strategy to overcome the sudden legal roadblocks from Beijing. They immediately began building relationships and connections within the government to explain their business model and position. Finally, the government made some concessions allowing direct selling through independent sales people, as long as Amway opened physical stores and signed labor contracts with their sales people. Under the concession, sales income could only be based on a person's individual sales and not on the sales of people they recruited into the company. Amway then invested US$29 million dollars in 100 stand-alone stores, which also functioned as distribution centers for Amway sales people and by 2003 the company had sales of approximately US$700 million dollars in China.[10]

Another example of unpredictable disruption occurred in 2007 when the Chinese government suddenly began to enforce a 36-hour-a-month maximum overtime policy along with new rules on the duration of employer service contracts. The net result of these new enforcements, together with an appreciating RMB and rising fuel costs was a dramatic increase in factory expenses and an unprecedented rate of factory closures, particularly in South China. In addition to the labor law challenges faced by factories, new product safety inspection standards were implemented due to incidents involving lead paint in toys, melamine found in pet food, and faulty product design issues, making 2007 a very difficult year for China manufacturers. By the end of 2008, an estimated 4,000 toy factories in Guangdong Province, many owned by Hong Kong companies, had closed. Prior to these closures, approximately 80 percent of the world's toys were being produced in China.[11] These instances of rapid change in Chinese government policy and business regulations highlight the importance of building resilience into the China supply chain, and being prepared for almost anything when doing business in the mainland.

Mattel provides another valuable lesson of what can go wrong in China. On August 2, 2007, Mattel voluntarily recalled 83 Fisher Price products affecting approximately 1.5 million toys that were made in China and sold around the globe. The reason for the recall was the use of lead paint. Mattel followed up with seven more recalls due to lead paint, and also a design problem involving loose magnets that could be swallowed by children. Lee Der Industrial, the factory involved with the lead paint situation, lost its export license over the incident. On August 11, Cheung Shu-hung, the co-owner of Lee Der Industrial, hanged himself after paying his employees their final salaries and a bonus. Then on August 14 Mattel initiated another voluntary recall for lead paint involving an additional 436,000 toys from a different China supplier, Early Light Industrial, which also had a long history of working with Mattel.[12]

There are several key lessons that can be extracted from Mattel's China experience of 2007. Lesson one is that it is common practice in China for primary contracted suppliers to outsource portions of their manufacturing, material purchases, and paint requirements to other subcontracted suppliers. Those subcontractors may turn around and outsource to additional subcontractors. Mattel was aware of this common vendor practice. In fact, Mattel required their primary vendors to notify the company when subcontractors were being used, so that Mattel could inspect the subcontractors separately for safety compliance.

In the first instance, Lee Der Industrial was a long-time trusted Mattel vendor; however, they purchased their paint from a company called Dongxing New Energy, who was not on Mattel's approved paint supplier list. Mattel inadvertently missed the fact that Dongxing New Energy was purchasing yellow pigment over the internet that came with a fictitious lead-free certificate. In the second instance, Early Light Industrial who was another long-time trusted Mattel vendor discovered that one of its subcontractors was not buying Mattel approved paint. When the subcontractor's toys were tested, lead was again discovered. Building a resilient supply chain in China requires that all contractors, sub-contractors and upstream suppliers be properly identified, verified, and kept in compliance over time.

As if lead paint was not enough of an issue for Mattel in 2007, the company was also forced to recall 18.2 million Chinese-made toys, because they contained small magnets that could be swallowed by children. Unlike the lead paint scenario, the loose magnets were actually a Mattel design flaw and not caused by subcontractor negligence. Understanding the importance that Chinese society places on the concept of saving face, Mattel acknowledged to the head of China's General Administration of Quality Supervision Inspection and Quarantine the fact that many of the recalled toys were due to Mattel's design flaw, and not caused by the negligence of Chinese vendors. This example highlights an important point: some attributes of a resilient supply chain in China could be cultural.

The positive impact of this acknowledgment by Mattel to the Chinese cannot be underestimated. The political climate and public opinion regarding China back in 2007 was not favorable, particularly in the United States. China was being publicly embarrassed internationally because of several product safety issues, including contaminated pet food, as well as tampered toothpaste and tampered cough syrup. Mattel's acknowledgment of the toy design problem gave China major face, and clearly demonstrated Mattel's grasp of the important role that relationship plays in China business.

What do you do when your business is selling chicken dinners, and the Avian (Bird) Flu breaks out? That's the dilemma Yum! Brands faced with its KFC restaurants in China in 2005 when the "Bird Flu" infected 133 people and killed 68. Poultry is a staple in the Chinese diet and has been traditionally purchased in outdoor wet markets, where birds can be more susceptible to the spread of Avian Flu. To address public concerns, Yum! Brands went on a marketing offensive, positioning their supply chain as the safe alternative for poultry, and publicly announcing supply chain contingency plans. In addition, KFC provided the Chinese with consumer education on why their poultry was safe.

Yum! Brands' Bird Flu contingency plans included comprehensive guide-lines for how poultry was to be handled and processed prior to it getting into the KFC supply chain. The chickens, for example, were enclosed to keep other birds from infecting the chicken population. Other measures included food safety audits with KFC suppliers to check on sanitary conditions and temperature requirements. Finally, Yum! Brands created a global food security task force to address food safety issues in the supply chain.[13] Yum! Brands was able to deal with Avian Flu concerns in China by educating the public on their supply chain processes, and by addressing public concerns head on.

Resilient supply chains in China require a clear understanding of the cultural, political, and financial nuances of the country itself. Global corporations must make an honest risk assessment of the likelihood and potential downside impact of a major disruption in China. They must build contingency plans that are flexible enough to deal with changes on the ground, and include a review of contractors, subcontractors, and the potential for unforeseen changes in government regulation. Proper training of company management and general staff based overseas is critical to success when things go wrong. Greater cooperation and engagement between LSPs and their clients in this area could create more dynamic and actionable contingency plans in-country, to help mitigate supply chain risk.

SUPPLY CHAIN SUSTAINABILITY IN CHINA

Achieving a sustainable supply chain is a popular topic with many companies visiting the Asia-Pacific region today. Areas of business concern in China include CO_2 emissions, labor conditions, recycling, and waste reduction. The concern over sustainable supply chains has finally reached the boardroom on both sides of the Pacific and LSPs are being asked to take a more active role in reducing their environmental footprint around the world.

Cargo transportation is an energy-consuming, carbon-producing industry, and it is a business that stretches around the globe. Adding to the problem is the fact that low-cost sourcing strategies often include dealing with developing countries whose priorities on the environment might not be as high as our own.

There is no question that China has a problem with pollution. It is now the largest emitter of CO_2, due in large part to a heavy reliance on coal. But before the Western world publicly scolds China on its environmental issues, it should consider the fact that 40 percent of China's energy consumption and related green house gas emissions actually goes into producing the products that go to Western markets.[14] With today's rapid transfer of technology and information we can anticipate that China will move through their industrial revolution in less time than it took Europe and the United States. Scolding China and causing them to lose face over environmental concerns is not the most constructive approach to the issue. Rather, the global community would be better served by ensuring that China has the latest in clean technologies and sustainable best practice to help them address their environmental issues.

Within the international supply chain, successful LSPs and their customers are proactively taking on sustainability initiatives together. In addition to environmental benefits, these sustainability initiatives can generate positive public opinion and positive financial benefits. As Lee Scott from Wal-Mart mentioned in his 2005 company speech, "being a good steward of the environment and being profitable are not mutually exclusive. They are one and the same."[15]

While there are tremendous opportunities in the area of supply chain sustainability, the biggest opportunities often reside with suppliers that are far away, in countries that may not place as high of a priority on environmental issues as we do. Establishing achievable sustainability goals with global suppliers, and accurately measuring supplier progress and compliance with issues such as labor conditions are major undertakings for any Western firm. Let's look at an example of one company's success in the area of supplier sustainability.

THE STARBUCKS EXAMPLE

Not surprisingly, Starbucks has been a leader in greening its supply chain and improving working conditions around the world. Faced with rapid business growth globally and an over-supply of lower-grade coffee in the market, Starbucks needed to figure out a way to support its expansion and at the same time help its coffee suppliers survive in a depressed pricing environment.

Starbucks runs a complex global supply chain involving family-owned farms for coffee production located in Latin America, the Pacific Rim, and East Africa. These farms in turn sell their beans to coffee processors, who then sell to export distributors, before the beans are finally sold to Starbucks. Taking the initiative to use its buying power for positive social change, Starbucks, together with Conservation International created C.A.F.E. (Coffee and Farmers Equity), which are stated best practices for suppliers in the Starbucks' supply chain. C.A.F.E.'s guiding principles are to ensure a sustainable supply of high quality coffee beans from a stable source of coffee farmers, who are free from exploitation. It is also important to Starbucks that these farmers use environmentally sound methods in the production of coffee beans, and that farmers live in healthy, secure, and supportive societies. A sample of some of the items covered by Starbucks' C.A.F.E. evaluation are shown in Table 9.1

Starbucks provides financial benefit to its suppliers to implement C.A.F.E. practices "through economic incentives and preferential buying status." The Coffee and Farmers Equity program seeks to build "long-term mutually beneficial contracts with suppliers to support Starbucks' growth" and to promote transparency and economic fairness within the coffee supply chain.[16]

Starbucks' suppliers are graded by an independent agency on social and environmental criteria including wages, diversity, worker health, safety, and living conditions. Suppliers who score above 60 are designated as "preferred suppliers" for future coffee purchases. Suppliers scoring above 80 are designated as "strategic suppliers" and they are rewarded with a "Sustainability Conversion Price Premium" per pound of coffee for one year. An additional premium per pound is available for suppliers who achieve a 10-point increase over an 80 percent score in the course of a given year.[17]

What's innovative here is the overall approach to creating sustainable business practices beyond the borders of corporate headquarters. The Starbucks model offers a framework for all companies who do business internationally, to play an active role in the health and sustainability of their suppliers and their service providers around the world.

The Starbucks framework is designed to reward the right behavior, rather than to punish the wrong behavior, and this is exactly the type of approach that works best in the Chinese culture. Many international companies that source in China have developed long-standing, mutually beneficial relationships with their key Chinese suppliers, and this partnership approach should increase the likelihood of success for corporate sustainability initiatives such as Starbucks'. Outside of China, as the global supply chain continues to expand into the world's more developing countries, implementing sustainability initiatives will be much more complex and much more necessary.

Table 9.1 Key Components of the C.A.F.E. Practices Self-Evaluation Checklist

Product Quality
- Green Preparation
- Cup Quality

Economic Accountability
- Demonstration of Economic Transparency
- Equity of Financial Reward
- Financial Viability

Social Responsibility
Hiring Practices and Employment Policies:
- Minimum/Living Wage/Overtime Regulation
- Freedom of Association/Collective Bargaining
- Vacation/Sick Leave Regulation
- Child Labor/Discrimination/Forced Labor

Worker Conditions:
- Access to Housing, Water and Sanitary Facilities
- Access to Education
- Access to Medical Care
- Access to Training, Health & Safety

Coffee Growing–Environmental Leadership
Protecting Water Resources:
- Watercourse Protection
- Water Quality Protection

Protecting Soil Resources:
- Controlling Surface Erosion
- Improving Soil Quality

Conserving Biodiversity:
- Maintaining Coffee Shade Canopy and Natural Vegetation
- Protecting Wildlife
- Conservation Areas and Ecological Reserves

Environmental Management and Monitoring:
- Ecological Pests and Disease Management and Reducing Agrochemical Use
- Farm Management and Monitoring Practices

Coffee Processing–Environmental Leadership
Water Conservation:
- Minimizing Water Consumption
- Reducing Wastewater Impacts

Water Management:
- Waste Management Operations/Beneficial Reuse

Energy Use:
- Energy Conservation/Impacts

Waste Management:
- Waste Management Operations/Beneficial Reuse
- Energy Conservation/Impacts

Source: Starbucks C.A.F.E Practice Evaluation Guidelines, Version 2.0, March 2007
See: http://www.scscertified.com/retail/docs/CAFE_GUI_EvaluationGuidelines_V2.0_093009.pdf

Building a resilient and sustainable supply chain is dependent upon having an enabled and supportive corporate culture, along with an informed and action-minded leadership team. Resilience and sustainability must be imbedded in the DNA of the entire organization. Also critical to building a resilient and sustainable supply chain is understanding the cultural nuances as well as the political and economic realities faced by third world countries within the supplier network. Oftentimes, Western businesses forget about the cultural and political sensitivities that their suppliers face. Successful resilience and sustainability initiatives overseas can be achieved by understanding and embracing cultural and political differences and then working within those differences to implement constructive and positive change.

PRODUCT PACKAGING REDESIGN

The World Packaging Organization estimates the global market for product packaging to be US$500 billion. "It is further estimated that one third of all municipal solid waste in the United States is packaging waste. That's 800 pounds of packaging per person annually" just in the United States alone.[19] One of the fastest growing areas of interest for many leading logistics companies is around package re-design initiatives in China.

> Shipping Point: "Best should not be the end point, but rather the starting point for innovation."
>
> *Larry Page - Google*

A typical supply chain optimization process for an LSP involves first optimizing the client's purchase order, ensuring that the right orders will arrive at the right place, on the most cost-effective mode of transport, and in the right quantity. The next step involves maximizing the utilization of the ocean container by getting as many cartons inside the box as possible. While container optimization programs can provide substantial up-front cost savings, these initiatives have diminishing returns over time, as maximum utilization is ultimately achieved. This is where package redesign can take waste reduction and cost savings to the next level.

Reducing inner and outer carton dimensions for products made in China reduces the amount of paper used in packaging material, thereby reducing waste and lowering the overall cost of the packaging material used. A reduction in carton dimensions also provides additional opportunity to further increase the utilization of the shipping container (more cartons loaded per container). This in turn lowers the overall per unit cost of transportation by reducing the total number of containers shipped. In addition to the cost benefits of packaging redesign, there are the obvious green supply chain benefits as well. Less paper used in packaging material means less trees impacted, reduced CO_2 from fewer containers being trucked, and fewer containers on cargo ships crossing the world's oceans.

CEVA Logistics has been at the forefront of packaging initiatives on behalf of its clients for the last several years. But it has not been easy because getting to the value proposition in packaging design takes expertise in knowing where to look. Phil Trabulsi, CEVA's senior director of engineering, explains that "the cost of the packaging material is buried somewhere in the cost of the goods. You have to decouple the box."[20] Customer savings vary in packaging initiatives according to Trabulsi, but it is not uncommon to see up to a 10-percent reduction in material use, and with smaller, less dense cartons, importers can realize up to 20-percent savings in overall transportation costs. Pittsburg-based CombineNet, which specializes in packaging value chain and packaging optimization, explains that packaging value chain costs can typically be broken down as 10 percent secondary packaging materials, 20 percent warehousing and 65 percent freight. CombineNet notes that, "most companies focus primarily on the shipping container without regard to logistics impact—saving nickels by spending quarters."[21]

Packaging redesign can be a lucrative and environmentally worthwhile endeavor; however, some companies struggle with the internal coordination necessary to get this type of initiative off the ground. Product packaging can touch several stakeholders within an organization, such as procurement, finance, marketing and transportation. To be successful, the financial and social benefits need to be clearly articulated to all stakeholders in the organization, and support from senior management is critical.

When it all comes together the results can be impressive. Let's look at one example.

Wal-Mart re-sized packaging for its private label toy brand, Kid Connection, which resulted in a net decrease of 497 ocean containers totaling US$2.4 million in freight savings. Wal-Mart estimates this simple package redesign reduced the company's environmental impact by saving 3,800 trees and over 1,000 barrels of oil per year.[22]

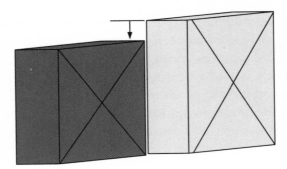

Source: Lyn Denend, "Wal-Mart's Sustainability Strategy" OIT-71, (Stanford Graduate School of Business, April 17, 2007) p.44

Wal-Mart's "Light and Sound Vehicles" Toy Packaging Reduction

A similar result was recognized by Wal-Mart when it redesigned its Shower Soother display to allow 21 units per pallet instead of just three, reducing the number of trucks needed to ship the item to stores from 196 trucks down to just 28. Freight costs were reduced by US$250,000, fuel consumption was reduced by 5,975 gallons, and 66 tons of CO_2 emissions were eliminated.[23]

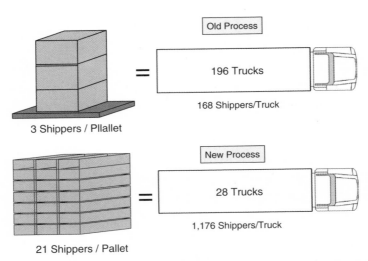

Source: Lyn Denend, "Wal-Mart's Sustainability Strategy" OIT-71, (Stanford Graduate School of Business, April 17, 2007) p.44

Impact of Wal-Mart's Smoother Package Redesign

Innovative LSPs like CEVA Logistics are breaking out of their traditional service offering and expanding into broader areas of value added services, that include package design. Combining previously unrelated services such as packaging, quality assurance, and finance into a more comprehensive and dynamic supply chain offering creates additional value for the client and at the same time improves customer satisfaction and retention for the LSP. To achieve transformational results for clients, LSPs must provide a consultative approach to break down internal and external barriers to change.

OCEAN TRANSPORTATION SUSTAINABILITY

The transportation industry overall has been taking an active role in developing cleaner, more fuel-efficient modes of transport. In the area of ocean shipping a significant amount of progress is being made. The international shipping industry carries approximately 90 percent of the world's trade.[24] Maritime shipping is responsible for approximately 2.7 percent of annual greenhouse gas emissions, with 25 percent of that coming from container ships.[25] Container ocean shipping is still the most environmentally friendly way to transport large volumes of goods from China around the world.[26] Figure 9.3 shows a comparison of CO_2 emissions and energy use by transportation mode.

The Container Shipping Information Service (World Shipping Council) notes that, "for every kilometer that a container ship carries a ton of cargo, it

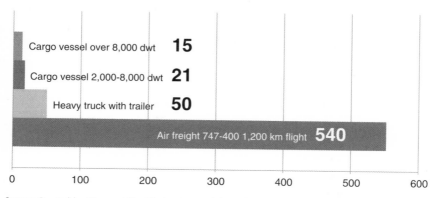

Source: Created by Margaret Li with data sourced from The International Chamber of Shipping[27]

Figure 9.3   CO$_2$ Emissions Comparison by Mode of Transport

is far more energy efficient and emits much less in the way of harmful CO_2 than any other type of freight transport, including airplane, truck and train." The service also notes that, "on average a container ship emits around 40 times less CO_2 than a large freight aircraft, and over three times less than a heavy truck." Container shipping is approximately two and a half times more energy efficient than rail transport, and seven times more efficient than road transport.[28] The ocean transportation industry continues to strive for greater improvements through vessel design and more stringent international standards. As noted in The Liner Shipping Industry and Carbon Emissions Policy September 2009, "carbon efficiency on a per mile per cargo volume basis has improved 75 percent in 30 years as a result of technological improvements and the utilization of larger vessels."[29] Let's look at some examples of technological improvements in the maritime industry that are having a positive impact on the environment.

Source: Courtesy of CMA-CGM

CMA-CGM's Environmentally Conscious Vessel *Christophe Colomb*

In November 2009, CMA-CGM took delivery of the *Christophe Colomb*, a new generation of cargo ship which measures 365.5 meters in length and has 13,344 TEUs of cargo capacity. In addition to its remarkable size, the *Christophe Colomb* is equipped with the latest in environmentally friendly vessel design technology. The ship contains an electronic injection system for the engine which reduces fuel consumption by 3 percent and oil consumption by 25 percent. The ship is fitted with a twisted leading edge rudder which optimizes the flow of water around the steering mechanism, reducing energy consumption and CO_2 emissions. The *Christophe Colomb* also has a new device called a pre-swirl stator, which alters inflow angles to the ship's propeller in order to maximize propulsion efficiency. This technology provides an additional 2-percent reduction in fuel consumption and a 4-percent reduction in greenhouse gas emissions. The *Christophe Colomb* is fully equipped with a fast oil recovery (FOR) system to help prevent marine pollution in the event of a vessel accident by allowing hydrocarbons to be rapidly recovered without having to go through the hull of the ship.

New vessel designs such as the *Christophe Colomb* are already making a positive environmental impact. Future vessel design will continue to incorporate the latest in technological innovation to help provide sustainable ocean cargo transportation.[30]

ORCELLE CONCEPT VESSEL

Ocean cargo vessels continue to get larger and more efficient. Today's largest container ship, the *Emma Maersk*, is 397 meters long with a 56-meter beam (too big to fit through the Panama Canal). It can carry up to 14,000 20-foot equivalent units at speeds of 25 knots. The ship's engine is close to seven stories tall. Modern naval architecture is improving the speed, capacity, and efficiency of container ships, but game-changing design innovation is just over the horizon.

Wallenius Wilhelmsen is at the forefront of environmentally friendly ship design with its concept vessel the *E/S Orcelle* (named after the Irrawaddy dolphin), which was initiated by the company in 2004. The initial design specifications call for a length of 250 meters with a 50-meter beam, a 9-meter draft, and a top speed of 20 knots.

The design also calls for a storage capacity equivalent to 10,000 automobiles with an adjustable cargo deck totaling 85,000 square meters. The ship's design includes 3 × 800 square meter solar panels, and 3 × 1400 square meter sails on deck. The *Orcelle* design uses renewable energy sources and fuel cell storage to generate ship propulsion with zero emissions into the ocean or the atmosphere. It uses energy that is readily available at sea: wind power, solar

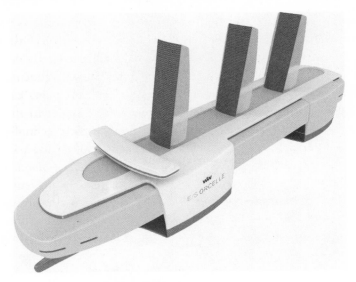

Source: Courtesy of Wallenius Wilhelmsen

Orcelle Concept Vessel

power, and wave energy to run its generators along with a fuel cell system that is powered by hydrogen.

The design allows for solar energy to be captured via photovoltaic panels inside the vessel's adjustable topsails that are also used to capture wind energy. Wave energy is generated through 12 fins located on the sides of the vessel that transform wave movement into hydrogen, electricity or mechanical energy. The fins themselves have a propulsion utility in the water that can be driven from other energy sources.

The *Orcelle* design also contains two electric propulsion systems at the bow and stern to complement the other propulsion systems. These units will be maneuverable to 360 degrees.

This vessel concept also eliminates the need for one of the biggest environmental threats to the world's oceans, ballast water. This is achieved through an innovative hull design called a "pantamaran," which eliminates the need for a propeller and rudder at the stern while maximizing the amount of cargo space available for transport.[31]

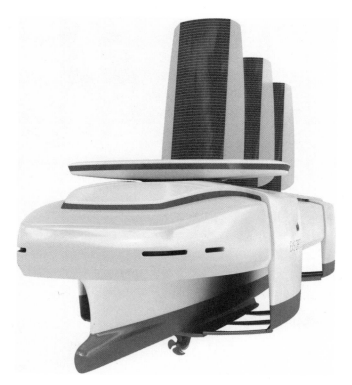

Source: Courtesy of Wallenius Wilhelmsen

Orcelle Concept Vessel

The hull would be made of aluminum and thermoplastic composite materials making it strong and lightweight with reduced maintenance. While the *Orcelle* concept vessel may never actually be built, the innovative concepts included in its design will help future naval architects to build more environmentally friendly cargo ships that can cross the oceans to and from China. It is a clear example of the transportation industry's concern and involvement with building more resilient and sustainable supply chains in the future.

Japanese flag carrier NYK Lines is also developing an environmentally friendly ship design in cooperation with MTI, Garroni Progetti, and Elomatic Marine. The vessel design is expected to emit 69 percent less CO_2 than existing container ships by using fuel cell-power, solar power, and wind power. Most of the technology is expected to be commercially viable by 2030.

Table 9.2 Comparison of Eco Ship 2030 to Today's Ship

	Conventional Vessel	NYK Super Eco Ship 2030
Length overall	338 meters	353 meters
Breadth	45.8 meters	54.6 meters
Draft	13.0 meters	11.5 meters
Main power (Fuel)	Diesel Engine (C heavy oil) 64 megawatts	Fuel Cell (LNG) 40 megawatts
Natural power	None	Solar: 1–2 megawatts Wind: 1–3 megawatts
CO_2 emissions	195 g/TEU-miles	62 g/TEU-miles

Source: NYK Lines

Source: NYK

The NYK SUPER ECO SHIP 2030 project is jointly formed by MTI, Garroni Progetti S.r.l., Elomatic Marine, and NYK Line

Building resilience and sustainability into the international supply chain will continue to be important corporate objectives throughout the next decade. Taking a blended approach to developing strategy in these areas and working with innovative LSPs to help execute those strategies will help facilitate success. Flexibility is key to both resilience and sustainability. Having a strategy that can alter course to meet the changing conditions on the ground is critical for successful implementation and execution of initiatives in places like China. The transportation industry understands the importance of sustainable shipping. We can expect more research and development in technology, fuels, and vessel design in the years ahead that will continue to reduce the supply chain's environmental impact on the world we live in.

NOTES

1   "The Return of von Clausewitz: The Fine Art of Being Prepared," *The Economist*, March 9, 2002, http://www.economist.com/node/1010336?story_id=1010336.
2   Stephen Flynn, *America the Vulnerable: How Our Government is Failing to Protect Us from Terrorism*, (New York: HarperCollins, 2004).
3   Yossi Sheffi, *The Resilient Enterprise, Overcoming Vulnerability for Competitive Advantage*, (Cambridge: MIT Press, 2007).
4   Ibid., 25.
5   Ibid., 25.
6   Ibid., 65.
7   William Paul, *Fundamental Immunology*, 5th ed. (Philadelphia: Lippencott Williams & Wilkins, 2003), 1273.
8   "Chinese officials ban direct marketing, ada-based Amway changing distribution," Associated Press, April 22, 1998, http://www.rickross.com/reference/amway/amway34.html.
9   Yang Yan, "Avon Given Direct-Selling Nod in China," *China Daily*, September 4, 2005, http://www.chinadaily.com.cn/english/doc/2005-04/09/content_432686.html.
10 Leslie Chang, "Once-Barred Amway Becomes Booming Business in China," *The Wall Street Journal*, March 12, 2003, http://www.rickross.com/reference/amway/amway56 .html.
11 David Hoyt, "Unsafe for Children: Mattel's Toy Recalls and Supply Chain Management," GS-63, (Stanford: Stanford Graduate School of Business, September 15, 2008).
12 Ibid.
13 Document 4, http:www.qsrmagazine.com/issue/82/birdflu.phtml 2005.
14 John Wharburton and Leo Horn-Phathanothai, "China's crisis: A development perspective, part one," *Chinadialogue*, October 25, 2007, www.chinadialogue.net/article/show/single/en/1418-China-s-crisis-a-development-perspective-part-one.

15   Lee Scott, "Twentieth Century Leadership," Wal-Mart Stores, October 24, 2005, http://walmartstores.com/sites/sustainabilityreport/2007/documents/21stCentury Leadership.pdf.

16   Stacy Duda, James LaShawn, Zeryn Mackwani, Raul Munoz, David Volk, "Starbucks Corporation, Building a Sustainable Supply Chain," GS-54 (Stanford: Stanford Graduate School, May 2007), 2-4.

17   Ibid., 5.

18   "C.A.F.E. Practices Generic Evaluation Guidelines," Starbucks Coffee Company, March 1, 2007, http://www.scscertified.com/retail/docs/CAFE_GUI_Evaluation Guidelines_V2.0_093009.pdf.

19   Lyn Denend, "Wal-Mart's Sustainability Strategy", OIT-71 (Stanford: Stanford Graduate School of Business, September 30, 2008), 32.

20   Bill Mongelluzzo, "New Dimensions in Savings," *The Journal of Commerce Magazine*, March 2, 2009, http://www.joc.com/logistics-economy/new-dimensions-savings.

21   J. Ampuja, J. Reddy, P. Stirling, "Packaging Value Chain Optimization" (2009): www .CombineNet.com.

22   Denend, "Wal-Mart's Sustainability Strategy," 43, 44.

23   Ibid., 43, 46.

24   The International Chamber of Shipping "Shipping, World Trade and the Reduction of CO_2 Emissions, United Nations Framework Convention on Climate Change (COP15), International Maritime Organization World Maritime Day 2009, Climate Change: A Challenge for IMO Too," see http://www.imo.org/KnowledgeCentre/ InformationResources/ClimateChangeandtheMaritimeIndustry/Documents/CO$_2$% 20Flyer.pdf.

25   The Liner Shipping Industry and Carbon Emissions Policy 2009, World Shipping Council, September 2009, p.6, see http://www.shippingandco2.org/LinerShippingand CO$_2$EmissionsPolicySeptember.pdf.

26   Container Shipping Information Service, http://www.worldshipping.org/benefits-of- liner-shipping/low-environmental-impact.

27   International Chamber of Shipping.

28   Container Shipping Information Service.

29   Liner Shipping Industry Policy.

30   Information on the *Christophe Colomb* is courtesy of CMA-CGM, Marseille France. Additional information can be found at http://www.cma-cgm.com/AboutUs/Press Room/Press-Release_CMA-CGM-CHRISTOPHE-COLOMB-100th-giant-of-the-seas- to-call-at-LE-HAVRE_10066.aspx.

31   "*E/S Orcelle*—Green flagship," Wallenius &Wilhelmsen Logistics (2008): http:// www.2wglobal.com/www/environment/orcelleGreenFlagship/index.jsp.

SUPPORTING THE DYNAMIC SUPPLY CHAIN

CHAPTER TEN

SCM LEADERSHIP IN CHINA

PROFESSOR STEVEN DEKREY

INTRODUCTION

In a remarkably short period of just over 30 years, China has transformed itself from a poor undeveloped nation into one of the most powerful economies in the world and there is little end in sight to its forward progress. In 2007, it overtook Germany to claim the third spot (in term of size of economy) and very quickly leaped to number two, outpacing Japan in 2009. While the United States remains a prodigiously bigger economy, and will hold the number one position for some time to come, China's rise has become an essential focus of study when considering how one nation can rise from seeming obscurity to global economic player. One thing is certain: this did not happen by accident.

While circumstance and opportunity have undoubtedly helped in China's transformation, a key factor of success has been effective leadership in all phases of the country's development and across multiple sectors. Decisions have been taken with clear goals in mind and an eye to the next step in the development path. These decisions have been driven not only by the leaders in Beijing, but by many other people in leadership roles in the Chinese government, state-owned enterprises, global companies doing business in China and start-up ventures, as well as leaders outside business circles.

Just what has made this leadership so effective? Many observers have searched for clues in China's unique history and cultural background. However, the circumstances suggest something more basic is at work. China has risen as a result of leadership "in" China, not "Chinese" leadership. While national organizations in the country had certain similarities before the country opened up, such as being more authoritarian and hierarchical, these elements are disappearing among the growing number of globally-oriented companies that are emerging in China. Leadership in China is becoming global leadership, and it has enabled the country to work across boundaries and respond rapidly to the opportunities in its path. Global leadership attributes will play a vital role in the development of supply chain management (SCM) in China over the next decade as the mainland evolves from a manufacturing economy into an international consumer-based economy.

THE LEADERSHIP QUESTION

In order to understand the impact of effective leadership on China's rise, we need to first consider elements of leadership in general. What qualities make an effective leader? The answer is a complex one and there are many theories and responses, as I have found in my own 30 years of personal encounters with this question.

I first became interested in leadership in 1979, when I read an article while researching my dissertation. The article, which I have no reference for, pointed out that the average grade point average (GPA) of Fortune 500 CEOs was only 2.0—the equivalent of a C. I was truly shocked. I had always understood that the better you do in school, the better you do in life. Yet here were results that clearly showed this was not always true.

My curiosity was piqued and so began my deep passion in understanding leadership. I wanted to know where these top leaders learned to lead and why this ability was not reflected in their college performance. How could they go on to such impressive career achievements, running the biggest companies in the world, having barely graduated from college? That article changed my career path: I have focused on leadership development ever since.

Over three decades or so, I have had plenty of experience teaching and studying leadership, selecting potential leaders for leadership development programs in the United States and Asia (where I have lived since 1996) and getting to know business leaders from across the globe. Leadership is a complex process, but I have come to a greater understanding and appreciation of its intricacies and how its application is developed.

You will surmise from my story about the C grades that I've found leadership to be about much more than the things taught in academic settings. Leadership does require interpersonal skills and characteristics which may be learned in school generally through peer-to-peer contact, social interactions and sports, but are generally not learned from teacher instruction. A well-known statement is that "leadership cannot be taught but it can be learned." It makes the point succinctly.

I have confirmed these findings repeatedly. While serving as admissions dean of a full-time MBA program in the United States, I conducted validity studies to predict success in our admissions decisions. We found that grades and test scores were both highly predictive of performance in MBA courses, but not career success as measured by first-year salary or number of job offers obtained. This was the outcome for both undergraduate and graduate results. We did find, though, that the admissions interview correlated with career success. As a result, we became the first top school in the United States to require such interviews of all applicants. It's a legacy I am proud of to this day.

So, having established that career and leadership success require something more than just good qualifications, the central question remains: just what is it that defines successful leadership and what attributes should international supply chain executives be looking for in order to meet their long-term objectives in China?

DEFINING QUALITIES

In speaking to students, business groups, and other audiences about leadership over the years, I am often asked to address particular circumstances. People want to know if they or their managers have the qualities of good leaders, how they can acquire them, and how they can address leadership problems in their organization. In any given audience, this means trying to address multiple leadership issues under a single umbrella—a truly difficult task given the highly complex and interactive nature of the topic.

Nevertheless, I have found there is value in working from a common definition of leadership that can be used as a benchmark for assessing a variety of situations. There are many definitions out there but here is one that I think best sums it up:

"Leadership is a process to influence others toward the achievement of an organization's positive goals."

Note that this definition mentions "influence" and focuses on the achievement of positive goals for the organization. Some definitions are leader-oriented and don't consider the broader impacts of leadership. This one, though, assumes a shared vision and implies that there is more than one leader. In fact, in most organizations there are multiple leaders to meet group goals. Taking these ideas further, you can see that serving the organization also means serving the leadership because the leaders represent the organization and its goals.

The focus on what's best for the organization also addresses a problem we're all aware of: the "bad people" leaders who are generally self-serving and not positive contributors to the organization. Our definition by using the word "positive" effectively eliminates them from the question of leadership because the focus is on organizational goals. While self-interest is a common and understandable motivator, a positive leader will be self-served if the organization's positive goals are achieved, because these achievements will yield recognition and advancement for the leadership.

Having set out the goals of leadership, how does it work in practice? Our definition implies that the job of the leader is to get others to do something for the benefit of the organization. The social psychologist, L.L. Bernard, provided a succinct framework for this in 1939, when he showed that leadership as a process was defined by the interaction of three major components: 1. Leader 2. Followers 3. Situation, as shown in Figure 10.1.

Bernard and his adherents, including many influential organizations and think tanks such as the Center for Creative Leadership, say that in order to understand a leadership activity, we must first understand the leader, the followers, and the specific situation that they face. This means that no two leadership events are alike—not only are the leadership situations unique, so too are the leaders and followers. This makes leadership complicated indeed and impossible to generalize. What we can say is that we know good leadership when we see it, but it is not easy to predict whether good leadership will be exercised in future situations.

Consider, for example, the differences between the president of a university and a financial services firm. The leaders of both organizations need to be

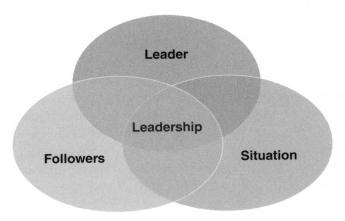

Source: Chart created by Margaret Li, based on L.L. Bernard's leadership framework

Figure 10.1   Leadership Interactional Framework

proven, senior and have highly developed leadership skills, yet the criteria for selecting them is very different.

I use the example of the president of my own university, HKUST. Professor Tony Chan was recently appointed to lead this prestigious research institution. HKUST was fortunate to find a candidate who meets all the dream criteria set out by the search committee. Our new president is passionate about education and holds significant academic credentials (a BS from California Institute of Technology and a PhD from Stanford University). He served as a dean for five years at a prestigious institution (UCLA) and has been a senior director of the largest research-funding source in the world, the U.S.-based National Science Foundation (NSF). On an interpersonal level, he is approachable, energetic, friendly, and of high character. He was an exceptional candidate for president and HKUST is fortunate to have attracted this distinguished scholar back to his home city of Hong Kong to take up the position.

The candidate for the presidency of a financial services firm, on the other hand, will need a very different background. Most likely he or she will require a strong credential, likely an MBA degree, and many years of experience in the finance industry. The candidate will have a finance leadership history and may already be in a senior leadership position in another firm or second in line at the target firm. Passion for the industry and an ability to attract future finance talent would both be critical.

What these two sets of criteria do have in common, though, is the expectation of relevant albeit very different experiences. In order to predict success, we like to see a track record of leadership in similar situations to the one we are seeking to fill. While it is unlikely the two presidents above could change positions with similar success, the best predictor of future leadership success is past experience and success in similar situations. Nowhere are these predictors more critical or more relevant than in the area of international SCM.

And yet, we know appropriate experience and credentials alone are not going to make a good leader. Something more is needed to help the prediction, and that is the most distinguishing facet of leadership: the candidate's character and cultural fit with the organization.

We know from work done by Jim Kouzes and Barry Posner, a groundbreaking team in leadership research for over 20 years, that there are certain characteristics most people like to see in their leaders. They are valued in different situations and by an extensive cross-section of followers and those who select leaders. The top four characteristics in order of importance are:

1. Honesty
2. Forward-looking
3. Inspiring
4. Competent

Kouzes and Posner contend that leaders with strengths on these characteristics are the most widely accepted by their followers and they are predisposed to lead. These results have been repeated consistently by the authors, even across borders, including China's. I have tested these characteristics myself in surveys of junior executives in Shenzhen, Shanghai, and Beijing and produced similar results. Most people agree these four characteristics matter the most in their leaders and across different situations.

As suggested by Posner, it comes as no surprise to know that these characteristics mirror several of those shown by social psychologists to be prerequisites of credibility—people who have these traits are considered to be more credible by others. The top two credibility-defining characteristics are trustworthiness and competence, which overlap with honesty and competence in our list. A secondary credibility quality, charisma (persuasiveness), closely approximates "inspiring." We can conclude from this that followers are more easily influenced, or led, by credible people, so an organization's goals are best achieved when followers are inspired by honest and competent leaders. If they trust the leader, they will listen and respond more to what the leader says. This is how influence is achieved.

The fourth characteristic of leaders on this list—forward-looking—defines not so much the leader but what they need to be able to do. International SCM organizations want credible, influential leaders to propel them forward in terms of growth, opening new horizons, resolving current challenges, etc. Credibility alone cannot achieve that goal. A good organizational leader needs the right characteristics and a vision for the future, as in the end leaders are about the future.

Let's bring this full circle to the question of how people develop into leaders. Things like honesty and trustworthiness are not something learned in school. In fact, they are rarely discussed or developed in leadership programs. Rather, it is through life experience and social influences that these traits are enhanced and reinforced. This shows most clearly that when considering leadership appointments or potential, we must look beyond the résumé and take into account the person's character.

WHO'S A CREDIBLE LEADER, THEN?

That's the most important question a leader can ask himself or herself. Your followers need to find you credible. Otherwise they will not take you seriously. And when we look at society as a whole, this is a particular challenge for business leaders.

The Gallup organization conducts periodic polls to determine the honesty and ethics—that is, the trustworthiness—of 22 professions. Sad to say, business people do not come out very well. Top of the list in 2009 were nurses and pharmacists and we need to go down to 15th place to find business executives, who are sandwiched between lawyers (at 14th) and advertising practitioners (at 16th). Most of the professions that place high on this list are in the service field. Surprisingly, it is not their leaders who get the credit but the professionals themselves. This is counterintuitive to me. Why are nurses so trustworthy? It's likely that the teachers and leaders in these professions have imparted and upheld a high standard, yet the leaders are not the ones who get the credit. The fact that business executives score so low shows a clear credibility gap with the public. What's worse, the gap has been getting wider. In 2001, 25 percent of respondents gave business executives a very high rating; in 2009 that rating had been cut to 12 percent.

While this is a U.S. survey, I have found similar results in my class of students in Shenzhen, China: business executives were ranked low on a credibility scale. I asked the students why this was so since most of them were business executives themselves. One student immediately responded: "I certainly trust myself but not those other guys." Business leadership is in need of professionalization to rebuild trust. Something needs to start within the ranks of business leaders themselves. We need trustworthy business leaders, we need credible business leaders, and we need to trust our business leaders. It is up to today's leaders—which may include you—to set an example for others.

LEADERSHIP IN ASIA

An interesting dimension of leadership is to consider whether there are differences across cultural settings—in other words, whether there are certain cultural characteristics to leadership situations. After moving to Asia in 1996, I was determined to discover the leadership secret for success in Asia. At that time the media was busy writing about the exceptional achievements of the four tigers of Thailand, Korea, Taiwan, and Hong Kong. These places were booming economically and it occurred to me that effective and exceptional leadership had to be responsible for so much success to be evidenced. While this turned out to be true, and the leadership I found here was special, I quickly learned that the special leadership was also unique. Asia is not one single place and certainly not composed of one situation, and there is no ideal or unique leadership style for Asia. As Kouzes and Posner have shown, similar characteristics are widely appreciated everywhere but, as I have discovered, there is no single generalized leadership style or approach associated with success.

Style is an interesting issue in leadership because it fleshes out the whole idea of what a successful leader does or how they act. While style is independent of credibility and not predictive of success in general, it does give an indication of behavior. Knowing someone's leadership style can be useful for subordinates and for helping leaders develop their capabilities. Some styles work better in certain situations than others.

Styles evolve out of basic personality traits so there are several types of leadership styles. The most effective approach for leaders may actually be to have multiple styles—to adapt one's style to the situation at hand. In contrast, while personality is a good predictor of a leadership style, multiple personalities are not!

Tools have been developed to assess leadership styles. In our MBA orientation programs at the HKUST Business School, we use one of the better leadership assessment tools developed by Professional Dynamic Process (PDP). This measure identifies five types of leadership styles, as shown in Figure 10.2.

We use the PDP measure to help our students develop self-awareness, understand the similarities and differences they have with their classmates, and develop additional skills that can further their leadership careers. Over the 10 years that we have applied the measure, a clear and profound result has emerged: all five leadership styles have been shown to be successful in Asian

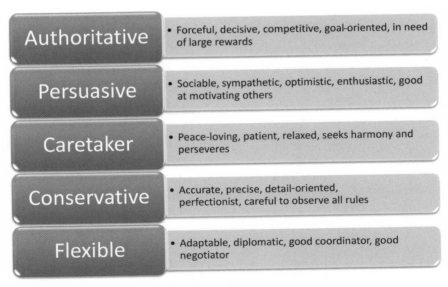

Source: Steven DeKrey. Chart created by Margaret Li

Figure 10.2 The Five Types of Leadership Styles

business careers, confirming the idea that there is no specific "Asian" style of leadership. Rather, as I've pointed out above, leadership depends on universal criteria—the followers, the situation and the credibility of the leader. We all prefer to follow credible leaders and it seems not that important what leadership style they use. This is a significant finding when we consider future SCM leadership needs in China.

Looking specifically at the Kellogg-HKUST EMBA program, which recruits high-achieving executives from across the region and is one of the most elite programs in the world (ranked number one by the *Financial Times* in 2007 and 2009), we found all styles of leadership being practiced by participants, broken down as shown in Table 10.1. Bear in mind that 56 percent were ethnically non-Asian and 75 percent held leadership positions in Asia, many of them in China.

Over the years I have conducted several studies to determine if any of the styles are more successful than the others. Using salary as a variable, I have found that leadership style is not predictive of income. It is not even predictive of EMBA grades, the industry that an executive comes from, or the position of authority they hold.

However, one interesting research finding concerns PRC nationals who study in our bilingual Mandarin/English-speaking EMBA program. Many of these executives are senior people in state-owned enterprises. They are given a Mandarin version of the PDP as part of their orientation but, while all of the styles are represented, a very small percentage of them practice a caretaker-type style and an inordinately large percentage (51 percent in a recent class) are authoritative leaders.

This should not be surprising considering the history of leadership in the PRC. These students represent leadership that is hierarchical and authoritative

Table 10.1 Leadership Style of EMBA Students as Measured by the PDP

Authoritative:	38%
Persuasive	29%
Flexible:	27%
Conservative:	13%
Caretaker:	12%

Source: Stephen DeKrey

and operates very much by command and control. They do not speak much English so have not been influenced by international practices, nor have they studied overseas. There is a definite tendency for the PRC leaders of state-owned enterprises, and government leaders in general, to adopt authoritative styles. It is a culturally accepted way to lead.

Having said that, there is an important point to keep in mind: leadership style is changeable. When we surveyed alumni of the Kellogg-HKUST MBA program five years or so after graduation, their styles had changed in an astonishing way. The authoritative, caretaker and traditional styles had almost vanished. These successful leaders in Asia had become more persuasive and flexible, as Table 10.2 shows.

I would like to think that their education at HKUST contributed to that change. Certainly, the environment they operate in has required different approaches. The demands in Asia and China mean they need to be open, innovative and persuasive to succeed. This is true of all global leaders.

And this comes to a crucial point: China is changing and so is its leadership. China as a whole is becoming a proving ground for global leadership practices and its leaders are evolving before our eyes. At the beginning of this chapter, I indicated that effective leadership had helped lift China out of poverty, connect it to the rest of the world, and elevate it to a world economic power. In order to succeed in the global marketplace, China's leaders have had to demonstrate the universal qualities of credibility, competence and vision that are the hallmarks of successful leadership. They have had to demonstrate that they are indeed global leaders. As we have seen with our students, there is no distinct "Asian" style of leadership and the future of SCM in China will depend upon the ability of SCM firms to attract and retain global leadership talent.

Table 10.2 Leadership Style Adopted ~ Five Years After Graduation

Persuasive:	49%
Flexible:	39%
Authoritative:	5%
Caretaker:	4%
Conservative:	2%

Source: Stephen DeKrey

GLOBAL LEADERSHIP IN PRACTICE

Being a leader in a globalized world requires the same set of leadership skills that I have described, but with a twist. It is not just about how you lead, but where your horizons lie. Stephen Kobrin, Professor of Multinational Management at Wharton, has pointed out that global leadership is about "operating in multiple environments trying to achieve a common objective. Global leadership is about managing an integrated enterprise across borders where you encounter different cultural, legal, regulatory and economic systems."

If we simplify that, we can amend my earlier leadership definition as follows:

"Global leadership is the process of influencing others toward the achievement of an integrated organization's goals across borders."

With a global perspective, what is important in Asia is also important in China and vice versa. To me, successful leadership in China is global leadership.

I've talked about credibility and style but there is one final crucial component to leadership success, and that is putting leadership strengths to best use. Kouzes and Posner developed five exemplary practices and I teach these practices in my classes. I am confident in recommending them to Asian leaders because they are in effect exemplary practices for global leaders.

Model the Way: Leaders establish principles concerning the way their peers, colleagues, customers, and other constituents should be treated, and the way goals should be pursued. They create standards of excellence that set the bar for others to follow. They understand that complex change can overwhelm people and stifle action, so they set interim goals that enable people to achieve small wins as they work toward larger objectives. They unravel bureaucracy when it impedes action. They put up signposts when people are unsure of where to go or how to get there. And, they create opportuities for victory.

Inspire a Shared Vision: Leaders passionately believe they can make a difference. They envision a future that creates an ideal and unique image of what their organization can become. Through their magnetism and persuasion, leaders enlist others in their dreams. They breathe life into their visions and get people to see exciting possibilities for the future.

Challenge the Process: Leaders search for innovative ways to improve the organization. In doing so, they experiment and take risks. And because leaders know that risk-taking involves mistakes and failures, they accept the inevitable disappointments as learning opportunities.

Enable Others to Act: Leaders foster collaboration and build spirited teams. They actively involve others. Leaders understand that mutual respect is what sustains extraordinary efforts; they strive to create an atmosphere of trust and human dignity. They strengthen others, making each person feel capable and powerful.

Encourage the Heart: Accomplishing extraordinary things in organizations is hard work. To keep hope and determination alive, leaders recognize contributions that individuals make. In every winning team, members need to share in the rewards of their efforts, so leaders celebrate accomplishments. They make people feel like heroes.

Global SCM leaders need to apply these practices to their organizations that operate in different countries and cultures, so it is imperative that they also think laterally about their organizations. Consider some specifics. While they still need to concern themselves with single-country issues like diversification, marketing, planning, and competitor analysis, they also need a broad understanding of the differences and commonalities of the various markets they operate in. And they need a vision of how the local and global perspectives can come together. What added value can their firm offer that will prove to be successful in other locations? How do they staff to stay competitive, and how do they lead people in a way that attracts and retains quality staff? How do they keep people motivated and committed in balancing appointments of the home office staff and locals? Decisions like these take careful planning, up-to-date market knowledge and, most importantly, exemplary leadership.

Wal-Mart is a prime example of a global company, which gets it right most times but stumbled badly as it crossed borders, particularly in Germany, South Korea, Japan, and even the United Kingdom. Miscalculations were made based on cultural misunderstandings and an insistence on keeping to the Wal-Mart way. As it turned out, the Germans did not like stores open seven days a week.

Global leaders should also consider the insight from Professor Kobrin, who says the best global leaders are the ones who can balance between extremes—who find the happy medium and understand that differences need to be respected, but that both differences and commonalities can enhance selling. Bringing that around to China and Asia, we can find numerous examples of leaders who manage complex supply chains that operate in different countries and operate across borders. The Asian success story has in many ways been built on this global approach to leadership and trade.

PROSPERING THROUGH INNOVATION

The recent economic downturn has been a serious and unprecedented challenge for leaders and it has called upon all of their skills to survive a harsh economic climate, let alone maintain credibility. Even the most admired and capable leaders have struggled in this uncertain environment, and many leaders have fumbled badly. Research done by one of our EMBA faculty, Ranjay Gulatti, has shown most firms (90 percent) either vanish or barely survive a recession and only 10 percent prosper. Here's the interesting thing, though: the firms that prosper are those that innovate.

Innovation requires forward thinking—one of the top leadership characteristics described by Kouzes and Posner. Leaders are not only there to hold the fort, but to help organizations adapt and thrive in new circumstances and with new ideas—to challenge the process when it needs shaking up. They also need persuasive powers to convince people to carry out their vision, and competence to follow through—qualities also cited among the top four leadership traits.

The importance of innovation is being recognized by many leaders in Asia today, as I've discovered in surveys of our Asian EMBA alumni. We polled them in 2008 and 2009—pre- and post-financial tsunami—and witnessed a significant shift in priorities. In 2008, while the economy was still booming, their top concern was the recruitment, selection, and retention of talent. After the downturn, innovation came out on top. Globalization and talent were still important, but the new economic climate amplified the need to find new solutions and ways of doing business.

SUMMARY AND CONCLUSION

China is encountering particular challenges and opportunities as it continues to evolve and grow. One sure way of dealing successfully with issues and getting the most of favorable circumstances is through effective leadership. Leadership concepts can be difficult to generalize, but we do know that followers prefer their leaders to be credible and forward-looking. These are the most important qualities needed to influence people and organizations, and prepare them for the future of international SCM.

Since China has become a place where international practices merge with local culture and where global business is dominant, it is natural to consider what kind of leadership style works best there. The simple fact is that there is no ideal leadership style and, indeed, multiple styles can be most effective, even within one leader. The ability to adapt style to situation has become especially important in the wake of the global financial crisis and the great lows and highs that it has spawned.

Innovation is a key feature of successful leadership in this environment. As supply chains become more complex and as the need for innovation continues, flexibility and openness to new ideas are now highly valued in leaders. China requires leaders who are rightly steeped in this forward-looking approach. They will need to complement that with multiple capabilities that enable them to juggle cultural and economic demands in a way that meets the future needs of domestic and international markets. No longer will it be good enough to copy leadership models based on what happens in the West. A new brand of SCM leadership is required—a global leadership capability—that can work across cultures and boundaries.

CHAPTER ELEVEN

DYNAMIC SUPPLY CHAINS

The Origin Consolidation Model

MICHAEL JACOBS

As the complexity of consumer retail relationships continues to evolve, the need for a more dynamic and flexible supply chain intensifies. China remains at the forefront of global retail sourcing. Its entry into the World Trade Organization (WTO) and its liberalized customs regulations have created new opportunities for retailers to implement more comprehensive distribution models at the manufacturing point of origin. To properly address this area of opportunity it is necessary to cover a comprehensive landscape of supply chain terminology and industry best practice in order to articulate the overall value proposition that exists. Specifically, this chapter will cover:

- Key terms used to define the business of importing from China
- Development of terms of sale for managing risk and payment options
- The scope of available services provided by key supply chain providers in China and measurements for success
- Importing technology along with other value added services and future trends

China's economic expansion since 1978 has been the fastest of any major nation. During 2001, as China was admitted into the WTO, the Chinese government made a commitment to further provide an environment of economic liberalization and deregulation. Incredibly, as of 2007, China's economy has expanded to now represent the second-highest gross domestic product (GDP) worldwide, as shown in Figure 11.1 (using purchasing power parity), led only by the United States. Its average annual GDP growth rate has been above 10 percent with a per capita annual average income growth of 8 percent.[1]

China's vast, low-cost labor-force coupled with an expanding skill base provides the foundation for massive production capability into the future. In addition, the Chinese government has been working to reform its economy to be more market-oriented and amenable to world trade. This momentum will drive future economic growth, assuming that the Chinese government continues to make the necessary infrastructure investments and social change to demonstrate its ability to provide a stable business atmosphere.

As China continues to expand its capabilities and economic growth, the ease of adaptability for foreign business to conduct global commerce will be critical for its success. As such, this chapter will examine the complexity of how to conduct a U.S.-based importing business using resources in China to optimize efficiencies, enhance speed-to-market, and provide confidence through transparency.

As Sunil Chopra and Peter Meindl point out in their book, *Supply Chain Management Strategy, Planning and Operations*, "the goal of every supply chain should be to maximize the overall value generated. The value a supply chain generates is the difference between what the final product is worth to the customer and the costs the supply chain incurs in filling the customer's request. For most commercial supply chains, value will be strongly correlated

Rank	Country	GDP (purchasing power parity) Billion $
1	United States	13,860
2	China	7,043
3	Japan	4,417
4	India	2,965
5	Germany	2,833
6	United Kingdom	2,147
7	Russia	2,076
8	France	2,067
9	Brazil	1,838
10	Italy	1,800

Source: IndexMundi

Figure 11.1   Country GDP Purchasing Power[2]

with supply chain profitability. A well-designed transportation network allows a supply chain to achieve the desired degree of responsiveness at a low cost."[3] As such, within this chapter, numerous techniques for mitigating supply chain variability along with methods to improve import efficiencies will be raised in a practical manner for field application.

THE ART OF THE DEAL

Conducting business in China can seem like a complex undertaking for foreigners. Often distance, language barriers, culture differences, and risk can deter foreign companies from doing business with enterprise China. By taking the approach of focusing on a business' core competencies (e.g. product selection and development) and then augmenting these internal capabilities with the right external partners, conducting business in China can be fairly simple and efficient. As Chopra and Meindl note, "To succeed in global markets, firms will need to be able to successfully access global suppliers and to assure that such selected suppliers will serve both the present and future needs of the firm."[4]

Once the Factory Is Selected for Production, the Importing Process at a Macro Level Can Be Summarized in Seven Steps.

- Product is sourced, terms of sale are established and purchase order contract accepted

- Using the letter of credit for financing, the factory sources raw materials and labor

- Factory produces product and makes booking with consolidator/ forwarder

- Contact is made with a Chinese customs broker to arrange for origin cargo clearance

- Product is trucked from factory to the consolidator or origin port

- Import documentation is transmitted to the destination country; goods are shipped

- Cargo arrives at the destination country and clears local customs

TERMS OF SALE

For an importer to be successful in negotiation, the fully loaded landed cost must be identified to ensure acceptable levels of risk and profitability. The total landed cost can be difficult to capture, however, depending on the terms of sale. This could include the cost of goods along with all related supply chain costs such as transportation, duty taxes, sourcing overhead, inventory-related costs, legal fees, customs brokerage fees, and freight forwarding charges.

The terms of sale are the agreed-upon obligations and rights of each party as they relate to risk and costs. The terms of an international sale are distinct to that of the terms of payment. There are 13 terms of sale as defined by the International Chamber of Commerce Terms of Trade (Incoterms 2000). Incoterms 2000 is the standard for international trade for determining delivery and transportation documentation, transfer of costs, and assumption of risk. Incoterms define the place where the delivery occurs, either at the factory door, the buyer's door, or any place in between.[5]

Group E Terms—Departure—Minimal seller risk:

1. **Ex Works (EXW)**—the exportable product is made available from the seller to the purchaser at the origin factory, warehouse or point of departure. The seller has no responsibility for any transportation or export clearance through origin customs. The buyer takes on all of the expense and risk associated with transporting the goods from the factory premises to the final destination. This term of sale represents the minimal logistics obligation for the seller.

Group F Terms—Requires the seller to deliver the goods for carriage:

2. **Free Carrier (FCA)**—the seller fulfills its obligation when the product is delivered in good order, cleared for export, delivered to the designated carrier at a pre-determined location in the country of origin.
3. **Free Alongside Ship (FAS)**—the seller fulfills its obligation when the product is cleared for export and is placed alongside a vessel or located at the port. Using this term of sale, the buyer takes on all the expense and risk of potential damage from the port of loading the container onto the vessel and beyond.

4. **Free on Board (FOB)**—the seller fulfills its obligation when the product is delivered in good order and it has passed over the ship's rail at the named port of origin.

Group C Terms—Requires the seller to contract the carriage to a named port or place:

5. **Cost and Freight (CFR)**—the seller agrees to pay the delivery costs and freight to have the product delivered to the port of destination. Using this term of sale, although the seller is responsible to deliver the goods to the destination port, all risks associated with damages as well as other costs become the responsibility of the buyer when the goods pass the ship's rail at the port of origin. The CFR term requires the seller to clear goods for export.

6. **Cost, Insurance and Freight (CIF)**—includes all of the terms included under CFR and the seller is obligated to provide marine insurance, against the buyer's risk of loss or damage for the product in transport. The CIF term requires the seller to clear goods for export.

7. **Carriage Paid To (CPT)**—the seller pays the expense of carriage to the agreed upon destination. The risks of loss as well as any other costs are passed on from the seller to the buyer after the product has been successfully delivered to the carrier. The CPT term requires the seller to clear goods for export.

8. **Carriage and Insurance Paid (CIP)**—the seller has the same obligation as under CPT. However, it is also responsible for securing marine insurance against loss or damage during transport.

Group D Terms—Seller responsible for arrival at the agreed-upon point of destination:

9. **Delivered at Frontier (DAF)**—the seller is obligated to deliver, clear for export, and have product made available at the named port, and located at the frontier (country of export) but before customs term of sale at the adjoining country.

10. **Delivered Ex Ship (DES)**—the seller fulfills its obligation when the product has been available to the buyer on board the ship and not yet cleared for import at the destination country. The seller bears all

of the expense and risk associated with transporting the goods to the destination country.

11. **Delivered Duty Unpaid (DDU)**—the seller fulfills its obligation when the product is delivered at a named place in the destination country. The buyer then assumes all cost and risk associated with bringing the goods into the destination country as well as managing customs clearance and documentation.

12. **Delivered Ex Quay (DEQ)**—the seller fulfills its obligation when the delivery duty unpaid (DDU) is achieved. However, the product must also be made available to the buyer on the quay (wharf) at a predetermined port of destination. The seller assumes all risks of costs including freight and other delivery charges.

13. **Delivered Duty Paid (DDP)**—the seller fulfills its obligation when the product is made available in the destination country. The seller assumes all costs and risk involved in bringing the goods into the destination country including customs clearance and related duty.

It should be noted that the EXW term represents the lowest level of obligation for the seller; however, DDP represents the maximum responsible for the seller.[6]

When Incoterms are incorporated into a purchase order (as discussed under the section Purchase Order Creation), the purchase order will clarify which party will manage various responsibilities and who in the transaction is subject to risk and cost. The title of the cargo passes from the seller to the buyer when delivery is made under the definitions provided under Incoterms 2000 as detailed in the purchase order or pro forma invoice.

At the time of writing, Incoterms 2010 was being finalized and publication was expected later in the year. The primary focus to this revision is to place broader responsibility on the importer to identify troublesome aspects of international transactions. The most notable changes to the Incoterms include the following:

The eliminations from Incoterms 2000 include:

1. DEQ (Delivery Ex Quay)
2. DAF (Delivery at Frontier)

3. DDU (Delivery Duty Unpaid)
4. DES (Delivery Ex Ship)

Additions to Incoterms 2010 include:

1. DAT (Delivered at Terminal). This will be used to replace DEQ.
2. DAP (Delivered at Place). This new term can be used in substitution for DAF, DDU or DES.

Incoterms 2010 will be the seventh update since the initial publication in 1936. After the publication of Incoterms 2000, the September 11 attacks in New York City resulted in a greater burden on import security for international trade. Since the purpose of Incoterms is to clearly define the roles of both the buyer and seller, Incoterms now incorporates a broad level of shipment security responsibility into its definitions.

Examples of Purchase Terms and Related Risk

A retailer that imports from China chooses to negotiate all products using "FOB Yantian, China" terms. This would mean that when delivery is made, the risk passes to that retailer when the container passes the ship's rail (a point) in the port of Yantian, China (a location).

A second option for this retailer to mitigate risk is to choose to purchase the same product but using "DDP Long Beach, California" terms of sale. This would define the location as cleared destination customs and delivered to a warehouse in Long Beach, California. DDP would mitigate inventory and transportation risk to the retailer (buyer) by allowing an easier import model whereby the seller assumes the full burden to import the product.

In this situation, the seller would assume all costs and risk involved in importing the product from China into the destination country.

PURCHASE ORDER (PO) CREATION

A purchase order (PO) is a legal agreement signed by a buyer requesting a seller to provide goods or services. POs normally list the amount of goods or services required and the terms and conditions of delivery and payment.

Overseas suppliers will usually ask for payment upon delivery or sight draft letter of credit terms (see section on Payment Terms for definition).

PO management can be both physical and electronic, requiring best-practice integration of well-defined procedures with sophisticated enabling technologies. PO management begins with the detail of the buyer's requirements and purchase terms. The collection and distribution of the PO is done in collaboration with the vendor and consolidator/forwarder. Often, a local Chinese sourcing office or consolidator will need to meet with the Chinese factory to provide the necessary level of education for proper execution of the PO. This service is performed to ensure that the factory has the necessary information for a seamless transfer of title and delivery of product.

There are numerous methods of distributing POs to vendors. Although it is not uncommon to pass on paper POs, the more sophisticated companies use electronic data interchange (EDI) and web portals for PO distribution.

EDI is an electronic exchange of structured business information that is distributed between a buyer's and seller's computer systems. Using a structured standard for business documents, it allows a common exchange of information to support international commerce. EDI increases the overall efficiency of commerce using a cost-effective technique. Increased productivity and the elimination of confusion can be achieved through the use of this universal language. Different transactions are identified using numeric codes. Examples of international document transactions are presented thus:

- EDI 850—Transmission of an electronic purchase order
- EDI 855—Acknowledgement and acceptance of the 850 purchase order
- EDI 860—Purchase order changes/updates
- EDI 810—Electronic invoice
- EDI 997—Functional acknowledgment of the receipt of an EDI transmission
- EDI 856—Advanced shipping notice (ASN)
- EDI 315—Ocean status details
- EDI 310—Ocean invoice/bill of lading (BL)
- EDI 214—Shipment status message (domestic or inland)

Another method of exchanging international documents is through the use of a web portal. Through access to the worldwide web, documents can be accurately and efficiently exchanged between international companies. A web portal allows supply chain partners to communicate and collaborate in an extremely efficient and cost-effective manner. Business documents are posted to and retrieved from a portal electronically. Email is used to alert supply chain business partners when new or changed documents have been posted to the portal. Each party can easily view, accept, or request changes to the portal documents. Although web security must be considered, these documents can easily communicate in both directions. Alerts as well as document amendments can be tracked electronically.

The foundation to build communication technology is a key factor for companies to overcome barriers of entry into new markets, as Chopra and Meindl observe in relation to Wal-Mart's success. "Wal-Mart has been a leader at using supply chain design, planning, and operations to achieve success. From the beginning, the company invested heavily in transportation and information infrastructure to facilitate the effective flow of goods and information."[7]

The development of an import purchase order can be complex when working to ensure that the product arrives on time. The lead time is significantly longer on an imported product compared with that of a domestically sourced product. Following is an example of the lead times of an average plastic-injected toy product being sourced in Shenzhen China and destined for New York.

Tables 11.1, 11.2 and 11.3 detail the steps from purchase order creation to delivery:

Table 11.1 Ocean Transportation Cycle Time From PO Creation

	Days
Sourcing raw materials, production, and safety testing	60
Booking and delivery to consolidator	3
Consolidation, exportation, and vessel loading—Shenzhen	4
Transport to the USA west coast (including customs clearance)*	14
Vessel unload and rail transit	9
Delivery to the warehouse and unload	1
Total Ocean Transport Lead Time in Days	**91**

Source: Michael Jacobs

Table 11.2 Air Freight Cycle Time from PO Creation

	Days
Sourcing raw materials, production, and safety testing	60
Booking and delivery to air freight forwarder	3
Cleared for export	1
Transportation to JFK Airport	2
Local customs cleared and pickup order	1
Delivery to destination warehouse and unload	1
Total Air Freight Transport Lead Time in Days	**68**

Source: Michael Jacobs

Table 11.3 Combination of Ocean and Domestic Air Freight

	Days
Sourcing raw materials, production, and safety testing	60
Booking and delivery to consolidator	3
Consolidation, exportation, and vessel loading—Shenzhen	4
Transport to the USA west coast (including customs clearance)	14
Vessel unload and transload product	2
Air delivery to the warehouse and unload	1
Total Ocean and Air Transport Lead Time in Days	**84**

Source: Michael Jacobs

Add an additional seven days if transporting product from Shenzhen China to New York by routing product all-water through the Panama or Suez Canal using ocean services directly into the port of New York. All-water service into the east coast of the United States is also referred to as "reverse inland point intermodal" (RIPI). Certainly, an all-water service into the east coast of the United States adds seven days to the product lead time; however, it also offers reduced transportation cost and, more importantly, can be used strategically to reduce risk. By diversifying the ports used, supply variability risks can be managed more effectively, as rail delays and other labor-related delays can be mitigated.

It is clear that purchasing product as a direct import has considerably more transportation lead time than if sourced domestically. Although this additional lead time creates business risk, the payback can be significant as product margin can be greatly enhanced.

Each of the example lead times presented must be considered into the initial PO, prior to confirmation of production. The fastest method of transportation is direct airfreight; however, this is the most expensive of the transportation alternatives. Even so, based on the value of the items being moved or the time-sensitive nature of an item, airfreight may be a good option. In the toy industry, however, airfreight is generally not a viable option because of the expense associated with the large volume and low value of the items. Refer to Airfreight section of this chapter for expense details and examples.

In the toy industry, ocean freight is most commonly used. Based on carrier selection and inventory value, ocean transport can offer a reasonable transit time and cost-effective service.

PAYMENT TERMS

The letter of credit (LC) is an essential component for protecting the foreign buyer by ensuring that the accepted terms of sale have been fulfilled prior to payment. It is a legal document issued by a financial institution as directed by a buyer of goods or services authorizing the seller to pay a specified amount, based on pre-determined conditions, within a specified time period. By employing the services of an independent third-party bank, an LC is a guarantee to the seller that the issuing bank will pay the factory on behalf of the foreign buyer provided that the factory has successfully met the essential terms and conditions (T&Cs) detailed in the LC. These terms and conditions reconcile to the accepted purchase order.

This method of bank payment is made based on the presentation of documents that clearly demonstrate the transfer of title as well as confirmation that the terms of sale have been met, as detailed in the LC and purchase order. The foreign buyer initiates the LC once the terms of sale are understood and accepted (the buyer is also known as the "LC applicant"). The factory or selling agent that ultimately will be receiving the payment is known in the LC as the beneficiary (the seller is also known as the "LC beneficiary"). Based on all conditions being met, the LC terms can offer an immediate payment or be dated to pay at a later time.

To establish and execute the LC, the bank charges fees to both the foreign buyer and local seller of the product being sold. All bank fees should be detailed in the body of the LC. The LC specifies all documents required by the foreign buyer and has an expiration date.

The LC may have different operating characteristics. For example, it can be revocable or irrevocable. An irrevocable LC cannot be changed or cancelled unless both parties agree. It is considered a binding agreement. A revocable LC can be changed by either party. A revocable LC may not be preferred as it introduces potential risk to both parties. When a change is made to an LC, it is known as an "amendment." Generally, bank charges are imposed for the initial LC set up as well as for amendments and correction of any discrepancies when the shipping documents are presented. Following are several commonly used LCs in international trade as defined by Network F.O.B. Inc.

- **Straight LC**—A letter of credit that contains a limited engagement clause, which states that the issuing bank promises to pay the beneficiary upon presentation of the required documents.
- **Revolving LC**—An irrevocable letter of credit issued for a pre-specified amount but which continually renews itself for the same amount over a given period. This type of LC is often used for bulk orders that are being fulfilled over a period of time.
- **Transferable LC**—A letter of credit that permits the beneficiary to transfer in whole or in part to another beneficiary any amount which, in aggregate, will not exceed the total value of the LC credit.
- **Restricted LC**—Contains a condition in the letter of credit limiting its negotiation to a named bank.[8]

A second option to pay for import product is the creation of an open account. Using an open account as a financial payment tool, the foreign buyer simply pays the factory or selling agent under pre-agreed terms commonly defined in a purchase order or contract. As the acceptance of an open account payment method is based on the creditworthiness of the foreign buyer and not guaranteed, it is frequently used by larger firms with a strong reputation and credit rating.

Another method of foreign payment is international consignment where goods are shipped to a foreign distributor but title remains with the exporter until the goods are sold. Companies such as Dell computers purchase components on consignment and take ownership in a just-in-time (JIT) manner. As Chopra and Meindl note, "Dell manages its cash flows very effectively. By managing inventories, receivables, and payables very closely, it managed a cash conversion cycle of negative 36 days in 2004. In other words, Dell ran its business on other people's money!"[9]

Separately, a countertrade arrangement is an international barter using goods or services between two parties, generally due to a trading partner's lack of foreign exchange. Companies like PepsiCo have historically used countertrade agreements in areas such as Russia due to the lack of a global foreign exchange. In exchange for Pepsi syrup and the secret recipe to produce Pepsi in Russia, PepsiCo receives Stolichnaya vodka for resale in the United States.

CONSOLIDATION SERVICES IN CHINA

At its simplest level, the word "consolidator" can be defined as "uniting or combining into one unit or to confirm into a single entity."[10] In the shipping industry, the consolidator is responsible for receiving less-than-container-load (LCL) quantities of freight from multiple China suppliers and sharing that space in a container to gain the cost advantage of full container load (FCL) pricing for the shipper. For the purpose of this discussion, "the shipper is the party that requires the movement of the product between two points in the supply chain. The carrier is the party that moves or transports the product."[11]

Once the freight consolidated into the container, the consolidator would act as a freight forwarder by booking the ocean cargo, arranging for pickup, as well as conducting the audits and the management of all shipping documentation. The consolidator is working for the foreign buyer, also called the shipping consignee, that is designated on the bill of lading (see Documentation section).

When product is consolidated into an ocean container, the goal is to optimize the shipping space and thus minimize the cost of transportation. Cargo is mixed from multiple factory sources to ensure that the best possible combination of container fill is achieved without increasing the risk of product damage to the merchandise. Areas containing a large number of less-than-container-load orders in geographically dense regions are prime locations for a consolidation point. In addition, by fully utilizing larger ocean equipment (see Equipment section of this chapter), a reduction in drayage (transportation) charges as well as demurrage and detention (container dwell time) charges can be realized. Reduction in cost per cubic meter is the primary reason to use the larger equipment.

Through standard operating procedures (SOPs), industry best practices, frequent communication, and document audits, consolidators in China can act as an extension of the foreign buyer or freight consignee as the control tower for import management. Through a rigorous selection process and with the right level of engagement, a Chinese consolidator can provide a wealth of market intelligence, vendor management, and bring best-in-class operating practices to a company.

As the control tower, consolidators offer a comprehensive range of services beyond simple consolidation and freight forwarding. Examples include:

- Management of standard operating procedures (SOPs) and vendor communication.
- Tracking of raw material and manufacturing production performance by purchase order.
- Issuance of the dock and cargo receipt to vendors delivering product in good order.
- Management of factory load programs to optimize container utilization.
- Preparation of the container manifest and advanced shipping notices (ASN).
- Product kitting, pick-and-pack, inspections, assortment creation, labeling, barcoding, and ticketing. This is the process where the consolidator adds value by managing items at the piece level. Individual items can be grouped, packed, and labeled to produce a customer-ready selling unit.
- Chinese-origin warehousing and trucking services.
- Document management and electronic scanning for customs clearance at the destination country.
- Software technology using EDI and web portals to provide full visibility to all operations in China as well as container movement (down to the item level).
- Reporting on key performance information.

- Certification for security and governmental programs (such as Customs Trade Partnership against Terrorism (see Security section).
- There are many other types of value added supply chain services. Examples could include DC by-pass and drop-ship programs, transloading operations, multi-country consolidation, supplier management, exception management and alerts, transit time guarantee, and non-vessel operating common carrier (NVOCC) services (see NVOCC section).

To understand the value of a consolidator, the cost structure of ocean freight must be clearly understood. Many experienced shippers do not fully understand the cost of ocean freight. There is good reason for this. Although most ocean containers from origin to destination contain a consistent base ocean rate, the carrier's price uses an "a la carte" approach by adding numerous arbitrary charges. An arbitrary charge is "a stated amount over a fixed rate from one point to make it to another point."[12]

Presented in Table 11.4 is an example of the components of ocean freight from Yantian, China, to Columbus, Ohio, on a 40-foot standard container.

Other costs not listed in the table could include (depending on the origin and destination of the cargo):

- Port Clean Air Act fees
- War risk charges
- Peak season surcharge
- Carrier security fees
- Currency adjustment factors
- Emergency fuel surcharge
- Canal fees
- Advanced manifest submission fee (AMS)

In addition to these costs, it is also strongly advised that a shipper or consignee obtain marine insurance. Marine insurance covers loss or damages sustained during the transportation of goods.

Chopra and Meindl state, "Within the United States the passage of the Ocean Shipping Reform Act of 1998 has been a significant event for water transport. This Act allows carriers and shippers to enter into confidential contracts, effectively deregulating the industry."[13] As ocean contracts are now

Table 11.4 40-Foot Standard Ocean Container Shipping Cost (USD)

Origin receiving charge (ORC)	$ 269
Base ocean rate 40-foot standard container	$ 1,750
Container yard destination delivery charge (CYDDC)	$ 169
Fuel adjustment factor (FAF) or bunker surcharge	$ 380
Port security fee	$ 100
Intermodal transport	$ 1,900
Trucking charge	$ 290
Total Cost	**$4,858**

Source: Michael Jacobs

confidential, when negotiating freight rates it is crucial to get an all-in rate to ensure full disclosure prior to signing a contractual minimum quantity commitment (MQC) to an ocean carrier. Although carriers state that they use a standard boilerplate for all contracts, as identified earlier in this chapter, there are hidden costs throughout the agreement.

Containerized ocean freight volume and weight is a significant variable for selection of the right container size. For example, the maximum U.S. Department of Transportation (DOT) gross weight limit placed on American highways is 80,000 pounds. This maximum weight includes the tractor, container, and cargo. Based on the weight of the first two components mentioned, the ocean cargo generally should not exceed 40,000 to 44,000 pounds.

The selection of the optimal container size and the utilization of the container's space are as critical as the rate paid for ocean freight. If weight is not a factor, a general rule is that the larger the ocean container, the better the utilization. Other factors that drive enhanced container utilization is product type and mix as well as consolidator experience.

Figure 11.2 presents the liquid space of an ocean container by size and type. It should be noted that no shipper will ever achieve utilization equal to the liquid volume of an ocean container; however, many shippers can achieve a minimum of 85-percent liquid space utilization.

When pricing the ocean containers, multipliers are applied to the base container size of a 40-foot standard. Although container multipliers can vary by ocean carrier, the standard multipliers for the U.S. market are as presented in Table 11.5.

Ocean Container Dimensions:

20-Foot DRY CONTAINER

INTERIOR DIMENSIONS	DOOR OPENING	TARE WEIGHT	CUBIC CAPACITY	PAYLOAD
Length: 19'5" 5.919m Width: 7'8" 2.340m Height: 7'9.5" 2.380m	Width: 7'6" 2.286m Height: 7'5.5" 2.278m	4,189 lbs 1,900 kg	1,165 cubic ft. 33.0 cbm	48,721 lbs 22,100 kg

40-Foot DRY CONTAINER

INTERIOR DIMENSIONS	DOOR OPENING	TARE WEIGHT	CUBIC CAPACITY	PAYLOAD
Length: 39'6.5" 12.05m Width: 7'8" 2.340m Height: 7'9.5" 2.380m	Width: 7'6" 2.286m Height: 7'5.5" 2.278m	6,799 lbs 3,084 kg	2,377 cubic ft. 67.3 cbm	60,401 lbs 27,397 kg

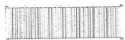

40-Foot HIGH CUBE CONTAINER

INTERIOR DIMENSIONS	DOOR OPENING	TARE WEIGHT	CUBIC CAPACITY	PAYLOAD
Length: 39'6.5" 12.056m Width: 7'8 1/4" 2.347m Height: 8'9.5" 2.684m	Width: 7'8" 2.340m Height: 8'5 3/4" 2.58m	6,393 lbs 2,900 kg	2,684 cubic ft. 76.0 cbm	65,256 lbs 29,600 kg

45-Foot HIGH CUBE CONTAINER

INTERIOR DIMENSIONS	DOOR OPENING	TARE WEIGHT	CUBIC CAPACITY	PAYLOAD
Length: 44'6.5" 13.582m Width: 7'8 1/4" 2.347m Height: 8'10" 2.690m	Width: 7'8" 2.340m Height: 8'5 3/4" 2.58m	9,061 lbs 4,110 kg	3,026 cubic ft. 85.7 cbm	62,589 lbs 28,390 kg

Source: "Container size and specifications," Beyond Freight Inc.

Figure 11.2   Ocean Container Dimensions[14]

Table 11.5 Expected China to U.S. Standard Average Container

Container Pricing Multiplier	Utilization in CBMs*
20-foot standard container = 0.800	26
40-foot standard container = 1.000	56
40-foot high volume container = 1.125	66
45-foot high volume container = 1.266	76

*Cubic Meters
Source: Michael Jacobs

Based on the container cost size multipliers, as indicated above, if a shipper has the ability to fully utilize the space of the ocean container, the larger the size container the lower the per unit landed cost. If weight is not a factor, based on the standard U.S. multipliers a 40-foot container is less expensive to move than a 20-foot container. Using the above multipliers as an example, the cost of a 20-foot ocean container is 80 percent of the cost of a 40-foot ocean container with less than half the expected utilization.

With the exception of the 20-foot container, although the multiplier itself is commensurate with the liquid volume measurements of the ocean container, much of the container's space is lost at the door. The gap needed to close the ocean container doors takes a material amount of space away from fully utilizing the space of the container. Therefore, if there is enough freight to fully utilize the space of two 45-foot containers, it will be less expensive than moving three 40-foot standard containers on a cost per cubic meter (CBM) basis.

There are scenarios whereby selecting a 20-foot container may minimize landed cost. For example, if the weight of the product being loaded into an ocean container exceeds that maximum allowed weight (heavy items such as imported marble or hard wood items), cubing out a larger container may not be possible. As such, a 20-foot container would be advantageous. In this particular situation, a consolidator may offer a strategic benefit. Consolidating heavy items and light product into a single container can optimize landed cost for the shipper.

Proper selection of equipment type in international ocean shipping is an important component to optimize the cost structure for the shipper. It is the consolidator's responsibility to manage container size selection to minimize transportation cost.

As a shipper of containerized freight, knowledge of the volume of the cartons being shipped along with how many cartons can fit on a container is a critical competency to optimizing container utilization. It is possible that a reduction of an inch on a master carton can translate into a 10-percent decrease in shipping cost per case. Once the shipper pays the cost of the ocean container, there are no incremental fees if additional freight can be loaded onto that box. The cost of moving the container is a flat fee regardless of the amount of cargo inside.

The following equation highlights the difference in the average factory load utilization (not through a consolidator): ((66 CBMs less: 56 CBMs)/ 56 CBMs). It should be noted that the actual utilization of containers is dependent on the commodity being loaded. The container utilization presented below is common but not an industry standard. For example, although there is 12.5-percent difference in the pricing multiplier between a 40-foot standard and 40-foot high volume container, the shipper can load on average 18 percent more cargo in this container.

Later on in this chapter, a discussion on pricing calculations will be presented to provide additional examples using ocean freight rates.

For China to U.S. shipping, standard multipliers are used to determine the cost of a container. Although there are exceptions, most ocean freight rates are either a dollar add-on or a multiplier of the 40-foot standard container rate. As such, the standard multiplier for the 40-foot standard container is equal to "one."

Shipping cost of ocean freight (Base Ocean Rate + CYDDC + ORC + FAF)/container utilization of larger (premium) ocean container equipment must be compared to the incremental cost associated with consolidation expense to determine the best solution for minimizing landed cost.

Using the cost example above on the 40-foot standard container, the calculation of moving a 45-foot container is detailed in Table 11.6.

This is a basic example of the financial value of using premium ocean container equipment to import product. In this example, the shipper will save US$8.08, or 9 percent per cubic meter by using a 45-foot ocean container versus a 40-foot standard container. Based on the type of product being consolidated, the container utilization numbers presented in this example should be obtainable. The higher the container utilization, the lower the shipper's landed cost per unit.

Table 11.6 Ocean Container Costing By Size (USD)

	40-Foot Standard		45-Foot High volume
Origin receiving charge (ORC)	$ 269	Flat rate by size	$ 340
Base ocean rate	$1,750	By multiplier	$2,188
CYDDC	$ 169	By multiplier	$211
FAF or bunker surcharge	$ 380	By multiplier	$475
Port security fee	$ 100	Flat rate	$100
Intermodal transport	$1,900	By multiplier	$2,375
Trucking charge	$ 290	Flat rate	$290
Total Cost of the Container	$4,858		$5,979 + 23%
Average Container Utilization	56		76 + 36%
Cost Per CBM	$86.75		$78.67 - 9%

Source: Michael Jacobs

As shown in the photo below, space is needed at the tail of the ocean container so that the doors may close easily without damaging the product inside.

Using a consolidator can further optimize container utilization and thus minimize landed cost. As discussed earlier in this chapter, when moving

Source: Michael Jacobs

Maximum Container Utilization

freight, a decision must be made regarding having the factory load, also called a container yard (CY), delivered or having loose freight transported to a container freight station (CFS) to be managed by the consolidator. The CFS is a shipping dock where cargo is consolidated or de-consolidated from containers.

If the freight is loaded into the container by the factory, the freight will have two less handling points than if brought to a consolidator. The handling points saved include the product unload by the consolidator at the CFS delivery point and the reload of the freight into the destination ocean container. The reduced handling can be translated into reduced cost by the factory (in China it is a standard practice for the factory to pay the consolidation fees). In addition to the savings on the incremental handling, with less touch points in the supply chain there is less potential product damage.

The second option is to have the less-than-container-load quantity (LCL) delivered to the CFS for consolidation. If the volume of product purchased is LCL, there are several options including the use of a non-vessel operating common carrier (see section on the use of NVOCC) or delivery to a consolidator.

The consolidator has numerous methods of reducing the landed cost of the product. As vendors/factories from many locations are delivering freight to a single point, the consolidator has the ability to mix product from multiple vendors into ocean containers. By mixing large cartons with smaller cartons, the consolidator has an advantage over that of the factory to gain better overall container utilization and also use larger premium equipment. In addition, if moving heavy freight, the consolidator has the option of mixing lighter freight with the heavier freight to gain the benefit of balancing the weighted product over multiple containers to offset the restrictions and also utilize the larger premium equipment. It is not uncommon for a consolidator to average 10-percent better container utilization than that of a factory-loaded container.

Based on the ocean freight example provided, a 9-percent saving was realized by moving a 45-foot container over the cost per CBM of a 40-foot standard container. If the consolidator achieved an average of a 10-percent container utilization improvement over that of a factory-loaded container, this would represent a 19-percent saving on the landed cost per CBM. Based on an all-in container cost of a 40-foot standard container of US$4,858, a 19-percent saving would be US$923 less the cost of consolidator-related expenses. If the shipper loaded 1,000 units of product on the ocean container, a saving of US$0.92 per unit would be realized.

To gain this level of savings, consolidators use sophisticated tools to enhanced utilization such as container optimization software. This software is designed to examine the liquid volume dimensions of the ocean container and compare that with the volume of the freight available to be loaded.

The software (in this example, TOPS Maxload) works as if trying to solve a puzzle comparing variables of different container sizes with available freight.[15] As noted below, the application uses algorithms to maximize container utilization based on pre-set stacking rules and equipment dimensions. The plan provided by the software mixes different product in the container to optimize the utilization. The software uses color codes to highlight the different products being stowed in the container, the exact location in the container, and the manner that it must be loaded in a step-by-step format, as shown in Figures 11.3–11.8.

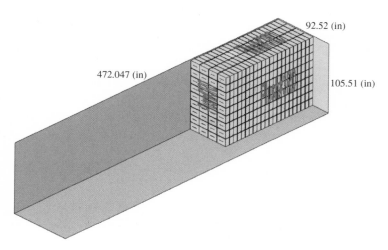

Figure 11.3   Container Utilization

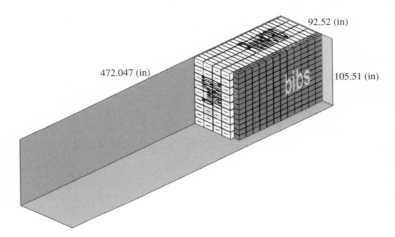

Figure 11.4   Container Utilization

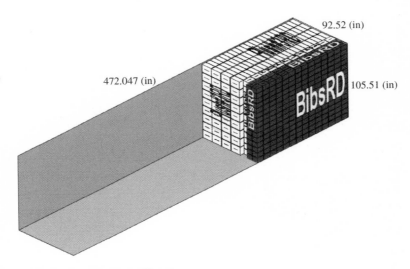

Figure 11.5   Container Utilization

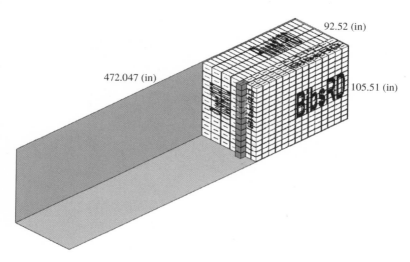

Figure 11.6   Container Utilization

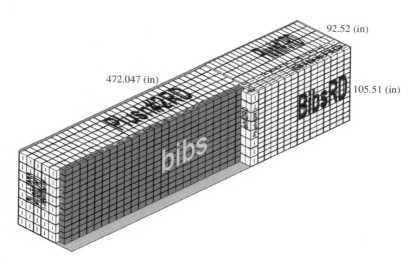

Figure 11.7   Container Utilization

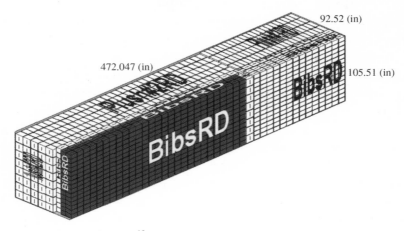

92.52 (in)

472.047 (in)

105.51 (in)

Source: Michael Wiggins, DHL- ISC[16]

Figure 11.8   Container Utilization

CONSOLIDATION MANAGEMENT AND VISIBILITY TOOLS AS PROGRAM ENABLERS

At the core of the success of a consolidation operation is the development and maintenance of standard operating procedures (SOPs). The SOPs capture the responsibilities and goals of the consolidation program for all stakeholders associated with the consolidation process. The SOPs have seven primary components:

- Purchase order management
- Vendor management
- Carrier management
- Container freight station (CFS) and factory load (CY) management
- Supporting processes and decision tree models
- Forwarder services and documentation management
- Key contact information

Consolidators and forwarders offer fully hosted, web-based portals that provide their clients import-container visibility. The core of these systems consists of modules that work via EDI or online access. These systems have become quite comprehensive in that they can track product from PO acceptance, the manufacturing process, consolidators and forwarders, through the ports, onto and off the ship, customs clearance, rail, truck, and ultimately to the receipt at the final destination (warehouse, store, or even to the door of a customer). These systemic tracking tools have many important features that are designed to mitigate supply variability and provide exception management, such as:

A: On-demand access relating to a specific ship, ocean container, purchase order and item. When asked the question, "Where is my shipment?" or, "Will my product make the ad date?" the answer is consistently available through the tracking system.

B: The reporting system not only contains a report writer tied into shipment visibility but also a much wider view of information including such items as volumes, shipment cost, merchandise value, vendor compliance levels, and transit time information. Most consolidators and forwarders provide standard reports that are used commonly across their client base. Over the past few years, the reporting capabilities of these systems have become more advanced with customization abilities to provide ad hoc reports as needed by the client. These systems can also provide a high, as well as detailed, level of decision support to measure vendor and carrier compliance.

C: Within the visibility tool, supply chain exceptions can be defined. Using this capability, automatic exception notifications can be sent to provide real-time reporting when a variance occurs from the original supply chain transit plan. If managed properly, this can be a very powerful decision support tool.

An example of this could be that container KEAU3372215 containing advertised product is scheduled to be loaded onto a specific vessel. An EDI transmission that the container was loaded onto the vessel is not received from the ocean carrier; however, the vessel departure EDI transmission was received. An exception report would be automatically generated stating that container KEAU3372215 was not loaded onto the scheduled vessel. The consolidator and the shipper would be notified of an operating exception using email. Immediate action would be taken to re-route that container to the next possible ship.

As described in this example, these visibility systems contain sophisticated exception management capabilities that identify potential operating issues very early in the process thus creating a new level of supply chain efficiency to minimize variability. These exception and alert functions continually monitor a shipper's (also known as the consignee's) supply chain information against a pre-determined transit time plan. In many cases, monitoring the shipments can be close to real time. These alert functions are systemically driven and the notifications to key stakeholders are automatic. Examples of exceptions could include:

- Vendor misses a ship window for product delivery
- Vendor delivers cargo to the wrong location
- Delays to shipment in transit
- Customs processing delay
- Missing the scheduled intermodal connection
- Container is not picked up at the railhead
- Product is not received by the warehouse in a timely manner
- Product was received after the ETA identified in the purchase order

These tools can also be used to report on key performance indicators (KPIs) and service-level agreements (SLAs) with suppliers throughout the supply chain. In addition, the detail of each alert can be put into a report for performance reviews with vendors and carriers. These reports can also become a powerful tool in holding supply chain partners accountable for the commitments that are made.

CFS VERSUS CY

The purpose of employing a consolidator beyond simply forwarding responsibilities is to minimize import costs regardless of order size and maximize speed to market. To achieve this goal, SLAs such as container minimums must be established. An ocean container can be loaded at the consolidator's container freight station (CFS) or loaded directly by the factory and delivered to the container yard (CY), as presented in Figure 11.9. If there is enough freight to meet the minimum container utilization, then the ocean container will be loaded directly by the factory to optimize costs by minimizing touches to the freight.

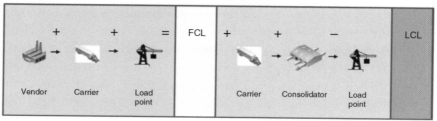

Source: Michael Jacobs

Figure 11.9   FCL and LCL Flow

For a CY-loaded container, the minimum cubic volume must be established in the standard operating procedures. After the PO is created and the product is manufactured, a booking is made by the vendor identifying the shipment as a factory load. Using container optimization software, the consolidator provides a product load plan to the vendor, validates the earliest ship date, chooses an ocean carrier to optimize speed to market and reserves the correct container sizes for the shipment.

Separately, for CFS freight, if the shipment is being delivered to the consolidator LCL for consolidation into an ocean container, the vendor books the delivery of product to the consolidator. Upon receipt, the product is de-consolidated from the factory's truck or container and entered into a bonded warehouse in China where it is measured and weighed. All available LCL freight from multiple vendors that is delivered to the CFS is entered into the container optimization software and a load plan is created.

Whether freight is moving FCL or LCL, the following is a list of variables and complexities when consolidating product into an ocean container:

- Lead-time standards required to make the PO ETA. Dwell time at origin can be as significant a variable as container utilization and must be factored into the operating procedures
- Number of freight touches to minimize handling and storage costs
- Purchase terms and related documentation requirements
- Sailing schedules of the contracted ocean carriers and related vessel cut-off dates
- Ocean freight costs

- Client allocation and contracted volume commitments by ocean carrier
- Optimized container size for the freight versus carrier equipment availability

VALUE ADDED SERVICES (VAS)

The consolidator offers many value added services (VAS) beyond basic consolidation and forwarding. One example of a consolidator VAS is the DC by-pass program (also known as a direct ship program). This service is designed to reduce inventory-holding costs and provide faster supply chain speed-to-market. Through systemic integration, the consolidator can segregate the cartons into a container by store location. By providing this level of service, product is now stowed in the container and ready for delivery by retail outlet. The benefits of the DC by-pass program include:

- Improved speed due to direct-to-store routing and a reduction in handling at the destination country
- Reduction in pipeline inventory levels due to the time saved through the DC by-pass
- Reduced cost due to a reduction in carton touches
- Improved inventory turnover

DC by-pass can be especially beneficial when managing special programs such as high volumes of seasonal product like large volume furniture or Christmas promotions.

Consolidators (such as DHL ISC) have extensive experience with the DC by-pass solution. Figure 11.10 demonstrates how DHL ISC distributed to over 500 stores from seven entry ports into the United States from China.

Since many retailers' products are seasonal in nature, domestic DC processing does not add value to the supply chain other than storing the products.

Using a specific case study, DHL ISC first examines multiple scenarios using different combinations of entry ports to reduce the domestic travel distance as well as filling full containers to each port. Once the criterion is established, DHL ISC determines seven ports to use located across the west coast, east coast and also the Midwest. At the origin CFS, vendors bring the

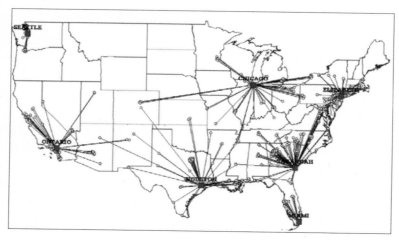

Source: Toys"R"Us

Figure 11.10   DHL ISC Pool Distribution Plan to 500 Toys"R"Us Stores

products into CFS for temporary storage. These products are then sorted by store location prior to being loaded into ocean containers, in accordance with the retailer's EDI distributed purchase order (DPO). When the container arrives at the destination port, the freight moves directly to a less-than-truckload (LTL) terminal and final delivery is handled by the LTL carrier.

DHL ISC's engineering team uses a comprehensive approach to capture all supply chain costs and support the business case. The cost elements include origin handling cost, transportation cost (ocean and domestic), and destination handling cost (DC and cross-dock). Using this innovative solution, the retailer is able to achieve a 17-percent saving compared to the current practice. In addition, it dramatically reduces the space and resource pressure at the DC level.

The most critical component of a successful DC by-pass solution is the order lead time to stores or customers. Sufficient time has to be allowed to ship products from overseas to the final consignees, which extend the delivery time a few weeks if inventory is available. Therefore, the solution usually works well with push or seasonal products where delivery quantities are known far in advance.

Another VAS provided by consolidators is transit guarantees. This service provides expedited ocean/air combinations to minimize the extreme expense associated with using air services directly from China (see Transit Schedule section).

One example of a consolidator providing an ocean/air option is American President Lines Logistics (APLL). APLL provides a service called "Ocean Guarantee Continental."[17] Coming out of any one of three major China ports, APLL can provide a port-door service to anywhere in continental United States. APLL will guarantee delivery anywhere in the United States within five business days of the vessel's arrival on the west coast. This offering provides airfreight reliability at a fraction of the cost while ensuring that an in-ware-house date or customer promise is achieved. If the guaranteed date is missed, a percentage of the freight cost is refunded to the shipper.

A third VAS is the ability to act as a third-party warehouse to work with suppliers to delay the transfer of inventory to the retailer. Often suppliers want to source their raw materials and finished goods close to the shipping point to minimize transportation and handling expense. By working directly with the sourcing community for a client retailer, a consolidator can hold inventory on behalf of the supplier for the client retailer. When product is required for replenishment by the retailer, communication is transmitted systematically. The consolidator then would act as a neutral party to transfer the inventory from the supplier to the retailer without any incremental trucking costs.

By taking these steps there is a two-sided benefit: a reduction in supply uncertainty and inventory-holding cost for the retailer; and for the supplier, a reduction in transportation costs, handling costs, and potential charge-backs for delays in delivery or documentation.

Another VAS is multi-country consolidation (MCC). This program can be used by larger shippers to combine multiple LCL Asian-origin shipments at a single consolidation point to minimize overall importing costs. The consolidator will conduct a feasibility study to determine if an MCC mode option is optimal to reduce overall freight costs. Working with the consolidator and ocean carrier, the ocean freight expense is reduced as the carrier uses prorated FCL rates and not LCL rates. Although somewhat complex, the consolidator coordinates the shipment with the carrier and manages all documentation to ensure an expeditious clearance through customs. Several of the larger MCC points in Asia include Singapore, Kaohsiung, and Hong Kong. Benefits of the MCC program include:

- Reduction in freight related expenses
- Faster transit times than LCL
- Lower destination delivery expense

- Minimizes risk as LCL travels with other shippers' cargo. Utilizing MCC, the container will carry the freight of a single shipper
- Reduces the potential need and costs associated with trans-loading import product at the destination country

Today, many consolidators and ocean carriers provide trucking services throughout China. At one time considered a difficult and complex process, trucking in China is now a viable option.

As an importer, there are benefits to taking on the burden of product ownership and trucking at the factory to have greater supply chain visibility as the goods enter the shipper's network earlier in the importing process. In addition, often the vendor develops the markup on product based on the total cost. If origin trucking is included in the vendor's cost structure, markup is often automatically applied. Although retailers have not aggressively used origin as a technique to reduce cost, it is becoming clear that this VAS will become an increasingly important factor in the years to come.

As described in this chapter, there are numerous VAS provided by consolidators. Several other services that are notable include barcode labeling and scanning; C-TPAT/ISO28000, 10 + 2 certification security compliance, program systemic and procedural support; kitting which requires piece pick, pack and sorting; certification of weights and measures; and raw materials importation, and bonded warehouse services (a warehouse authorized by customs for storage of freight of which payment of duties can be deferred until the goods are moved).

When selecting a consolidator, bundling of services must be considered. Bundling of services is when a single provider has the capability to provide a variety of services. As different consolidators have varying levels of experience and expertise in providing the menu of VAS, a shipper must consider which VAS will be most critical to its business prior to selecting the consolidator. By bundling services with a single consolidator, the shipper will build scale with the consolidator. This scale will potentially provide a platform for the consolidator to reduce its overall margin on its services. Using a bundling strategy, a win-win business partnership can be achieved by providing both the consolidator and shipper with a competitive cost advantage in the market.

NON-VESSEL OPERATING COMMON CARRIER (NVOCC)

As an alternative to a consolidator or freight forwarder, the non-vessel operating common carrier (NVOCC) is an international ocean carrier that does not operate their own vessels but signs a contract with one or more ocean carriers. From this commitment, the NVOCC guarantees that they will ship with the ocean carrier a given number of containers per week. The NVOCC signs as a large shipper and as a result is able to secure wholesale ocean rates. The scope of services include taking the booking, issuing the B/L, publishing tariffs, and generally conducting itself as an ocean carrier, except that they do not provide any terminal services or own assets. In many cases an NVOCC will even clear the goods through customs. The NVOCC provides a competitive rate structure for FCL and LCL services.

In the case of LCL, the NVOCC will provide a consolidation service to load multiple shippers in the same container, prepare all documents as a forwarder, act as the customs broker, and then de-consolidate the shipment at the port of destination. The NVOCC will charge a cost per cubic meter for these services and will build in a markup for each of these services to secure a profit.

An NVOCC can be very cost effective for the small- to medium-size shippers. The flexibility of the NVOCC pricing could provide the shipper savings as the landed cost could be better optimized due to the economies of scale associated with using the larger-sized container and leveraging the NVOCC's purchasing power. It is also a very easy solution for new importers as it is a one-stop shopping experience, with easy to understand all-in pricing to import goods from China.

It should be noted that almost all consolidators also provide NVOCC services as they have the LCL freight on-hand and can manage this process for the shipper extremely efficiently. In many cases, the consolidator can also provide a bundled solution for the shipper as noted thus:

Origin trucking → NVOCC service → customs brokerage →
trans-load → domestic trucking → shipper destination → warehouse
    delivery

AIRFREIGHT

Although this chapter focuses primarily on ocean freight, if enhanced speed-to-market is required, moving product via airfreight from China is an option. To airfreight a product from China or Hong Kong to the west coast of the United States, the process will average between three and six days. The pricing of airfreight is mostly quoted in kilograms and subject to minimums (see Table 11.7).

Table 11.7 International Airline Cargo Tariff All Commodities: Hong Kong to US West Coast: Currency in USD$ Rates Per Kilogram

				Rate/Kg in USD					
Origin	Destination	Currency Used	Min	−45 Kg	+45 Kg	+100 Kg	+500 Kg	+1000 Kg	+2000 Kg
HKG	LAX	USD	60.37	$1.72	$1.72	$1.64	$1.64	$1.64	$1.64

It should be noted that rates are airport-to-airport and do not include trucking fees/pickup, delivery, forwarding fees, and customs clearance.

To convert pounds into kilos divide the weight of the shipment into 2.2046. Let's assume that an importer had an airfreight shipment of a quantity totaling 200 books that weighed 190 pounds. First, a conversion of pounds to kilos would be calculated (190 lbs/2.2046) and then rounded up to 86 kg. As this weight is greater than the minimum air shipment rate of 45 kg and less than 100 kg in the tariff rate structure, the minimum rate in the table would not apply. As such, to calculate the airfreight expense on this shipment we would use the table rate of US$1.72 per kg × 86 kg to equal a total cost of US$148. Since the US$148 calculated airfreight charge is higher than the minimum charge of US$60.37, the minimum charge would not apply to the movement of the 190 pounds of books.

A second component to the calculation of airfreight is dimensional weight. Dimensional weight applies to air shipments of cargo that do not have as much density.

Using the example above, we will change one variable and the importer will no longer be shipping books but instead will use airfreight to transport 200 large dolls. Due to the large display boxes that carry these dolls, although the weight will remain at 190 pounds, the shipment dimensions would increase to 60″ × 60″ × 60″, so it is now a large volume shipment. The air carrier cannot provide this level of space on the airplane and charge a total cost of US$148 (as in the first example shipping books weighing 190 pounds). The shipper must now pay a minimum freight charge based on the cubic size of the shipment.

The shipper must now calculate the dimensional weight of this air shipment of dolls. This is accomplished by multiplying the height by the length by the width to determine the volume size of the shipment.

(length × height × width)

(60″ × 60″ × 60″ = 216,000 cubic inches)

Divide the 216,000 cubic inches by 166 to convert the cubic inches into a factor that will define the minimum dimensional weight (dim weight) the importer would be charged for this shipment.

(cubic inches/166)

(216,000/166 = 1,301 pounds)

Finally, divide the 1,301 pounds by 2.2046 to convert to 590 kg then multiply by the airfreight rate based on Table 11.7 or US$1.64 per kg (as displayed in the tariff as greater than 1,000 kg).

(total pounds/kilo conversion factor) × (airfreight rate)

The cost of the air shipment of dolls is US$968.

It is clear that shipping high-volume, light-weight dolls under dimensional weight is more costly using air transportation than shipping denser items like books of equal weight (US$968 versus US$148).

Airfreight represents one of the faster but most expensive shipping options for an importer. Products like toys, as shown in this example, clearly illustrate the negative financial impact that transportation options have on product profitability. Based on shipping 200 units, to airfreight the dolls will cost US$4.84 per unit whereas the cost per book is US$0.74 per unit. Based on the different combinations of cube and weight as well as the conversion factor used, the calculation for the break-even for dimensional weight application will vary by product.

MEASURING SUCCESS

To be successful in managing China operations, key performance indicators (KPIs) and service-level agreements (SLAs) must be established to track progress, ability to meet committed goals and standards, as well as to identify underperforming areas of the supply chain. The KPIs are often performance-, financial-, speed- and service-based. Although there are many KPIs that are meaningful to measuring importing success, at a high level there are four major KPI categories.

1. Vendor performance:
   a. Raw material procurement
   b. Human rights compliance
   c. Production tracking
   d. Production quality assurance

e. Production defect rate and safety testing compliance

f. On-time delivery performance (exportability)

g. C-TPAT compliance (see Security section)

2. Financial performance:

a. Vendor cost-plus pricing (raw materials, production labor, fixed expense, markup)

b. Carrier selection and compliance to negotiated commitments*

c. Container size and utilization

d. Duty rate

e. Landed cost

3. Speed-to-market tracking information:

a. Product receipt to consolidation into the container

b. Consolidation to onboard the vessel

c. Vessel transit time on the ocean

d. Customs clearance

e. Vessel arrival to rail departure

f. Rail departure to ramp arrival

g. Ramp arrival to truck pickup

h. Truck pickup to warehouse receipt

4. Quality and safety testing:

a. Actual defect rate

b. Certificate of compliance (COC) safety acceptance

*It should be noted that although there are different-sized ocean containers, for reporting purposes, all containers destined to the United States are reported as a 40-foot standard container, which is also called a 40-foot equivalent unit (FEU). In Europe, it is reported as a 20-foot equivalent unit (TEU). By reporting in this manner, the shippers' volume is clearly understood by the ocean carrier and the shipper. The FEU and TEU reporting method is used by the ocean carriers during contract negotiations to define a commitment of volume for a pre-defined rate level.

Presented below are examples of measurements that can be tracked during the import process from China.

1. Vendor performance:

a. Inventory accuracy—the master carton label and product do not reconcile.

b. Volume accuracy—the volume submitted by the supplier on the PO does not reconcile to the actual receipt. This can lead to incremental ocean freight per unit if the volume is actually larger than planned in the purchase order.

c. Order accuracy—the supplier's actual shipment is over or short from the commitment made on the PO.

d. On-time performance—was the shipment received and exportable within the receipt window by the consolidator.

e. Product damage—percentage of product received damaged and not in sellable condition (wet, crushed).

2. Consolidator:

a. Volume by origin—CFS and CY.

b. Equipment selection—when using a consolidator, the container size should be maximized whenever possible. Container size is measured in feet and can be 20-foot, 40-foot, 40-foot high volume and 45-foot high volume. Assuming the consignee has enough freight, the larger the container size, the higher the level of container utilization the consignee will achieve.

c. Container utilization—CFS and CY and by container size (FEU and TEU).

d. Container manifest and ASN accuracy to the actual receipt at the destination location. Discrepancies are reported on an over, short and damaged report (OS &D) at the destination location.

e. Number of days to loading container—speed of processing at the CFS origin location.

f. Number of days to sailing—speed of the carrier's vessel cut-off to ship departure.

g. Operations logs—rejected bookings by carrier, rolled containers off booked vessel, unavailable container equipment.

h. Eight-week volume forecast—a forecast of equipment needs as provided to the ocean carriers to ensure the premium equipment is available when needed.

3. Carrier:

a. Carrier commitment vs. performance reporting—carrier space, cut-off times and equipment availability based on the negotiated agreement.

b. Transit time—published ocean transit versus actual performance.

c. EDI accuracy—rejected EDI transmissions for product tracking.

d. Rejected bookings.

The consolidator is the critical link between all supply chain stakeholders from the vendor to the destination delivery point. The KPIs and SLAs provided by the consolidator serve as a forum for evaluating performance, compliance, efficiency, service levels, speed-to-market, and benchmarking. The KPIs are also the basis for continuous improvement.

VENDOR MANAGEMENT IN THE CONSOLIDATION MODEL

Merchandise vendors and factories play a prominent role in the supply chain process. As detailed in the purchase order section of this chapter, if the lead time from Yantian, China, to New York is 91 days via ocean transit, the vendor's production time is responsible for 60 days or two-thirds of that cycle time. As vendors are responsible for booking and product delivery as well as many export/import documents, taking a proactive approach to vendor education is a critical step to ensuring success when importing from China. The local consolidator in China can add value in this process by taking a leadership role in the education process as language and distance is not a factor. The result of this effort will be a clear understanding of requirements and processes, as well as the vendor's roles and deliverables.

The key to a successful relationship with any merchandise vendor or supply chain service provider is transparency to the operations. Using the shipper's PO for information, the consolidator will be in a position to monitor each vendor's performance. Key VAS that can be provided by the consolidator/forwarder to monitor vendor compliance levels through an established web portal include:

- Timely raw material procurement and delivery
- Factory production tracking
- Vendor booking performance—timely and accurate
- Physical delivery—level of completeness, damages, and vendor-agreed VAS (UCC128 barcodes, radio-frequency identification (RFID), carton markings)
- Carton volume/weight verification

- Product quality check
- Document audit results—completeness and accuracy

By having factories in China integrated into the consolidator's systems, vendors can be easily managed even when they are located hundreds of miles away from the port or consolidation point. Through the use of common systems, a vendor with multiple factories can receive compliance reporting in total or by origin location. This integration is critical to ensure consistency in quality of the operations as well as provide a database on the strength of operations across China. This information can be used as a basis for determining where to source product as well as the vendor's ability to achieve the goals of the shipper/customer.

RECORD RETENTION COMPLIANCE

Documentation is critical for importing product from China. Just as critical, however, the importer-of-record has a legal obligation to maintain complete and accurate records relating to all international trade transactions. These legal requirements have assumed increasing importance since September 11, 2001, because of the emphasis on homeland security and related regulatory requirements. In addition, as the volume of imports has continued to increase over the last decade, the automation of the documentation process has become an operating necessity for customs. The burden of volume has led to numerous customs initiatives to assist in expeditiously clearing imported products for shipment to final destination while maintaining control as containers pass through the ports.

Under the U.S. Customs Modernization Act, customs agreed to allow electronic filing of entries. Although this Act was established to facilitate trade, the importer's legal responsibilities relating to the accuracy and reconciliation of documentation, fraudulent information, proper valuation, record retention and descriptions, as well as proper classifications increased substantially. Under the Customs Modernization Act, the responsibility as an importer and related penalties for non-compliance became substantially more significant directly to the importer.

U.S. Customs has issued a *Record Keeping Compliance Handbook* that details the importer's responsibilities and proper record keeping methods, as well as the requirement for importers to designate a point of contact for administration and issue resolution. The importer must use "reasonable care" in determining value, classification, and admissibility.

DOCUMENTATION[18]

Regardless of the items being exported from China, documentation is a requirement of international trade. Documentation will be required by U.S. Customs as well as other federal, state, and local governmental agencies. In most cases, the factory, freight forwarder, and consolidator will prepare and scan the necessary documentation. Presented below are several critical documents necessary to import product from China.

1. The **commercial invoice** (Figure 11.11) is a record of the transaction between the seller and the buyer as a requirement of passing the title of the goods manufactured. The commercial invoice is used as the reconciling document for the value of the product delivered in compliance with the purchase order and letter of credit. There are two special requirements of the commercial invoice. First, it must state the terms of sale (i.e. EXW, FAS). Second, the country point of origin (where the product was produced) must be clearly displayed.

2. The **packing slip** (Figure 11.12) has a similar format to that of the commercial invoice, however, it does not display the price of the goods. The purpose of this document is to detail the commodities being shipped and how the goods were packed by the factory. For example, an importer's packing slip could state 20 cartons of 12 DVD players per carton, numbered 001 through 012.

3. The **bill of lading** (B/L) (Figure 11.13) is a contract to procure transportation services between the shipper and the carrier. The B/L also provides proof of delivery that the container has been accepted by the carrier. There are three types of B/Ls: ocean, truck, and airway bill.

   According to Network F.O.B., "The B/L is considered to be a clean bill of lading for freight that is issued by the carrier with an indication that the goods were received in good order and condition without damage or other irregularities. If no notation or exception is made, the B/L is assumed to be clean."[19]

Commercial Invoice

Exporter

Date:

PO Number:

Order Number:

Terms:

Ultimate Consignee

Commercial Invoice Number:

Pro Forma Invoice Number:

Consignee Phone Number:

Customer Account Number:

Exporting Carrier:

Loading Pier/Terminal:

Intermediate Consignee

Point of Origin (FTZ No.):

Ultimate Destination:

Product Code	Qty.	Product Description	Harmonized Code:	Price	Sub-Total

Ex Works Value:

Inland Freight Fees:

Handling Fees:

Consular Fees:

Insurance Fees:

Other Charges:

USD Total:

Title:

Authorized Signature:

Figure 11.11   Commercial Invoice

4. The **certificate of origin** is a document required by the U.S. government that certifies the origin of the manufactured product. U.S.
   Customs uses the certificate of origin to determine the applicable
   duty rate and determine the legality of the imported project based on
   anti-dumping tax or quota restrictions.

   Take, for example, a 100-percent cotton jacket manufactured in China
   and then shipped to the United States where a value added service is performed by placing a label inside the jacket. The jackets are then exported
   to Canada for sale. These jackets would have a China certificate of origin.

PACKING LIST

SHIPPER:	CONSIGNEE:	
	NOTIFY:	
VESSEL:	P.O. NO. REMARKS:	
DATE:	INVOICE NO.	

PKG NO. & TYPE	CONTENTS	NET WT. EACH	GROSS WT. EACH	TOTAL NET WEIGHT	TOTAL GROSS	DIMENSIONS Height × Width × Length	TOTAL CUBIC FEET

TOTAL GROSS WEIGHT: _____   NET WT: _____ CUBE: _____ NO. PCS: ____

Figure 11.12   Packing Slip

If that cotton fabric was manufactured in China and then shipped to the United States to be manufactured into a jacket and then exported to Canada, the certificate of origin would be a U.S. certificate of origin.

5. The **container manifest** is a document that displays the contents in the ocean container.

6. The **dock receipt** is a document signed by the container terminal or transfer station confirming receipt of the full container load or less-than-container-load product under the consignment of the carrier. If the goods are spread over multiple containers, the dock administrator will not acknowledge the receipt until the packing list of each of the containers is confirmed. The dock receipt is proof of delivery to ensure the issuance of the bill of lading from the shipping company.

7. **Forwarder's cargo receipt**—is a transport document that is issued by the consolidator or freight forwarder to acknowledge the full receipt of goods. This document is used by the issuing bank as a critical document to execute the payment of the LC.

SECURITY

Port security has become of increasingly significant importance to the United States government. Since September 2001, new importer requirements and legislation have been introduced to ensure national security. Presented is a list of several significant security initiatives.

Ocean Bill of Lading

Exporter (Name and address including ZIP code)	Document Number	Booking Number
	Export References	
Consigned To	Forwarding Agent (Name and address)	
Notify Party	Point (State) of Origin of FTZ Number	
	Domestic Routing/Export Instructions	

Pre-Carriage By	Place of Receipt By Pre-Carrier	
Exporting Carrier	Port Loading Export	
Foreign Port of Unloading	Place of Delivery By On-Carrier	Type of Move

Number of Packages	Description of Commodities in Schedule B Detail	Gross Weight (Kilos)	Measurment

There are: [   ] pages, including attachments to this Ocean Bill of Lading

FREIGHT RATES, CHARGES, WEIGHTS AND/OR MEASURMENTS

DATED AT _____

BY _____
Agent for the Carrier

Mo	Day	Year
	B/L No.	

I certify that the above information is true and correct to the best of my knowledge

Figure 11.13   Ocean Bill of Lading

Customs-Trade Partnership Against Terrorism (C-TPAT)

C-TPAT is a voluntary government-business program to build a cooperative relationship to improve the security of the overall international supply chain and most importantly U.S. borders. C-TPAT recognizes that U.S. Customs and

Border Protection (CBP) can provide enhanced cargo security through a close cooperative relationship with key members of the supply chain such as importers, carriers, consolidators, licensed customs brokers, and manufacturers. Through this initiative, CBP is working with business, on a voluntary basis, to ensure the integrity of their practices and physical operations comply with recommended security guidelines.

C-TPAT offers business an opportunity to play an active role in the war against terrorism. By participating in this first worldwide supply chain security initiative, companies audit both themselves and key suppliers to ensure a secure supply chain. Beyond the security benefits, if an importer successfully meets the requirements of C-TPAT, CBP will offer other benefits including:

- A reduced number of CBP inspections as containers enter the United States
- Priority processing when CBP inspections are required
- Assignment of a C-TPAT supply chain security specialist (SCSS) who will assist the business to validate and enhance security
- Potential eligibility for CBP importer self-assessment program (ISA) that emphasizes self-policing

ISO Standards

ISO28000 requires the use of a security management system for security assurance across the supply chain. According to U.S. Customs, ISO 28000 was established in 2007 and was put in place to:

1. Establish, implement, and maintain a security management system
2. Assure conformance with stated security management policies
3. Demonstrate such conformance to others
4. Seek certification/registration of a security management system by an accredited third party body or
5. Make a self-determination and self-declaration of conformance with ISO 28000:2007

There are legislative and regulatory codes that address some of the requirements in ISO 28000:2007.[20]

Seal Security

Most ocean shippers use number-coded bolt seals to secure freight inside an ocean container. With the emphasis placed on port security, companies are beginning to test the value of RFID seals.

The RFID seal is numbered as a control; however, it is also programmed to track the container as it passes selected points throughout the supply chain. In addition, the RFID seal can provide more timely feedback to the shipper if the seal is tampered with in any way.

The U.S. Department of Homeland Security has discussed the potential of using these seals as a mandate for shippers. If these seals were consistently used, it would provide a platform for the use of e-seals to assist in the automation of the seal security process in U.S. ports.

10 + 2 Program

U.S. CBP has created two sets of data requirements for importers and ocean carriers to follow regarding the management of information 24 hours before the vessel is loaded at the port of origin. The new rule was so-named because carriers will now have two additional data sets on top of current requirements under the 24-hour rule of 2003. Importers will be required to transmit and file 10 data sets in addition to the data already provided by their customs broker. The 10 + 2 transmission is known as the importer security filing (ISF). It is the importer's responsibility to obtain the required ISF information and ensure that customs has successfully received the transmission 24 hours before the vessel is loaded at the port of origin.

The 10 data elements are:

1. Manufacturer's name and address
2. Seller's name and address
3. Container stuffing location
4. Consolidator name and address
5. Buyer name and address
6. Ship-to-party name and address
7. Importer of record number
8. Consignee number
9. Six-digit commodity HTS classification number
10. Country of origin

CUSTOMS CLEARANCE

To ship goods from China into any destination country, they must be cleared by customs. In all cases a licensed customs broker must be engaged to clear the product. The license is issued by the Treasury Department. According to the U.S. Customs website, "There are approximately 11,000 licensed customs brokers in the United States Customs brokers are private individuals, partnerships, associations, or corporations licensed, regulated, and empowered by U.S. CBP to assist importers and exporters in meeting Federal requirements governing imports and exports. Brokers submit necessary information and related payments to the CBP on behalf of their clients and charge a fee for this service.

Brokers must have expertise in the entry procedures, admissibility requirements, classification, valuation, and the rates of duty, applicable taxes and fees for imported merchandise."[21]

Once cleared, the goods may enter the United States. It is common for goods to clear prior to the arrival of the vessel if the items being imported are low risk and all documents are submitted in a timely and accurate fashion. In addition, if successfully accepted into the security programs discussed earlier in this chapter including C-TPAT, ISO28000, and the 10+2 program, pre-clearance of goods through customs can become a common practice.

FUTURE TRENDS IN IMPORTING AND
THE CONSOLIDATION MODEL

For the future, there is much innovation ahead that will impact importing from China as well as the consolidation model. Examples include:

1. In China, different regions or zones often have their own customs clearance points. As trucks travel from zone to zone in China, the ability to clear product into the next zone can be inconsistent in process. Many consolidators are working to minimize the trucking complexity in China. As importers change purchase terms and take on the responsibility for the movement of freight earlier in the supply chain, by conducting multi-stop pickups, greater efficiency will be realized as well as a reduction in supply variability. This step will also allow CFS facilities to operate in a more efficient manner with stronger control on inbound flow into the facility.

2. Systemic product visibility is currently not on a real-time basis. Most visibility systems, as identified earlier in this chapter, are achieved through EDI transmissions and internet updates. As RFIDs are placed on ocean containers either using RFID tags or through the use of global positioning tracking systems, updates will move closer to real time for enhanced automated exception management. As consolidators manage the CY and CFS container loading and sealing processes, they will become a driver for embracing newer technology. Real-time visibility will improve reporting speed and assist to minimize supply variability.

3. Today most online commerce is done in the destination country. Using warehousing in China and delaying retailer ownership, consolidators can act as an intermediary between the manufacturer and retailer. Goods will be manufactured closer to the actual sale and thus the transfer of ownership from the factory to the retailer can occur after the sale. This could serve as both a centralization and postponement strategy to mitigate the impact of demand uncertainty and inventory-holding costs.

4. As importing from China is now beginning to mature and services have become very reliable, more piece-type work such as labeling, ticketing, and kitting will be performed in China by the consolidator and closer to the need of the customer.

Author's note: I would like to offer my appreciation for the support of Professor John E. Stevens and Penn State University. During our work together on this project, Professor Stevens was instrumental in the writing of this chapter by providing untiring support through proofing the material and challenging the results. His mentoring and time invested helped turn my ideas into this chapter.

NOTES

1   Country Comparison—GDP (Purchasing Power Parity) (January 1, 2009): http://www.indexmundi.com/g/r.aspx?t=10&v=65.

2   "Economy of the People's Republic of China"—Wikipedia Encyclopedia, http://en.wikipedia.org/wiki/Economy_of_the_People%27s_Republic_of_China.

3   Sunil Chopra, S. and Peter Meindl, *Supply Chain Management Strategy, Planning and Operations*, 3rd ed. (New Jersey: Prentice Hall, 2006), 5, 395.

4   Ibid., 169.

5   Incoterms 2000, ICC Official Rules for Interpretation of the Trade Terms, International Chamber of Commerce (September 1999).

6   "Terms of Sale—Glossary of Freight Terms," Network F.O.B., www.networkfob.com/glossary_of_freight_terms.htm.

7   *Supply Chain Management Strategy*, 7.

8   Glossary of Freight Terms—Network F.O.B.

9   *Supply Chain Management Strategy*, 8.

10   The Free Dictionary; http://www.thefreedictionary.com/consolidator.

11   *Supply Chain Management Strategy*, 386.

12   Glossary of Freight Terms—Network F.O.B.

13   *Supply Chain Management Strategy*, 391.

14   "Container size and specifications," Beyond Freight Inc. (2003): http://www3.sympatico.ca/mnrele/oltools/ocdimensions.htm.

15   DHL Consolidation Operations provided all examples used for consolidation optimization. Graphs prepared by Michael Wiggins of DHL, April 2009; software used—TOPS Maxload; http://www.topseng.com/MaxLoadFeatures.html.

16   Michael Wiggins, Interview on DC By-Pass Study, DHL – ISC (April 22, 2009).

17   American President Lines Logistics (APLL), Ocean Guaranteed Continental Service (2008): www.apll.com.

18   All document examples obtained from http://resources.alibaba.com/article/30/Shipping_documentation.htm.

19   Glossary of Freight Terms—Network F.O.B.

20   ISO28000 Abstract, International Organization for Standardization (2007): http://www.iso.org/iso/catalogue_detail?csnumber=44641.

21   US Customs Border and Patrol, "Becoming a Customs Broker," http://www.cbp.gov/xp/cgov/trade/trade_programs/broker/brokers.xml.

CHAPTER TWELVE

THE ROLE OF CHINA CUSTOMS

PETER LEVESQUE

Many of the customer questions that arise when discussing supply chain management processes in China have to do with the various export customs procedures and warehouse classifications that exist in the mainland. This topic can be confusing, since China's customs regulations are not uniformly administered across the country and many issues must be dealt with in an adhoc manner depending upon which province has jurisdiction. To reduce costs and avoid delays it is critical for supply chain managers to understand the function of customs and the application of China's value added tax (VAT). VAT, and more specifically VAT refunds, drive the behavior of most export manufacturing vendors in China. It is worth having a more in-depth look at this subject in order to better understand the concerns of vendors in China when it comes to implementing new supply chain programs.[1]

DEMYSTIFYING CHINA'S VALUE ADDED TAX (VAT)

China began charging VAT back in 1984. The tax system was overhauled in 1993 when the State Council of China enacted The Provisional Regulation of the People's Republic of China on Value Added Tax, which is still in use today. VAT is administered by the State Administration of Taxation. Seventy-five percent of VAT tax revenues go to the central government and local governments receive the remaining 25 percent. A significant portion of the central government's annual revenues (about 33 percent of total tax revenues in 2007) come from VAT.[2] According to the government, "all enterprises and individuals engaged in the sale of goods, provision of processing, repairs, replacement services and import of goods within China shall pay VAT."[3]

The Chinese Government imposes a range of VAT usually around 17 percent. VAT is charged on each input that goes into the manufacturing of an item at each stage of the product's flow, from raw material to trading company, to finished export.[4] The tax is generally applied to the gross margin of a product as it is bought and sold across the supply chain. On certain products that are manufactured and exported out of China, the government allows for a refund on a percentage of the VAT paid. The difference between the input VAT tax and the export refund tax is the portion kept by the government. As an example, let's say a Chinese toy manufacturer pays 17 percent VAT on the inputs needed to manufacture a specific toy and the VAT refund allowed by the government for that toy is 10 percent. The manufacturer would apply for a rebate of 10 percent and the government would keep 7 percent.

The actual VAT refund varies by product classification as outlined by the Harmonized Commodity Description and Coding System (HS codes). Each product and component part has a Harmonized System number (HS number) and this allows for a standardized classification of goods in international trade. Depending on how the product or component part is classified, it will have a corresponding HS number assigned to it and this helps determine the proper VAT refund. The Chinese government uses the VAT mechanism to provide incentives for producers to manufacture certain kinds of higher-value goods in the economy. A 17 percent VAT refund on microwave ovens, for example, might provide enough incentive for a factory to move away from manufacturing cell phones in favor of making microwave ovens in order to receive the higher VAT refund.

Obviously the VAT process in China can be difficult to quantify. Some Chinese exporters may become victims of a sudden change in government tax policy that creates a VAT refund deficit. These exporters will then seek to recoup this loss in their cost of goods sold. Other exporters may leverage local relationships with the tax bureau to influence their product classification, and thereby achieve a higher VAT refund. Most overseas buyers would not be privy to such arrangements which can inflate the true margin a vendor is actually achieving.[5]

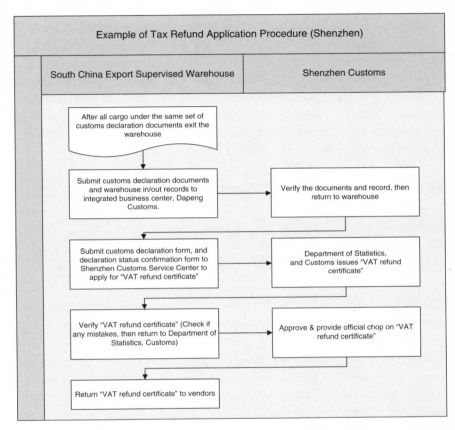

Source: Created by Margaret Li with data from China Customs and CEVA Logistics

Figure 12.1 Typical Value Added Tax Refund Process

Most cross-dock consolidation or other export-related supply chain programs in China depend upon the successful facilitation of the VAT process for suppliers. The inability to support a rapid VAT process for suppliers can derail an otherwise attractive supply chain initiative for both the 3PL and the end customer.

CHINESE EXPORT WAREHOUSE LICENSING

There are two primary international supply chain flows that involve China Customs. The first is finished product exported from China to other countries, and the second is product or raw material imported from other countries into

China. As discussed in chapter one, the special zones established by Deng in China were originally developed primarily for the Chinese export business. As China migrates from a manufacturing economy to a consumer economy, the government has had to adapt these zones to meet the needs of export and import operations. Over the years, five main designations for customs import and export logistics operations have been established across China with varying levels of functionality. We will describe several levels of customs designations available in China today from the least functional to the most functional.

Export Customs Supervised Warehouse

The Export Customs Supervised Warehouse (ECSW) designation allows 3PLs to store cargo that has already been cleared for export by customs, as well as perform bonded distribution and basic value added services. There are two types of ECSW: The first is an export-oriented facility whose function is to temporarily warehouse goods already cleared for export by customs. The second type functions as a domestic transfer facility that can provide storage for export cargo that will first be transferred to another customs zone. In general, the ECSW designation is authorized to offer storage for export shipments under general trade, processing trade, and transferred shipments already cleared by customs from other specially designated zones. A more comprehensive list of warehouse functionality by category can be found in Figure 12.2.

Non-Bonded Facilities in China

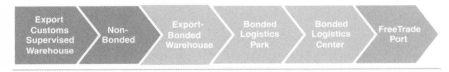

Non-bonded warehouse operations are usually the least expensive option in China; however, they have no on-site customs functionality and they are

Warehouse Types and Functionality in China

	Export Supervisory Warehouse (ESW)	Bonded Warehouse (BW-Import)	Bonded Logistics Park	Free Trade Zone (FTZ)	Free Trade Port (FTP)
Processing of goods (change HS code and assembling)	No	No	No	Yes	Yes
Goods flow (China domestic distribution)	Inbound from China, from overseas is also possible Outbound - 100% overseas - export only	Inbound from overseas only	Inbound & outbound no restriction	Inbound & outbound no restriction	Inbound & outbound no restriction
Repackaging, kitting (HS code unchanged)	Yes	Yes	Yes	Yes	Yes
Tax refund	Upon entry of goods	NA	Upon entry of goods & receipt of payment from consignee	Upon goods being completely loaded onboard vessel	Upon entry of goods
Export consolidation for multiple consignors	No	No	Yes	Yes	Yes
Time limit for storage	6 months	12 months	No limit	12 months	No limit
Imports declaration from overseas into facility—lead time	NA	8 days from arrival at port	5 days from arrival at port	3-4 days from arrival at port	3-4 days from arrival at port
Import into China from facility—lead time	NA	2 weeks	3 days	3 days	3 days
Multi-countries consolidation (MCC)	Restriction on consolidation-mix	Restriction on consolidation-mix	Restriction on consolidation-mix	Restriction on consolidation-mix	Less restriction (more than 90% from overseas)

Source: Shirley Pang, Modern Terminals Limited

Figure 12.2   Chinese Warehousing Capability by Category

typically used for domestic distribution services (i.e. non-export-related business). Non-bonded facilities may be used for export shipping; however, vendors delivering to the facility cannot clear export customs at the time of delivery to the facility and therefore must wait to file for their VAT refund until the cargo has been physically exported.

Non-bonded facilities can be useful for logistics programs that include the consolidation of multiple products into store-ready display units. This type of logistics value-added process is complicated from a regulatory perspective, because multiple suppliers deliver individual product categories into the facility, which are eventually mixed with other suppliers' product categories and then exported in a combined category store display unit.

If the normal customs export procedure were applied to this type of program it would be administratively complex, because what the supplier originally declares for customs export may change once it is combined with other products. One solution for this type of operation is inserting an import/export buying agent or trading company into the non-bonded warehouse process. The trading company actually purchases the goods from suppliers, suppliers then deliver to a common warehouse facility and the trading company sells the consolidated products to the end customer in a back-to-back transaction. This reduces the work needed for export declarations by allowing for one set of consolidated export paperwork rather than processing what could be thousands of individual export document sets.

Once the consolidated store display units ship out of China, the trading company then collects the total VAT refund and distributes the money back to each supplier on a prorated basis. The non-bonded facility allows the LSP to inspect and return faulty products to the factory without customs intervention. This is less complex than using a bonded logistics park for example, where once a product enters the bonded zone, it is considered to be exported. Any return of faulty products after entering the export-bonded zone would need to go through the importation process, including tax and documentation in order to be returned to the factory for repair. This can be costly and time consuming. The non-bonded option using an import/export trading company as an intermediary offers a viable solution.

Export-Bonded Facilities

The next level of customs functionality is the export-bonded designation. This is a common type of license used in warehouse facilities operated by most international logistics companies in China. The export-bonded facility is, as its name implies, designed specifically to facilitate export trade out of the mainland. There is typically a China Customs office at the warehouse location that is capable of making export clearances on behalf of suppliers who deliver into the bonded facility. Suppliers can choose to clear customs at their local customs office and then truck the cargo "in bond" to the export-bonded warehouse, where a customs transfer is performed as shown in Figure 12.3. Or, a supplier may choose to clear export customs directly at the export-bonded facility itself. The question of where to clear customs is influenced by the supplier's blue book procedure. Suppliers must present customs officers with an official factory record of imported raw material used in the manufacturing process, against the outbound finished product to be exported. More simply put, the materials into the manufacturing process must reconcile with the finished goods being exported in order to qualify for the VAT refund. The factory blue book plays a vital role in the supplier's ability to complete the export process.

Losing a blue book can actually force a factory to shut down. For this reason many factories may choose to clear customs locally (the blue book stays local) and then transfer customs at the LSP's export-bonded facility afterward. The export-bonded operation is the most common type of facility for international retail freight consolidation programs as described by Michael Jacobs in chapter eleven. This type of warehouse facility allows suppliers to deliver cargo and immediately apply for the VAT refund because the cargo is considered to be out of China. Value added services can be performed inside these types of bonded facilities. The drawback to the export-bonded process is that products that fail to pass a quality inspection,

Export-Bonded Process Flow

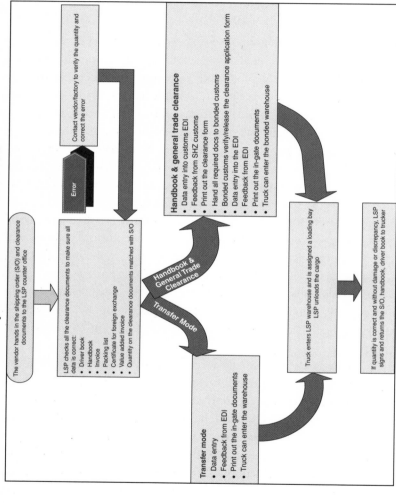

The vendor hands in the shipping order (S/O) and clearance documents to the LSP counter office

LSP checks all the clearance documents to make sure all data is correct:
- Driver book
- Handbook
- Invoice
- Packing list
- Certificate for foreign exchange
- Value added invoice
- Quantity on the clearance documents matched with S/O

Error

Contact vendor/factory to verify the quantity and correct the error

Handbook & general trade clearance
- Data entry into customs EDI
- Feedback from SHZ customs
- Print out the clearance form
- Hand all required docs to bonded customs
- Bonded customs verify/release the clearance application form
- Data entry into the EDI
- Feedback from EDI
- Print out the in-gate documents
- Truck can enter the bonded warehouse

Handbook & General Trade Clearance

Transfer Mode

Transfer mode
- Data entry
- Feedback from EDI
- Print out the in-gate documents
- Truck can enter the warehouse

Truck enters LSP warehouse and is assigned a loading bay LSP unloads the cargo

If quantity is correct and without damage or discrepancy, LSP signs and returns the S/O, handbook, driver book to trucker

Source: May Ma, Ceva Logistics

Figure 12.3 Export-Bonded Process

for example, must go through the importation and tax process to get these products back to the factory for repair. Export-bonded facilities have more functionality than non-bonded facilities and they will typically have a higher operating cost than non-bonded facilities.

Bonded Logistics Park (BLP) and Bonded Logistics Center (BLC)

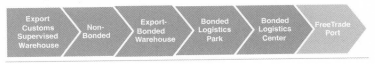

A bonded logistics park (BLP) is a customs-supervised area that is approved by the State Council in order to develop modern international logistics capability. BLPs seek to link bonded warehousing and manufacturing with port operations in a common location. Waigaoqiao Bonded Logistics Park (WBLP) was the first to open up in Shanghai and has proven to be very successful. Cargo entering a BLP is considered exported from China and the VAT refund process can begin upon delivery into the BLP with proof that the buyer has actually paid for the goods. BLPs offer multi-level customs functionality including import distribution capability, bonded storage, simple assembly, value added services, quality controls and repair, as well as international transshipment. They will typically be more expensive than non-bonded and export-bonded facility operations.

A "bonded logistics center" designation, such as the recently opened Taicang Bonded Logistics Center north of Shanghai, has all the functionality of a bonded logistics park with the additional capability of allowing both bonded and non-bonded operations to occur in the same area. An example of a China bonded logistics center and a description of typical BLP process flows are shown in Figures 12.4, 12.5 and 12.6.

Free Trade Port

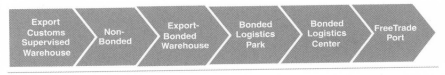

A free trade port (FTP) is a special area that is approved by the State Council to adapt to the more complex requirements of modern logistics programs.

Source: Modern Terminals Limited

Figure 12.4   Taicang's Bonded Logistics Center

An FTP is the latest and most comprehensive China Customs designation whose primary function is to integrate ocean port processing, free trade zone capability, export processing, and bonded logistics park functionality. Import and export cargo can be declared for customs in the same location and cargo being traded within the bonded port area is exempt from VAT. Major functions of an FTP include international transshipment, international distribution, logistics hub capability, and export processing trade. There are bonded port locations in Shanghai's new port of Yangshan as well as Xiamen, Yangpu, Yianjin, Meishan, Qingdao, Chingqing, Dalian, and most recently at Qianhai in Shenzhen.

The China customs process can be difficult to understand given the fact that rules are not uniformly applied across the country. There are as many nuances to the customs process as there are customs offices in China. The trend over the last several years has been toward more liberal customs reform in China, which is intended to increase business flows into and out of the country.

Outbound Flow From a China Supplier Through a Bonded Logistics Park (CHINA BLP EXPORT)

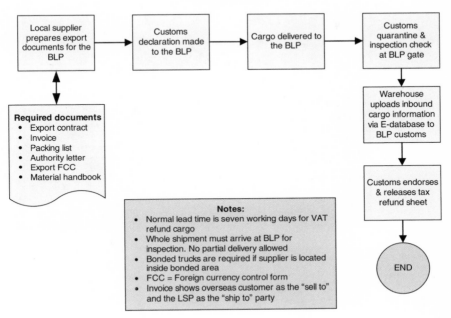

Source: May Ma, Ceva Logistics

Figure 12.5   Inbound Flow to a BLP

The development of BLPs and FTPs is geared toward more integrated full-service customs capability. The continued liberalization of China Customs will mean more opportunity for retailers and their LSPs to perform higher-level value added services at origin, and to construct more sophisticated supply chain models that can facilitate the distribution of products in and out of China.

Understanding a bit more about the nuances of China Customs is critical to making more informed decisons when choosing a 3PL service provider. As supply chain programs become more complex, knowing what type of facility and licensing are required for specific programs will save time and money. Because Customs regulations are not uniformly applied across the mainland there will always be a level of ambiguity to the process, and mistakes will inevitably occur. Experienced LSPs that have taken the time to build strong

Inbound Cargo Flow Through a China Bonded Logistics Park into China Market (CHINA BLP IMPORT)

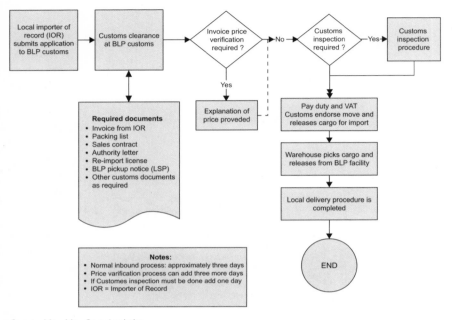

Source: May Ma, Ceva Logistics

Figure 12.6   Outbound Flow from a BLP

working relationships with local customs offices are usually able to resolve problems quickly in order to keep the goods flowing.[6]

NOTES

1   "Major Revision to the Chinese VAT Export Refund," PricewaterhouseCoopers (September 2006).

2   "Briefing of VAT Under China's Tax System," Ministry of Finance, Tax Policy Department (October 25, 2010): www.china.org.cn/english/LivinginChina/202770 .htm.

3   Richard Hoffman, "China's VAT System," *Beijing Review*, August 6, 2009, www .bjreview.com.cn/business/txt/2009-08/03/content_210354.htm.

4   Mike Bellamy, "China Tax, Understanding the China VAT Rebate," Smart China Sourcing (February 13, 2008): www.Smartchinasourcing.com/index2.php?option= com_content&task=view&id=43.

5   "China VAT Alert," PricewaterhouseCoopers (September 2003); Dr. Mark Sche-
     mitsch, "VAT Refund Filing—A Momentous Mistake," HK.org; Mike Bellamy,
     "China Tax: Understanding the China VAT Rebate".
6   Two major resources were used for customs information and customs procedures in
     China: May Ma of Ceva Logistics, and Shirley Pang of Modern Terminals Limited,
     both based in Hong Kong. They have a combined 40 years of experience with logistics
     and China Customs procedures, and their insight as to what actually happens on the
     ground in China with regard to Customs was invaluable.

CHAPTER THIRTEEN

INNOVATIVE RETAIL SUPPLY CHAIN PROCESS FLOWS

PETER LEVESQUE

There are three main export retail supply chain flows that are most common out of China today and each of these flows has varying degrees of complexity. The most common program is the outbound origin consolidation process, which Michael Jacobs describes in great detail in chapter eleven. This export consolidation procedure typically utilizes an international LSP to manage the export business process using the retailer's purchase order data as the driver of the physical export operation. A description of the most common outbound consolidation process flow is shown in Figure 13.1.

DIRECT-TO-STORE FLOW

After the basic export consolidation program, the next level of complexity for retail SCM in China is a distribution center (DC) bypass or a direct-to-store model, as shown in Figure 13.2. This supply chain process calls for the building of store-ready containers at the manufacturing point of origin that contain a proper mix of products as required by an individual retail store location. The retailer utilizes the ocean carrier's inland IPI pricing leverage to create a low-cost store-door delivery option.

ORIGIN DIRECT TO CUSTOMER

The most advanced retail supply chain process from China, as shown in Figure 13.3, is the direct-to-customer model, which requires that retailers tap

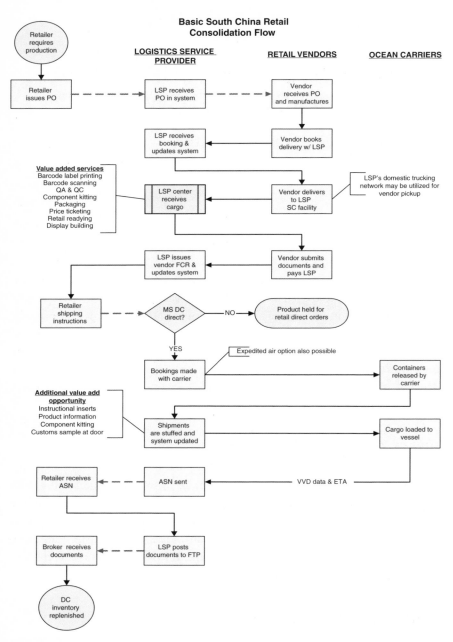

Basic South China Retail Consolidation Flow

Source: Peter Levesque

Figure 13.1 Basic Consolidation Flow From China

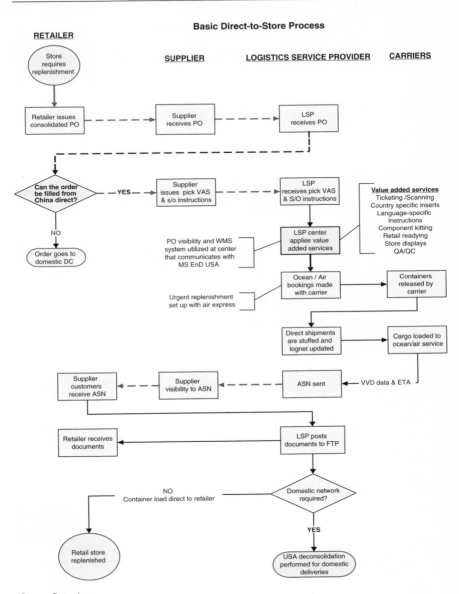

Source: Peter Levesque

Figure 13.2   Direct-to-Store Flow

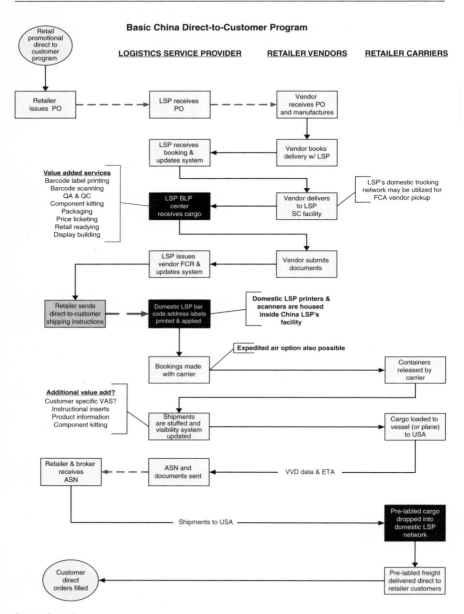

Source: Peter Levesque

Figure 13.3 Direct-to-Customer Process Flow

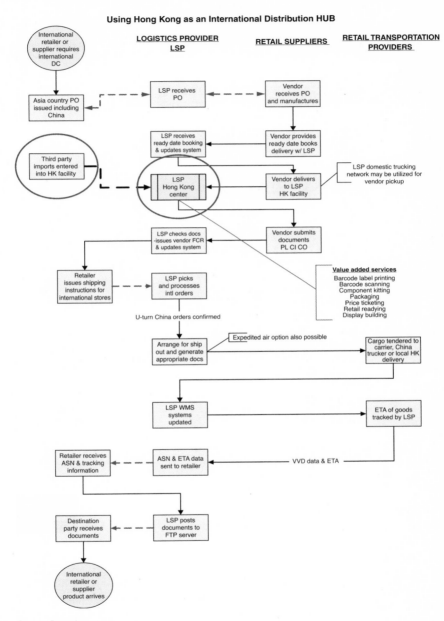

Source: Peter Levesque

Figure 13.4   Hong Kong as a Global Distribution Center

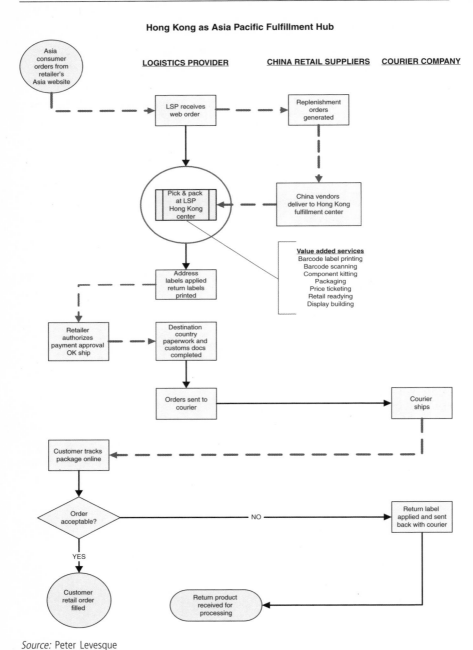

Hong Kong as Asia Pacific Fulfillment Hub

Source: Peter Levesque

Figure 13.5   Hong Kong as an International e-Fulfillment Center

into the LSP's domestic home delivery expertise on the last-mile delivery part of the process. Customer-specific address labels are printed and applied to products at origin in China, and these products are then consolidated and shipped via ocean container into the destination country's closest port of entry. Products are customs-cleared and drop-shipped into the LSP's domestic delivery network for last-mile home delivery.

HONG KONG AS A REGIONAL DISTRIBUTION CENTER

Hong Kong still maintains a competitive advantage over China in certain areas of supply chain execution. Hong Kong's free port status, for example, makes it a perfect global distribution hub for international retailers and retail suppliers, as shown in Figure 13.4. Products from China can be bundled with products from other countries and re-distributed without the bureaucracy and complexity of China's free trade zones or bonded logistics parks. Hong Kong's free port status offers customers fast and efficient international distribution capability.

HONG KONG AS A GLOBAL E-FULFILLMENT CENTER

International internet fulfillment is possible (including distribution into China) using Hong Kong's free port status to facilitate warehousing and package distribution as shown in Figure 13.5. Retailers can customize their brand websites with popular Asian SKUs that are made in China but stored at a Hong Kong fulfillment center. Orders are received and shipped (with country-specific power cords and proper language instruction inserts) via international courier services to the customer's door. Returns are facilitated via a return label which is inserted in the shipment packaging.

EPILOGUE

PETER LEVESQUE

As this book goes to print, the U.S. stock market has been able to claw its way back to more respectable levels, and priorities around job creation have taken center stage in American politics after the Republican mid-term election victories. Skepticism remains

Shipping Point:
"See the wind . . .
turn the rudder."
Chinese proverb

about the sustainability of a jobless recovery, given America's dependence on consumer spending. As the global economic situation continues to improve, China seems poised to lead the way out, having surpassed Germany as the leading global exporter. And in a reversal of the 2009 layoff situation, South China factories have even begun offering workers new incentive plans to lure alienated migrant employees back to the assembly line.

It is difficult to fully comprehend the scope and scale of the changes taking place in China today. The same can be said for understanding the dramatic shifts taking place in the consumer retail space. It is critical, however, for LSPs and their retail clients to grasp how these two seemingly unrelated themes intersect, and how the dynamics of their crossing paths will directly impact global supply chain strategy in the years ahead.

A discussion on China's future is easier to comprehend when prefaced by some insight on where China has been. Putting China into historical perspective helps explain the reasoning and motivation behind many of the initiatives underway in the country today. We know that China's great civilization state led the world leading up to the 18th century, only to be left behind by the rise of the West, which sent China and its cultural notion of and sending China into its self described "century of humiliation." These events had a profound impact on China in the years leading up to the 21st century. Today, we are experiencing China's historic re-emergence as a key player on the world stage, surpassing Japan as the world's second largest economy and firmly establishing itself as an emerging superpower.

As China climbs the ladder of sophistication from simple manufacturing into more complex areas such as research and development, technology, fashion design, and consumer retail, the business dynamics of the country continue to evolve. The Chinese are no longer satisfied with simply producing the designs of the West. They are now designing their own brand name products, and selling those products in their own retail stores. Some Chinese brands like Haier and Lenovo have already gone global, and this trend will only intensify. Opportunities abound for international brands and LSPs willing to invest the time necessary to build strong business and governmental relationships in order to capture the potential of China's emerging domestic markets.

Transportation in China can no longer be thought of in terms of bicycles and pushcarts. A more accurate portrayal of China today includes Maglev high-speed trains and new superhighways. The most recent government stimulus programs in China will increase spending on infrastructure projects to an astonishing level. China is now set to overtake India as having the second largest rail network in the world, and China began construction on 111 new expressways in just the first half of 2010.[1] China's dramatic development is directly related to the government's view that infrastructure will help facilitate national goals and give the country additional competitive advantage in the years ahead. The concept of social harmony also plays a key role in China's infrastructure development, specifically around bridging the gap between populations in the hinterland and China's urban centers. As product sourcing migrates to the northern and western rural areas of China, road and rail infrastructure projects will help ensure that manufacturers have distribution capability to both international and domestic markets. The growth opportunity for innovative LSPs will be in providing the transportation assets, logistics technology, and supply chain process expertise to facilitate the distribution of products to and from these developing rural locations.

Like China, the global consumer retail industry is also undergoing significant change as Western consumers with an overabundance of "stuff" begin to search for meaning. Customers, whose choices were once limited to what retailers had on the shelf, are today playing an active role in the design and functionality of the products they purchase. Mass-market retailers and LSPs must eventually adjust to the complexity involved with serving markets of one.

The convergence of social networking and consumer-enabled design puts the power of product development into the hands of end users, which significantly alters the supply chain dynamics for both retailers and their logistics service providers. Consumers want what they want, when they want it, and retailers who can't deliver that experience will feel the displeasure of the social network through lost customers. Retailers will need to differenti-ate less on product and more on process. Rather than strategies set in stone, retailers will need to work with their LSPs to be able to put almost any strategy into place to meet the changing requirements of the market. Traditional point-to-point transportation will be replaced by more dynamic, flexible, and modular supply chains capable of being rapidly deployed across geographies.

There are still plenty of opportunities to unlock supply chain innovation and create value if the mechanisms are in place within organizations to encourage new ideas. As we discussed, new ideas need not be complex to have game-changing results. Sometimes all it takes is a new way of thinking. The transportation industry, for example, could potentially benefit by moving away from the traditional "tit for tat" pricing strategy of old, and adopting a more mutually beneficial index-based pricing structure that promotes longer-term working relationships.

Oftentimes it can be difficult to generate new ideas without some sort of a structure for discussion. Creativity heuristics such as "identifying the inverse," "adding or combining features," "changing the scale," and "controlling the variance" are tools that can be employed to help look at things from a new perspective. While there are many ways to foster innovation, there are also many ways to kill it. We discussed the "Parmenides Fallacy," which is one such trap that might prevent an organization from making the right decision on innovation based on the erroneous notion that taking no action equates to the status quo. In reality, the competitive playing field is constantly changing, and taking no action may in fact have negative consequences when viewed in terms of a rapidly changing competitive landscape.

In chapter eleven, Michael Jacobs discussed the development of retail origin consolidation models in China along with the features and benefits of employing this type of program. Better container utilization through purchase order and vendor management can provide retailers an opportunity to lower overall transportation costs at the beginning of the supply chain. These consolidation models are more dynamic and modular today; capable of being deployed wherever they are needed. In addition, many consolidation programs today include value-added services such as kitting, labeling, packaging and store displays, all of which increase the potential for additional cost efficiencies.

In chapter seven, Chris Robeson discussed the benefits of postponement and delayed differentiation strategies. These supply chain models will continue to expand in scope and complexity over time, and will reduce supply chain cost by preventing the wrong product going to the wrong place at the wrong time. Delaying decisions on the final configuration of products to meet the tailored requirements of the end user takes cost out of the supply chain by reducing instances of stock-outs, lowering excess inventory levels, and eliminating re-distribution costs. Most postponement models are designed to operate at destination, close to the end-user market. Being able to postpone product differentiation, at the manufacturing point of origin in China, is the holy grail of supply chain process improvement, and with the liberalization of China Customs regulations, and enhancements in supply chain visibility technology, the holy grail is becoming a reality.

We discussed the migration of business process outsourcing to China and the opportunities that this trend is presenting in the area of SCM. The level of sophistication with regard to the types of jobs being outsourced today is a cause for concern in places like the United States and Europe, but it opens up new areas for revenue growth, geographic expansion, and partnership opportunities for those international businesses that wish to harness the value of Chinese skill sets.

As important as supply chain technology has become to global business, it is human capital that will make or break SCM in the years ahead. More sophisticated skill sets will be required to manage more dynamic and complex logistics processes, and this will drive the need to develop more highly trained logistics experts. Talent development will need to include left-brain analytical skill sets that can gather and interpret data, along with right-brain creative skill sets that can recognize patterns, make connections, and orchestrate complex logistics solutions. The most important attribute of logisticians moving forward will be the ability to look beyond the computer screen, to evaluate dynamic situations, and make common-sense decisions on the ground.

Supply chain technology will continue to play an important role in global transportation. While truly integrated systems have been slow to materialize, new web-based neutral platforms are beginning to bridge the gap that existed between heritage proprietary systems. Companies such as GTNexus and TradeCard are helping to facilitate the full spectrum of supply chain activity, including purchase order management, landed cost calculation, milestone tracking, and trade finance functions. Technology such as RFID and Bokode tags will also be interesting to watch over the next several years.

The importance of building resilient and sustainable supply chains cannot be overemphasized, particularly as it relates to China. A focus on prevention is important, but so is the need to prepare for when prevention fails, by developing contingency plans that are flexible enough to adapt to almost any situation. The Concentric Vulnerability Map highlighted in chapter nine is a useful tool to highlight the many areas that need to be considered when trying to understand what can potentially go wrong in order to build contingency plans for when things do go wrong.

Building sustainable supply chains is a top priority for many international companies today. Looking beyond the usual menu of possibilities are ideas such as packaging re-design and vendor sustainability scorecards. Keeping in mind the importance the Chinese place on saving face when advocating these types of sustainability initiatives in China, it is a good idea to provide incentive for compliance, as opposed to issuing punishment for non-compliance. There is a great deal of focus on China's environmental issues these days. Rather than pointing fingers at China, the best thing the world community can do to help the situation is to ensure that the latest in green technologies and sustainable business practices are made available to the Chinese people. They will take it from there.

There is an old Chinese proverb, "See the wind, turn the rudder." International retailers and LSPs that see the wind, will realize that the rise of China, and the changing face of consumer retail, represent opportunities for monumental expansion and growth. The greatest opportunity, and hence the greatest challenge, will be the ability of retailers and LSPs to turn the rudder and create more dynamic partnerships and supply chain business models capable of exploiting these lucrative new market opportunities in the 21st century.

NOTE

1   Jamil Anderlini, "Rule of the Iron Rooster," *Financial Times*, August 25, 2009.

SELECTED BIBLIOGRAPHY

PETER LEVESQUE

Aimi, Greg and W. McNeill. "Logistics Service Providers: Landscape of the Leaders' Demand-Driven Capabilities." AMR Research, 2008.

Capgemini State of Logistics Outsourcing Third Party Logistics, 2007.

Capgemini State of Logistics Outsourcing Third Party Logistics, 2008.

Christensen, Clayton, S. Kaufman, and W. Shih. "Innovation Killers." *Harvard Business Review* (January 2008): 1–8.

Collins, Jim. *Good to Great, Why Some Companies Make the Leap and Others Don't.* New York: HarperCollins, 2001.

Dekrey, Stephen and D. Messick. *Leadership Experiences in Asia, Insight and Inspiration From 20 Innovators.* Singapore: John Wiley & Sons Inc., 2007.

Denend, Lyn. "Wal-Mart's Sustainability Strategy." SGS No. OIT-71. Stanford Graduate School of Business, 2007.

Duda, Stacy, James LaShawn, Z. Mackwani, R. Munoz, D. Volk. "Starbucks Corporation, Building A Sustainable Supply Chain." SGS No. GS-54. Stanford Graduate School of Business, 2007.

Farrell, Diana, E. Beinhocker, U. Gersch, E. Greenberg, E. Stephenson, J. Ablett, M. Guan, and J. Devan, "From 'Made in China' to 'Sold in China': The Rise of the Chinese Urban Consumer." McKinsey & Company, 2006.

Flynn, Steven. *America the Vulnerable, How Our Government is Failing to Protect Us From Terrorism.* New York: HarperCollins, 2004.

Fukuyama, Francis. *The End of History and the Last Man.* New York: Free Press, 1992.

Fung, Victor, W. Fung, and W. Yoram. *Competing in a Flat World, Building Enterprises for a Borderless World.* Upper Saddle River: Wharton Publishing, 2008.

Garder, Daniel L. *Supply Chain Vector, Methods for Linking the Execution of Global Business Models with Financial Performance.* Boca Raton: J. Ross Publishing, 2004.

Hansen, Motern and J. Birkinshaw. "The Innovation Value Chain." *Harvard Business Review,* (June 2007): 1–12.

Hoyt, David. "Unsafe For Children: Mattel's Toy Recalls and Supply Chain Management." SGSOB No. GS-63. Stanford Graduate School of Business, 2008.

Hoyt, David and A. Silverman. "Crocs: Revolutionizing An Industry's Supply Chain Model For Competitive Advantage." SGS No. GS-7. Stanford Graduate School of Business, 2007.

Jacques, Martin. *When China Rules the World, The Rise of the Middle Kingdom and the End of The Western World.* London: Penguin, 2009.

Johnson, Fraser. "Supply Chain Management at Wal-Mart." IBS No. 907 D01. Richard Ivey School of Business, 2006.

Lal, Rajiv, C. Knoop, and I. Tarsis. "Best Buy Co., Inc: Customer-Centricity." HBS No. 9-506-056. Boston: Harvard Business School Publishing, 2006.

Landers, David S., *The Wealth and Poverty of Nations—Why Some Are So Rich and Some So Poor.* New York: W.W. Norton & Company, 1999.

Lin, Yifu J., F. Cai, and Z. Li. *The China Miracle—Development Strategy and Economic Reform.* Hong Kong: Chinese University Press, 1998.

McAfee, Andrew, V. Dessain, and A. Sjoman. "Zara: IT for Fast Fashion." HBS No. 9- 604-081. Boston: Harvard Business School Publishing, 2007.

Menor, Larry and C. Ramasastry. "Dabbawallahs of Mumbai." IBS No. 904 D11. Richard Ivey School of Business, 2004.

Messick, David, and R. Kramer. *The Psychology of Leadership, New Perspectives and Research.* Mahwah: Lawrence Erlbaum Associates, 2005.

Moore, Geoffrey. "Darwin and the Demon." *Harvard Business Review* (July-August 2004): 1–6.

Murnighan, John, K. and John C. Mowen. *The Art of High-Stakes Decision-Making, Tough Calls in a Speed Driven World.* New York: John Wiley & Sons Inc., 2002.

O'Marah, Kevin. "Remake Your Supply Chain to Support Innovation." *Harvard Business Review— Supply Chain Strategy* (2005): 3–5.

Pink, Daniel H. *A Whole New Mind, Why Right Brainers Will Rule The Future.* New York: Penguin, 2006.

Prahalad, C. K. *The Fortune at the Bottom of the Pyramid, Eradicating Poverty Through Profits.* Upper Saddle River: Wharton Publishing, 2006.

Prahalad, C.K. and M.S. Krishnan. *The New Age of Innovation: Driving Cocreated Value Through Global Networks.* New York: McGraw-Hill, 2008.

Rietze, Susan. "Case Studies of Postponement in the Supply Chain." Master of Science in Transportation Thesis. MIT, 2006.

Rizza, M. "Best Practices for Disaster Recovery & Planning in the Supply Chain." AMR Research PowerPoint presentation. AMR Research, 2006.

Robinson, Ken. *The Element—How Finding Your Passion Changes Everything.* New York: Penguin Publishing, 2009.

Sheffi, Yossi. *The Resilient Enterprise: Overcoming Vulnerability for Competitive Advantage.* Cambridge: MIT Press, 2007.

Sorkin, Andrew R. *Too Big To Fail.* New York: Viking, 2009.

Tenet, George, *At The Center of the Storm, My Years at the CIA*. New York: HarperCollins, 2007.

Ton, Zeynep, V. Dessain, and M. Stachowiak-Joulain. "RFID at the METRO Group." HBS No. 9-606-053. Boston: Harvard Business School Publishing, 2009.

Tunzelmann, Alex von. *Indian Summer, The Secret History of the End of an Empire*. New York: Henry Holt, 2007.

U.S. Department of Transportation and Federal Highway Administration. "Freight and Intermodal Connectivity in China." May, 2008.

Yergin, Daniel and J. Stanislaw. *The Commanding Heights, The Battle for the World Economy*. New York: Simon & Shuster, 2002.

Zakaria, Fareed. *The Post American World*. New York: W.W. Norton, 2008.

CHRIS ROBESON

Anand, Krishnan S., and H. Mendelson. "Postponement and Information in a Supply Chain." *IDEAS: Economics and Finance Research*. (22 March, 2009): <http://ideas.repec.org/p/nwu/cmsems/1222.html>

Barney, Jay. "Product Differentiation." In *Gaining and Sustaining Competitive Advantage* (3rd Edition). Upper Saddle River: Prentice Hall, 2006.

Bowersox, Donald J., and N. J. Lahowchic. *Start Pulling Your Chain! Leading Responsive Supply Chain Transformation*. Port St. Lucie, Fla: OGI Enterprises, 2008.

Cooper, M. C., and J. D. Pagh. "Supply Chain Postponement and Speculation Strategies: How to Choose the Right Strategy." *Journal of Business Logistics 19*, no.2 (1998): 13–33.

Copacino, William. C. *Supply Chain Management: The Basics and Beyond*. Boca Raton, Fl: St. Lucie Press, APICS, 1997.

Feitzinger, Edward and H. L. Lee. "Mass Customization at Hewlett Packard: The Power of Postponement." *Harvard Business Review 75*, no.1 (1997): 116–22.

Fisher, Marshall. "What is the Right Supply Chain for Your Product?" *Harvard Business Review 75*, no.2 (1997): 105–16.

Pine, Joseph. "Joseph Pine on what consumers want" Video on TED.com. *TED: Ideas worth spreading*. (12 Feb. 2009): <http://www.ted.com/talks/joseph_pine_on_what_consumers_want.html>

Robeson, James F., and W. C. Copacino, eds. *The Logistics Handbook*. New York: The Free Press, 1994.

Shen, Ting "A Framework for Developing Postponement Strategies." MIT Research Paper. MIT Center for Transportation and Logistics. (15 Dec. 2008): <http://ctl.mit.edu/metadot/index.pl?iid=6183>

Wanke, Peter F. and W. Zinn. "Strategic Logistics Decision Making." *International Journal of Physical Distribution & Logistics Management 34*, no.6 (2004): 466–78.

INDEX